Plays,

Movies,

and

Critics

PLAYS, MOVIES, AND CRITICS

Jody McAuliffe,

Editor

Duke University Press

Durham & London 1993

© 1993 Duke University Press   All rights reserved
Printed in the United States of America on acid-free paper ∞
Typeset in Pilgrim by Tseng Information Systems, Inc.
Library of Congress Cataloging-in-Publication Data appear on the last printed page
of this book.
The text of this book originally was published without the present introduction,
afterword, and index as Volume 91, No. 2 (Spring 1992) of the *South Atlantic
Quarterly*.

"The Rapture of the Athlete Assumed into Heaven," Copyright © 1990 by Don
DeLillo. First performed by the American Repertory Theatre (Cambridge, Mass.) in
April 1990. First published in *The Quarterly*, Vol. 15, 1990. "Reinventing American
Theater," Copyright 1992 by Robert Brustein. "What the Streets Mean: An Interview
with Martin Scorsese," Copyright 1992 by Anthony DeCurtis. This is an expanded
version of "Martin Scorsese: The Rolling Stone Interview" by Anthony DeCurtis from
Rolling Stone #590, 1 November, 1990. By Straight Arrow Publishers, Inc. Copyright
1992. All Rights Reserved. Reprinted by Permission. "An Interview with Stanley
Kauffmann," Copyright 1992 by Bert Cardullo. Portions of this interview, which was
conducted in New York City in July 1987, were originally published in the *New
Orleans Review*, *Literature/Film Quarterly*, and *Tulanian*. Thanks to the editors of
these journals for permission to reprint.

Contents

Plays,

Movies,

and

Critics

Introduction

Jody McAuliffe

First of all we must recognize that the theater, like the plague, is a delirium and is communicative.—Antonin Artaud

*lays, Movies, and Critics* begins with a play by Don DeLillo. This play takes the form of an interview, the subject of which is a tennis champion, a visionary athlete or athletic visionary in a state of exaltation, the supreme psychological warrior, whose body and soul are being taken up into heaven. The Tennis Player never utters a word; he is frozen in a pose of apotheosis. His moment of triumph, like that of mystical experience, is beyond language, ineffable. If the Player spoke at all it would have to be in tongues. The Interviewer, speaking into a hand mike, revolves like a moon around the frozen player and fades into shadow before she finishes speaking her one long statement (not a question). The Player, a sun surrounded by darkness, blazing in

intense light, lingers like an afterimage before black. What kind of signal is this actor sending us through the flames of his celebrity?

DeLillo's play fulfills Artaud's dictum that the spectacle of theater must produce a vibration in the actor and the audience. It must leave an image that will never be erased. *The Rapture of the Athlete Assumed into Heaven* functions as the keynote of this collection. Not only does it embody the major concerns of this book, but also it works as a kind of paradigm of the theatrical or cinematic event. The Interviewer (read audience) demands of the Player (read actor/director): Athlete of the heart: answer my questions about love and death; reflect my image back to me; take me on the set of your mind and make the movie. Let me be reborn in you. Audience can be characterized as desirous of rapture, desirous of the secret vision of someone else's undiscovered country and thereby maybe its own. The word rapture is derived from the root rape.

DeLillo's interview play is accompanied in this collection by three more conventional interviews. One is with Roberta Levitow, a theater director from Los Angeles in transit from theater to film and from Los Angeles to New York; the next is with Martin Scorsese, the film director from New York with a Chekhovian predilection for basing drama in reality, on what would really happen as opposed to what happens in conventional literature and film. Critic Anatoly Koni's comments about Chekhov's *The Seagull* might just as easily be applied in a different register to Scorsese's *Mean Streets*: "*The Seagull* is a work whose conception, freshness of ideas, and thoughtful observations of life raise it out of the ordinary. It is life itself on stage with all its tragic alliances, eloquent thoughtlessness, and silent sufferings— the sort of everyday life that is accessible to everyone and understood in its cruel internal irony by almost no one." The final interview in this volume is with Stanley Kauffmann, who is most distinguished among critics writing about both theater and film.

What is it about the interview that it has replaced the epistle as an instrument of self-revelation? In his review of *Malcolm X* in *The New Yorker* Terence Rafferty expressed Spike Lee's aesthetic philosophy, shared with Oliver Stone, as *koppelo ergo sum* ("I appear on 'Nightline,' therefore I am"). Lucy Winer, a documentary filmmaker I consider expert in interviewing, recounted to me an insight she had during the filming of *Rate It X*, her documentary on pornography. Wearing her white gloves and holding her microphone, she is consistently concealed and revealed in the film, though we never see anything but those eternal gloves. She offended programmatic feminists by seeing herself reflected in her subjects ranging from an art house exhibitor with a tendency toward films like *Blood Sucking Freaks*, which are extremely violent toward and exploitative of women, to the cartoonist who wrote Chester the Molester for *Hustler* magazine. Much to feminist distress, she did not come right out and accuse the cartoonist, who insisted he loved his four-year-old daughter, of encouraging child molesting by making a joke out of it. She didn't have to make an accusation; it was obvious. Her unbiased questions allowed him to reveal his true nature, let him implicate himself. I wasn't surprised to hear some years later that he had been arrested for molesting his beloved daughter.

In Michelangelo Antonioni's film *The Passenger*, the journalist's questions are much more revealing about himself than the African tribal leader's answers would be about himself. Only when the subject turns the camera on the journalist can the interview proceed. The point of view of the interviewer inevitably colors the interview. Errol Morris bent the rules of documentary filmmaking with his revolutionary *The Thin Blue Line* by staging, filming, and editing dramatizations of the crime and surrounding events from multiple points of view. The drama surrounding the crime became the audience's obsession. Documentaries and interviews are now no longer the exclusive terrain of journalists; they involve acts of imagination. Sandra Bernhard applauded Jodie Foster's Academy Award winning performance in *The Accused*, the fictional film of a true story, by saying: "She was so good, it was like a fucking documentary."

Two visionary modern playwrights studied herein facilitated the artful confusion of truth and illusion. Chekhov helped destroy linear storytelling, and Pirandello drew attention to the blurred borders between fiction and reality. Brecht, of course, used narrative devices in the theater to disrupt our identification with characters, and Godard reconceived Brecht's techniques for film. Woody Allen borrows from Godard in *Husbands and Wives*, leaving us with the harrowing prospect that we're all condemned to explain ourselves to an invisible interviewer until it, the movie or life, is finally over. Allen's movie ends with the miserable hero's plea to his interviewer for mercy: "Can I go, is this over?"

Though it is often said that the vitality of theater is measured by the quality of its playwrights, I think it is measured also by the quality of its visionaries, playwrights or directors or both. The chapters on Chekhov and Shaw in this volume consider them during the early periods of their playwrighting careers. The essay on *Mean Streets*—an anthropological, autobiographical work—is about Scorsese as a new director. Scorsese lends his mature personal perspective to the work in his interview with Anthony DeCurtis.

When I was a graduate student in directing at the Yale School of Drama, Lloyd Richards advised my class that we should "come in on the coattails of a playwright." This coming in on the coattails seemed to me at the time an insult. The conventional perception in the theater world had been that artistic collaboration was like a triangle with the playwright, director, and actor on three corners. The playwright stood securely at the apex. However, successful auteur directors had embraced Artaud's call for no more masterpieces, and tipped this triangle on its side. I was educated by Lee Breuer, a writer-director who came on his own coattails to the American theater via Europe and the art world. Breuer was one of the Big Four; the other three were Robert Wilson, Richard Foreman, and Richard Schechner.

In fact many directors of my generation, including Roberta Levitow, who is interviewed here by Mame Hunt, did break into the heavily director-staffed regional theater scene on the long coattails of new writers. Unlike England, where new directors cut their teeth on classics, here artistic directors cracked their doors open for new directors to do readings, staged readings, and productions of new plays. Readings were low front-end investment auditions with potential for future development. New plays were hot; classic plays were plums for artistic and associate directors or heavily sought after, experienced freelance directors. The forbidding economics of large casts in classic plays, along with a sincere desire on the part of producers to infuse blood into the theater with new plays, dictated these conditions.

Ten years after he had started Playwrights Horizons, dedicated to the development of new playwrights, Bob Moss thought the time had come for a Directors Horizons. The closest thing I've seen to that is Jim Nicola's New York Theatre Workshop. In developing this collection on the state of theatrical and cinematic art, I liked the idea of a critic as the third corner of that creative triangle. Maybe someday there will be a Critics Horizons, too.

In his essay celebrating the health of American theater, Robert Brustein deplores the dearth of intelligent, literate reflection on theater. In fact it was Brustein who commissioned DeLillo's short play about the athlete's rapture as part of an evening of short plays. He catalogues important voices and takes stock of the vital signs of the eternally invalid theater. When the profits become elusive the visionaries go underground and a kind of guerrilla movement develops, a revolution motivated by art and not by profits. The theater is perpetually reinvented by its visionaries.

And Chekhov is a prime example of one such revolutionary. About *The Seagull* he wrote, "I started it forte and ended it pianissimo, against all rules of dramatic art. . . . I'm more dissatisfied than satisfied and, reading through my newborn play, I'm more convinced than ever I'm no playwright. . . . Be sure you don't let anybody read it."

One of the pleasures of criticism is that if a critic falls in love with a particular writer, in this case Richard Gilman with Chekhov, the romance can last a lifetime. The critic is reflected in his alterego; he grows along with him over a critical career.

I had assisted Brustein on his production of *The Seagull* at Yale Rep in 1979. He carried out an idea of Serban's, the originally scheduled director of the play, that the play should be set *in* the magic lake. Michael Yeargan designed a waterlike mylar flooring and the surreal world that evolved reminded me of Paul Delvaux's hallucinatory mermaid paintings.

Chekhov's first major work, the product of his incipient vision, is preoccupied with the state of theater, the making of art and the life of both art and the artist. Here is a voice in formation. Treplev, the new writer in the play, says, "After all that talk about new forms in art, I'm starting to slip into a rut myself. . . . I'm still rushing about in a maze of dreams and images with no knowledge of who or what any of it is for. I have no faith. I don't know what my calling is." Chekhov was Treplev's kindred spirit after the dismal opening of *The Seagull*: "I roamed the streets, I sat. I couldn't simply forget about the performance. If I live seven hundred years, I'll never give a theater another play. When it comes to theater, I'm doomed to failure."

The theater almost lost Chekhov, and Shaw came to it late. What excited me about Stanley Kauffmann's essay on Shaw was that it is concerned with how Shaw found his voice as a playwright, how he found his medium. That Shaw's arrival occurred so late in his life gives me hope and faith in the future of theater. Just as the forces clustered at the end of the nineteenth century produced a Shaw, the forces at our current political/spectacular/spiritual crossroads might engender another thinker who could travel down an Ibsenian road of ideas straight into the heart of the next century.

> Then the theatre was changed
> To something else. Its past was a souvenir.
> It has to be living, to learn the speech of the place.
> It has to face the men of the time and to meet
> The women of the time. It has to think about war
> And it has to find what will suffice. It has
> To construct a new stage. It has to be on that stage
> And, like an insatiable actor, slowly and
> With meditation, speak words that in the ear,
> In the delicatest ear of the mind, repeat,
> Exactly, that which it wants to hear, at the sound
> Of which, an invisible audience listens,
> Not to the play, but to itself, expressed
> In an emotion as of two people, as of two
> Emotions becoming one.
> Wallace Stevens, *Of Modern Poetry*

From Chekhov to Shaw to Pirandello, a kind of eclectic modern progress was taking its course. Mary Ann Witt's essay looks at Pirandello's theatrical oeuvre in light of the connection between modernism and fascism. Wagner, Shaw's inspiration, has been identified with fascism, Shaw with socialism, and Pirandello with fascism. Wagner and Pirandello tried to make myths, tried to take theater back to its religious/political roots. Pirandello's theatrical ideas altered the cultural consciousness of the twentieth century, thanks to his vigorous pursuit of the modern impulse to unfix forms.

Good plays invent consciousnesses in the face of crises. *Henry IV* is a good play I have fallen in and out of love with for the last fifteen years. In *The Making of Modern Drama* Gilman writes, "The point is that in Pirandello's work consciousness plays back and forth between feeling and idea and is the very result of their relations, their reciprocity and tension. We know what we feel and feel what we know, he is saying, or rather, we can *think* our feelings and feel our thoughts." Pirandello helped me appreciate this seeming contradiction at the heart of the human sensibility. Henry IV anticipates the later twentieth-century American character of Port in *The Sheltering Sky*, a film by Pirandello's countryman Bernardo Bertolucci. Neither Henry IV nor Port can live in his own time, in his own country. Both refute the modern century and their life is a death in a spiritual desert.

David Wyatt's essay helped me appreciate a play I had not appreciated in production: *A Lie of the Mind*. I had considered it a poor man's *Long Day's Journey Into Night*, the nemesis play for all serious American playwrights, the Joe Louis they all have to fight. Sam Shepard takes Pirandellian ideas of identity into the conflict between the sexes. Paul Bowles takes up this confusion again in *The Sheltering Sky*, where the female protagonist, Kit, becomes a man-woman. So for this collection, Shepard, a maker of images in film as well as theater, is a bridge. In fact, this playwright has created characters whose very consciousnesses have been structured by film.

Shepard's conception of identity is distinctly influenced by Pirandello. These twentieth-century men—Henry IV, Jake in *Lie of the Mind*, and Port in *The Sheltering Sky*—believe and become their parts. The individual can no more survive the tyranny of democracy than the construction of fascism.

In her interview with Mame Hunt, Roberta Levitow says that in the American West (Shepard's home country), we are inventing and reinventing ourselves. Hunt and Levitow were right when they thought I was looking for a representative (I won't use the word token) woman director, someone of my generation—twenty years after the pioneers of regional theater—somebody who had experienced the perils of freelancing, worked with new plays, and worked on the West Coast, a decidedly different scene than New York. Like me Levitow crossed over to film through the Directing Workshop for Women at American Film Institute.

Any study of film criticism would be incomplete without the presence of André Bazin, who articulated the progression from the moral to the theological in his criticism. According to Kauffmann, Bazin believed the filmmaker's function was to celebrate God's miracle— the miracle of the world and human existence in it—by presenting it to us without Eisensteinian or any other kind of manipulation. He was interested in art, not political correctness.

Bazin's critical stance sets the stage for Hosney's, Wollman's, and Engdahl's spiritual reading of *Mean Streets* and prompts further examination of *The Last Temptation of Christ*. And Scorsese's deliberate confusion of sexual and religious ecstasy and desire for martyrdom take me back to DeLillo's play. This synthesis of religious and aesthetic passion, coupled with the rejection of conventional narrative forms, is a theme which permeates this book. During the time surrounding his writing of *The Seagull* Chekhov testified to the perennial confusion between spirituality and theater, art and ecstasy: "If monasteries accepted the irreligious and permitted abstention from prayer, I'd become a monk."

Like Charlie in *Mean Streets*, Port in *The Sheltering Sky* suffers the confusion between sexual and religious ecstasy and desires martyrdom. My essay on *The Sheltering Sky* came about because I happened to go to an empty multiplex, one of our very own urban desert spaces inhabited by people in the dark, and saw the film the day after I'd seen a production of *Waiting for Godot*. I was struck by the similarities between the four characters in Beckett's play and the two couples in Bertolucci's film. The ignorant Americans in the film, who don't belong in Africa, learn the power of the desert the hard way. After a storm of sensational pre-publicity the picture came out with a whimper. After I saw it I thought audiences must not have known how to read it. I wanted to reclaim it.

I like to think of all these auteurs of theater and film—Chekhov, Shaw, Shepard, DeLillo, Scorsese, Bertolucci, and Pirandello—as artists "in a kind of tumultous internal exile," to borrow DeCurtis's description of Scorsese. *The Seagull* leads to *Mean Streets, The Sheltering Sky* to *The Rapture of the Athlete Assumed into Heaven*. Put Treplev in Scorsese's world and he's another victim of romantic rejection. Joyce Carol Oates wrote a beautiful book on boxing in which she argues that boxing plays the role in contemporary society that tragic theater played in ancient Greece. Scorsese is right that "the ring becomes an allegory of whatever you do in life." Brecht knew it, too. One of my favorite metaphors applied to *Long Day's Journey* is that the fourth act for Tyrone is like the fifteenth round of a heavyweight bout. For after all it's the body that suffers, it's the body that pays.

In the final interview with Kauffmann we can see the evolution of a critic, his rigorously informed subjectivism. In his *After the Film Generation*, Kauffmann describes having been haunted by "two intelligent young women who were surprised that there had been a Dreyer, that a film could be exalting." From the ecstasy of Joan of Arc in Dreyer's film *Passion of Joan of Arc* to *The Rapture of the Athlete Assumed into Heaven* the distance is not so great. The internal landscapes of both Joan and the Athlete vibrate deliriously in images of aesthetic and spiritual exaltation as perfectly communicative as music.

The Rapture of the Athlete Assumed into Heaven

Don DeLillo

ENNIS PLAYER, a man in his early twenties
INTERVIEWER, an older man or woman
The TENNIS PLAYER, *all in white, falls to his knees at the moment of triumph—head thrown back, eyes closed, arms raised, one fist clenched, the racket in the other hand. He is frozen in this pose, his body glowing in strong light, with darkness all around.*
At the sound of the INTERVIEWER'S *voice, the* TENNIS PLAYER *begins to rotate as if on an axis, completing a single 360-degree turn in the course of the play.*

The INTERVIEWER *carries a hand mike and walks out of the darkness about five seconds after he begins speaking. He circles the* TENNIS PLAYER, *moving in the opposite direction, stopping occasionally, making as many revolutions as the monologue allows.*

INTERVIEWER: How special it must feel, Bobby, finishing off a career in this fashion, it must feel like a culmination you could only dream of years ago, growing up without a role model, without a high school on a hill, using a borrowed racket that smelled of someone else, it must feel like a vindication, an affirmation, winning the big one at last, the one that's eluded you all these years and in all these ways until today, playing before the Queen, the King, the Jack, the Ace, growing up without a blond girl in a Buick, without a girl with long and tawny legs who rocks beside you on the porch swing, coming from behind to win the match they said you'd never win, the doubters and skeptics, the pundits, the clever little men with bad bodies, how sweet it must be to reach your goal at last, so many disappointments, so much sorrow, growing up without sideburns or a personal savior, totally missing the point of rock and roll, undersized and out of breath but determined to prevail, it must feel like a restoration, an eternalization, growing up without a mom in flat-heeled shoes, finding a racket in the bracken and taking it to bed, obsessed, depressed, a boy without a girl in a blue Buick, how transforming it must feel, a blond girl with a tawny body slightly shiny in the moonlight, answering your critics at last, the naysayers and doomsayers, the gloom purveyors, the nihilists and realists, playing before the Queen Mother, the Gay Father, the Battered Wives, tell us quickly how it feels, growing up without a junior year abroad, so many failures, so much sadness, we're desperately eager to hear, it must feel like a permutation, a concatenation, growing up without a girl in a tawny field, a sunlit blond in a summer dress who lets you put your hand, who lets you touch, who says shyly in the night, growing up without an old covered bridge nearby, how super it must feel to achieve your biggest thrill as an athlete on the last day of your life, to know the perfection of the body even as your skin loses heat and energy and hair and nails, and now we're all enfolded in your arms, you are the culture that contains us, we're running out of time, so tell us quickly, time is short, tell us now.

The INTERVIEWER *fades into shadow before he finishes speaking.*
The TENNIS PLAYER *completes his rotation.*
He remains motionless in intense white light for five seconds.
Black.

Reinventing American Theater

Robert Brustein

he theater, usually at odds with reality, seems to be imitating nature in one important regard: its cycles of death and rebirth. Something seems to be dying, and, as with all seasonal changes, something new is struggling to be born. The death of the theater has been celebrated so many times now that nobody bothers to mention it anymore. Instead, the print and broadcast media are behaving as though grass is already growing on the grave. In the past, the state of the theater's health would be argued in intellectual magazines, popular newspapers, and trade journals, in living rooms and bars, even in the songs of Simon and Garfunkel. Today, the question is treated with a vacuous and rather bored silence. The Arts and Leisure section of the *New York Times*—who remembers when it was once called the Theater section?—can barely squeeze out an article about the stage once every two or three weeks on its front page. Nor does discussion often focus on the American theater. Instead, we find Frank Rich or Benedict Nightingale celebrating the riches to be found in London, and when

Mel Gussow does a follow-up review of some item of the Broadway season, that is usually an English import, too. The *Times* has three full-time reviewers, and another two or three part-time contributors; but considering how seldom they appear in the daily cultural pages— once or twice a week at most—it would be more economical to pay them an hourly wage.

Newsweek has drastically reduced the space of its regular theater critic, Jack Kroll, so that he rarely appears in print unless covering some monumental event—like Peter Brooks's *Mahabharata* or the London theater season. *Time* magazine is more generous to its reviewer, William Henry III. But most New York newspapers feature reviews that read like telex copy, not much different in kind from the encapsulated asides of the coiffured pundits of TV. The *Village Voice* still makes an effort to cover most New York theater events (so does *Variety* from another perspective), and its writers constitute the largest reviewing staff on any current newspaper. But even that lively enterprise is now buried under ads and personals, a considerably eviscerated effort in contrast to an era when half the paper was devoted to the stage.

As for the serious magazines, neither *Harper's* nor *Atlantic* has carried a theater article in years—an exception was David Denby's *Theaterophobia*, a savage attack on the stage. I'm still writing in *The New Republic*, but my once-weekly column now appears monthly, by editorial decree. John Simon continues to rage weekly at helpless moving objects in *New York* magazine, but that's less a species of criticism than a blood sport, to be recorded in the annals of bull-baiting. There was a time when every serious magazine reserved considerable space in order to examine what was happening in theater—when Mary McCarthy and Susan Sontag were reviewing for *Partisan Review*, when Elizabeth Hardwick was covering theater for the *New York Review*, when the *New Leader* featured Albert Bermel, *The Nation* had Harold Clurman (later Alan Schneider and Richard Gilman), and Wilfrid Sheed and Richard Gilman were writing for *Commonweal*. Even the *Hudson Review* had regular reviewers, John Simon among them, where he had the opportunity to be more reflective than reflexive. And *Commentary*—in the years before the editors began to see Reds in every dressing room—was noted for its sociological overviews of the American stage. Indeed, at one time virtually every American intellectual felt a compulsion to express an opinion on the state of Broadway theater.

Well, what happened? The chief thing was the decline of Broadway. We were having such a great time hurling stones at a seemingly invincible commercial target that we were unprepared when that muscular philistine fell flat on his face before the assaults. I'm not suggesting that it was our little slingshots that brought Goliath down. The issues were far more fundamental than that. But when you're flailing away against the mediocrity and meretriciousness of a powerful adversary, and it suddenly falls down, the effect can be disorienting. In any event, something unsettled many of the writers I've just named, because they abandoned theater criticism and returned to literary pursuits, thus ending that golden period, in the early 1960s, when literate theater critics were having an impact. The *New York Times* even asked me, a notorious high-brow, to become its daily drama reviewer, undoubtedly responding to the discontent then being expressed by the intelligentsia toward the newspaper's cultural personnel. I refused the temptation, pleading my inability to write coherent reviews in less than three days (the real reason was a hesitation to exercise instant life-and-death power over productions that took months to prepare). I recommended Stanley Kauffmann for the post. He held it for less than a year, and still hasn't forgiven me.

The end of concerted intelligent reflection on the state of our theater coincided with the deterioration of the commercial stage and the loss of a central platform for aspiring American theater artists. This left our New York-based critics with very little to write about, apart from the inferior quality of Broadway stagecraft. And how often can you write about that without falling into rage or repetition? Frank Rich is often assailed for destroying Broadway, and there's no question that sour critical judgments in the *Times* directly affect the barometric pressure of theater economics. But it's not necessary to agree with his opinions, or even his aesthetics, to conclude that his only critical alternative to ferocity is mendacity—or finding a less damaging place to express his views. Largely for money reasons, Broadway *has* degenerated into an arena for the tried-and-true: huge, numbing musicals; Neil Simonized comedies; or, at best, imports from Britain and transfers from American resident theaters. The new American play—once the proud staple of the commercial theater in the 1930s, 40s, and 50s—has virtually disappeared from producers' agendas, unless it can be marketed as a variant of affirmative action, alleviating liberal guilt toward minorities or the handicapped. And the day of the genuinely original American musical is over, too, eclipsed by such grinding British juggernauts as *The Phantom of the Opera* and *Les Miserables*.

Ticket prices are clearly the main issue. The high level of producers' greed, artists' royalties, expensive theater-leasing arrangements, and union featherbedding has made a couple of seats to a Broadway show—if you count in transportation, restaurants, parking, and baby-sitting—cost as much as a couple of shares of IBM; and when the evening's over, you don't even have a dividend to show for it. At such prices, any theatergoer is going to stay home unless he's promised a blockbuster. Consequently, what was once the theater center of the world no longer has a regular theater audience. Look around the Majestic or the Winter Garden the next time you visit Broadway and see if you can recognize anybody you know. It's an audience of tourists and expense accounters, commuters traveling via bridge and tunnel. The gabby, feisty, noisy, demanding New York audience that used to mob the Broadway box office is a thing of the past. Oh, you'll probably see a few natives at the revival of *Gypsy* or at *Cat on a Hot Tin Roof*. But most commercial producers recognize that they haven't the slightest notion who their customers are.

And it's for that reason, I think, that so much of the current Broadway product is trite and banal. Where the criterion for staging shows once was originality and surprise, now it is the capacity to repeat successful formulas from the past. Sometimes this works. All of Andrew Lloyd-Webber's big mechanical musicals sound exactly alike to people like me, but every one of them somehow manages to start a box-office stampede. The same is true of Neil Simon, each of whose recent hit plays is just another chapter in his romanticized autobiography, tinted with rose-colored water and studded with contrived gags. It is more likely, however, that any theater work based on some previous success will seem desiccated and tired, unless it has an infusion of new artistic energy. And that energy is just what frightens conventional Broadway producers these days. You don't risk four to ten million dollars on the unknown.

But in failing to trust their audiences, the Broadway producers have been encouraging audiences not to trust *them*, with the result that living-room conversation these days is never about the latest play; it's about the latest movie or mini-series. Attendance is down, though box-office income continues to rise, inflated by astronomical ticket prices. Each new season is pronounced more horrible than the last. For these reasons—and because there's so little youth, vigor, excitement, or new ideas on the Broadway stage—the theater as a whole is now considered moribund. And because the intellectuals have deserted it as well, no strong voice in this country is calling attention to the fact that, far from being dead, the American theater throughout the nation may today be more advanced and more dynamic than at virtually any other time in its history.

I realize this is a large and unsupported claim. But it might seem less preposterous once it is recognized that the idea of theater has undergone a profound change during the past two decades—in its definition, its structure, its purpose, its geography. Being a market for proven commodities rather than a source of new forms, New York has been among the last areas in this nation to acknowledge this fact. Until recently, the new theater has been seen only around the city's periphery—at the Brooklyn Academy of Music or at Ellen Stewart's La Mama or at the Kitchen—though the presentation of performing artists at Lincoln Center called "Serious Fun" suggests a growing awareness at its midsection.

But what a provincial village New York has become in regard to the arts. This is clear enough in opera, where the Met continues to roast old chestnuts and the City Opera is devoting more and more of its repertory to light opera and musical comedies of the past. If you want to see a new American opera, you have to fly to Chicago, Philadelphia, Santa Fe, Houston, St. Louis, Louisville, or—this is a bigger scandal—to the Netherlands and Germany, where most of Philip Glass's work has been premiered. The first-string music critic for the *Times*, who seems to believe that opera consists of divas clunking downstage, facing the audience, and warbling arias *in situ*, will invariably attack any operatic methods that depart in any way from conventional practices of composition and production. This may explain why a recent issue of the magazine *Daedalus* was wholly devoted to asking why New York has lost its place to Europe and regional American cities as a hospitable arena for new musical expression.

What is less commonly noticed is that the same thing is true of the stage. Decades ago, a number of theater leaders—Tyrone Guthrie and Zelda Fichhandler were the first—recognized that if theater were going to survive in this country, it was going to have to be decentralized and based on a system motivated by art, not profits. Fichhandler went to Washington and founded the Arena Stage. Guthrie—rejecting Boston because it was too close to New York—went to Minneapolis, where he not only founded a fine theater, but helped to make that city into the most progressive in the land for philanthropic support of the arts.

The earliest resident theaters in this country were formed on such British repertory models as the Old Vic, the Royal Shakespeare Company, and the National Theatre, staging staple classics mixed with the occasional new play, performed in an acting style influenced by the great English performers (Gielgud, Olivier, Richardson). But some of the newer companies were later to explore other forms of inspiration. The Theatre of Living Arts, founded in Philadelphia by André Gregory, developed a radical, boisterous approach to the works of Beckett and Anouilh; Joe Papp's New York Shakespeare Festival and Public Theatre, especially in their early days, encouraged new American plays and began experimenting with a peculiarly American Shakespeare, based on rough-hewn styles borrowed from broad movie farces. And, if I'm permitted to mention it, the Yale Repertory Theatre, after its founding in 1966, was turning to a blend of Brecht and cabaret in approaching little-known classics and satiric new works. At the same time, the Open Theatre and, later, Mabou Mines and the Wooster Group—performance groups reflecting the influence of the Living Theatre—were exploring a whole new approach to acting in their evolution of new works for the stage.

The 1960s and early 1970s were a high point for the resident theater movement, though it must be acknowledged that after a time—

largely as a result of a funding crisis caused by dwindling private foundation support and the too-slow growth of the National Endowment for the Arts—many of these theaters began to grow stale and conventional, losing their initial radical thrust. One of the proudest things about this movement in the early stages was its independence from the commercial New York stage. Now many were returning to an old role as tributaries, generating products for Broadway. Of course a good play deserves a longer life in many different venues, and there's no reason why New York should not be one of the pit stops. But this is different from actually choosing plays in order to move to Broadway, or restaging past Broadway and off-Broadway successes. A Chorus Line, though it saved Joe Papp from bankruptcy and enabled him for a while to preserve his dedication to unpopular new plays, was an early harbinger of the misalliance between nonprofit theaters and the commercial stage. Before long, resident theaters would be trying out the comedies of Neil Simon, or circulating productions of August Wilson and Into the Woods to other resident theaters as tryout stations on the way to New York.

This made good sound fiscal sense. It brought an infusion of royalties to hard-pressed institutions and created celebrity for its artistic directors, directors, playwrights, and actors. But as the media wheeled around to applaud this new breed of American theater people, and turn them into stars of the week, the institutions themselves began to sicken and even die. The first casualty was the idea of a resident permanent company. How could an ensemble remain together when so many of its members were performing in New York? As a result, there are not more than three or four major resident acting companies still in place in this country, because its members— once happy to join a group with lofty and clearly defined goals—have largely decamped for Hollywood and New York. Another casualty was the ideals and aspirations of these once-committed institutions. Institutional theaters originally devoted to developing their own style and their own artists began competing with each other over projects they thought might have the legs to walk to Broadway.

A little of this is understandable and probably inevitable. But it has presently grown so widespread and endemic that it is discrediting the entire movement. In a culture that worships success, few are prepared to cry out against this progressive deterioration. Quite the contrary, it is being encouraged, largely by critics interested primarily in results, with little interest in the process by which these results are achieved. The effects, however, are more noticeable in England, which currently provides so much fodder for our own commercial stage—and our noncommercial stage as well. The two large companies responsible for much that was forceful and original in English theater lost their prime artistic leaders a few years ago—Trevor Nunn of the Royal Shakespeare Company and Peter Hall of the National. Both were under fire for having abandoned their original purpose in order to profit personally by their commercial ventures. If anyone had said, a decade ago, that the leading purveyor of blockbuster musicals to Broadway and the West End was going to be the head of the Royal Shakespeare Company, he would have been pilloried for impugning the honor of British culture. Yet Trevor Nunn is now enriching himself with such factory items as *Cats* and *Starlight Express* and *Miss Saigon*, while Peter Hall is spinning off star-studded revivals of Shakespeare and Williams to Broadway. Meanwhile, the companies they once led are devoting more and more of their repertories to new and old musicals, and American producers and critics are shopping for new products along the corridors of established classical theaters. A *New York Times* article on this subject, noting the predominance of English talent in the American musical theater, was entitled "The Empire Strikes Back." A better title would have been "The Empire Strikes Out." Certainly, the American resident theater movement has also been striking out lately to the point where, in many cities of this country, it is barely distinguishable from the commercial theater in any way except its 501-C3 nonprofit designation.

Before I leave this rather depressing issue, let me cite one more possible reason for the disappointing record, recently, of the once-promising resident theater movement: time itself. The initial leaders of this movement were usually men and women who had founded their theaters and provided them with their structure and vision. Their enthusiasm managed to attract not only a group of like-minded artists, but patrons from the community ready to support their work in a crucial moral and financial way. Now that the movement is over thirty years old, many of its leaders have either died, burned out, or retired, with the result that power over the theater has shifted not to their artistic successors but rather to their managing directors and their boards. Board members hold the purse strings; they also hold the power to hire and fire. But whereas old warriors like Tyrone Guthrie, Joseph Papp, and William Ball usually had the capacity to keep a board at bay, if not productive and friendly (Adrian Hall once fired a board when it started to get rambunctious), their young artistic director replacements are considerably more subject to the whims and caprices of financial advisors. In most cases, this second artistic generation is composed of gifted and imaginative directors. But since they didn't found their theaters and, in most cases, have abdicated fundraising to development people, they are often much less involved with the fiscal health of the institutions they run. In economic terms, they are more like employees than independent leaders. In psychological terms, they are rather like sons and daughters who accept their allowance without feeling any particular responsibility for keeping the family bank account in balance.

Consequently, their jobs are always at risk if subscriptions falter or unearned income drops, and their theaters become accountable not to the exigencies of artistic exploration but rather to the vagaries of the box office. This puts the resident theater—to borrow a term from Jean Genet—back in the brothel, and explains why so many of its leaders have begun to lose heart and desert it. Adrian Hall, the brilliant artistic director of Trinity Rep and, later, of the Dallas Theatre Company, is only the latest casualty of the general anomie. An eloquent and dedicated spokesman for nonprofit companies, as well as one of our most imaginative creative artists, he has now abandoned the movement to seek personal satisfactions in free-lance directing and moviemaking. And who can blame him when the system proceeds, so remorselessly and inexorably, to suck the idealism and adventure—and pleasure—out of any promising theatrical venture?

I may be exaggerating the extent of the rot, but even if what I say is only partially accurate, it is a pretty depressing account of theater in this country. And, under these circumstances, you may ask, how in the world can I claim that American theater has rarely been stronger in the quality and vision of its creative artists? The conditions I have been trying to describe are hardly congenial for a renaissance of this beleaguered art. Yet something like a renaissance has nevertheless been brewing over the past five or six years—and perhaps the crisis has been partly responsible.

Take playwriting. Everybody remembers a golden time when the American theater could boast a succession of dramatists renowned throughout the world, beginning with O'Neill, and continuing through Odets, Hellman, Miller, Williams, and Albee. By contrast, today it is generally assumed that playwriting is in decline. I am nevertheless convinced that the young writers working on the contemporary stage have the capacity to equal, if not surpass, most of those I have just named. Admittedly, they are more obscure. Few have had a major success on Broadway. But that is more a condition of a faulty system than of their own intrinsic talents. Sam Shepard, for example, has contributed a body of plays—chief among them *Buried Child* and *True West*—that will stand comparison with virtually anything written in the last twenty years, though it is true that he spends less time writing these days than acting in such movies as *Baby Boom*. David Mamet—also a part-time Hollywood writer and director—is another major playwright of the period: *American Buffalo* and *Glen Garry Glen Ross* are masterpieces, but all of his plays come from the hand of a master. David Rabe's *Hurly Burly*—in its full-length version, not the truncated comic mechanism greased for the stage by Mike Nichols—can compete, in power and rage, with the late plays of O'Neill. Christopher Durang, a deadly scorpion with poison leeching into his writing hand, is one of the most powerful satirists our stage has ever seen. And Ronald Ribman continues to write with a surrealist bite and poetic penetration that make most of the domestic drama of the past look declarative, linear, and obvious.

Many other distinctive writers—Arthur Kopit, Craig Lucas, Howard Korder, David Ives, Tom Babe, Richard Nelson, Wendy Wasserstein, William Hauptman, Lanford Wilson, Eric Overmeyer, John Guare, August Wilson, Alfred Uhry, Harry Kondoleon, Alan Havis, David Henry Hwang, Marsha Norman, Wallace Shawn, Keith Reddin, A. H. Gurney, Charles Mee, Jr., dozens more—have all done redoubtable work. The numbers alone suggest that something unusual is happening, but the general intelligence and aspiration of their plays are the real measure. Because they so rarely have Broadway hits, few of these playwrights have been celebrated by the media, so their existence is not a significant fact in the public mind. But this may be why they continue to write with such obdurate intensity, with such astonishing unpredictability. Obscurity has advantages as well as disappointments, just as sudden fame can prove to be an enemy of promise—as it did with our more celebrated playwrights in the past, many of whom faltered in trying to repeat their early successes. Today's playwrights may not have as much chance as yesterday's to enjoy the rewards of American success. But they have a better shot at something more elusive and satisfying—to last the course with dignity, without exhausting their creative wills.

And most of them have found congenial directors—Jerry Zaks, Gregory Mosher, Ron Lagomarsino, Norman Rene—who mount their plays tastefully and faithfully, though the more interesting directors today are essentially auteurs who, following Peter Brook and Jerzy Grotowski, work best with material devised in concert with actors and dramaturges. The rise of the auteur director is another recent American theatrical phenomenon worthy of note—a movement that parallels, without often meeting, the movement in playwriting. The grandiose creations of Robert Wilson, just beginning to be recognized and appreciated in this country, though long celebrated in Europe, are among the most startling and original theater works ever devised by an American: *Einstein on the Beach*, created in collaboration with Philip Glass (a composer whose valuable contributions to the modern stage have yet to be measured); *Death and Destruction in Detroit*, parts 1 and 2; and above all, the monumental *The CIVIL warS*. These creations are making theatrical history at a time when the theater is no longer thought to have a history.

The work of Richard Foreman with the Ontological/Hysterical Theater, Lee Breuer and Joanne Akalaitis with Mabou Mines, Elizabeth LaCompte with the Wooster Group, Andrei Serban with a variety of theaters, Anne Bogart, Robert Woodruff, Peter Sellars, Des McAnuff, Julie Taymor, Ping Chong, and countless others—usually in collaboration with a cadre of gifted designers and composers and performance artists—testifies to an auteur vitality unique in our theater history. And with the probes of the dancer Martha Clarke into theatrical territory, in conjunction with the composer Richard Peaslee and the designer Robert Israel, the borders have been breached between theater and dance through such stunning creations as *The Garden of Earthly Delights*, though her subsequent works are admittedly less impressive. These artists, fighting for recognition and grants in our own country, have almost all been recognized in Europe and Asia as people who make our experimental theater the envy of the world—at the very moment when the funeral notices are being posted by our own critics and reviewers.

Two new departures should be noted: the growing interest of auteur directors in classical drama and, even more unexpected, new American plays. Lee Breuer was among the first to try his hand at such work, after experimenting with the short pieces of Beckett, first with his *Lulu* at the American Repertory Theatre (a compound of Wedekind's *Earth Spirit* and *Pandora's Box*), then with a controversial *Tempest* at the New York Shakespeare Festival, then with a modern adaptation of *Oedipus at Colonus*, adapted for gospel singers and retitled *The Gospel at Colonus*, and most recently, with a less successful deconstruction of *King Lear* with Ruth Malaczech in the title role. Joanne Akalaitis has also been working with texts, first from the modern period—with *Endgame* and *The Balcony* at the American Repertory Theatre—then with such classics as Buechner's *Leonce and Lena* and Genet's *The Screens* at the Guthrie, and then with Ford's *'Tis Pity She's a Whore* at the Goodman Theatre in Chicago. Also notable among recent auteur-driven classics are Richard Foreman's *Woyzeck* at the Hartford Stage and Robert Woodruff's *Baal* at Trinity Rep. A few seasons ago, I persuaded Robert Wilson to direct his first classical text—Euripides' *Alcestis*—preparatory to his work on the Gluck opera, *Alceste*. The results were strong enough to win a prize as best foreign production in France when the production traveled to the Festival D'Automne in Paris.

Andrei Serban, who has been working with classics all his creative life, undertook his first new American play some years ago—Ronald Ribman's *Sweet Table at the Richelieu* which, despite its idiosyncratic approach, the author declared the finest production his plays had ever had. In the same season, Richard Foreman turned for a moment from his own scenarios to direct a radical production of Arthur Kopit's *End of the World (With Symposium to Follow)*. These, along with other such ventures by experimental directors, while no doubt fraught with potential battles between authors and auteurs, promise to close up one of the few remaining gaps in our theater process—the once unbreachable division between living playwrights and independent directors.

Let me mention one more element in this new awakening—the public. Audiences, once either sleepy or pious before American efforts to create a serious theater, have suddenly come alive. There is a huge and growing following for the more radical artists in our midst, and once again, the audience at a play includes many young people who lend an air of freshness and vitality to the theater event. The New Wave Festival at BAM, featuring some of the most advanced art in the world, plays most of its performances to sold-out houses. And the American Repertory Theatre, in what is thought to be the rather staid and conservative area of Boston, has been playing almost to capacity with what are often considered difficult and challenging works. Not all experimental theaters can boast of similar success with the public. But it has become increasingly clear that those who keep faith with the audience's intelligence will ultimately win out with a little persistence. It is a far better gamble than cynicism or fear.

Two major problems remain for the American theater, one concerning actors, the other involving critics. Most American actors seem to have lost interest in the stage, and those that remain are riddled with uncertainty and self-doubt. All the pressures of our success-crazed society tell the actor he's a fool to remain with a profession that promises little money and less fame when those enticements are continually beckoning from LaLa Land. As a result, and with a great sense of sadness, the resident theater movement has watched some of its most gifted performers end up in a vapid TV series or, at best, a feature film, while the great stage roles go begging. What also goes begging is their creative spark in a meat market culture that values only their easily digestible personal qualities, and only for a moment, before they are left on the scrap heap, bemoaning the waste of spirit in an expense of shame.

And then there are those who evaluate our stage, leaving the only permanent record of an ephemeral art that disappears the moment the curtain falls. It may well be our critics and reviewers, a handful of honorable exceptions noted, who represent the major failure of contemporary American theater, though only history will be able to measure how much responsibility they bear for the lapses and failings of the art they continually belabor. For very few of our critics have adapted to the primary recent changes in our theater structure—its institutionalization and decentralization. The New York critics still remain largely in New York, where the structure is falling apart. And those few that travel, and even most of those who regularly work in other cities, still tend to evaluate production on a show-by-show basis, as if the resident theater were a commercial house with no identity of its own as an organic institution. As a result, most dedicated theater people feel they are laboring in a vacuum, which adds to their sense of frustration. How many theater critics are prepared to examine the relationship between one company production and another, or to admit they've seen a resident actor before in an entirely different kind of role, or to watch the development of a director, a playwright, a designer in a sequence of creations, or to prod a theater that seems to be failing its own declared purposes? No, the repertory critics who would spur the new movement—whose aesthetics and energies are tied to an entirely different form of alternative theater—have not materialized in any significant numbers, and, as a result, the American stage is currently being evaluated on the basis of minimal evidence and false cues.

Still, as I said, a large and growing public exists for the kind of work that I have been trying to describe, and that gives strength to us in difficult times. The public may be slow in responding to new developments, but with a little courage and patience on the parts of theater boards, audience members eventually come around. They must. For it is in the memory of the public that any lasting theatrical achievement will be recorded until that time when critics and reviewers again assume their full responsibilities to this provisional art.

The Seagull: Art and Love, Love and Art

Richard Gilman

ome preliminary notes, ideas, observations, questions, and reminders for an essay on the play.

Its title is the most nearly symbolic of those for any Chekhov play, but like its closest rival, *The Cherry Orchard*'s trees, the bird isn't symbolic in any pseudo-poetic or anxious way.

The chief "subjects" are art and love, never far from each other thematically. Or perhaps a better way of putting this is in the form of questions: What does it mean to be in love? What does it mean to be an artist? And to be both in love and an artist?

This is Chekhov's first play that doesn't have a dominant figure, a protagonist whose fate, and our interest in it, dwarfs all others, and so it is the first thoroughly to disperse action and sentience among a considerable number of people of whom, in this instance, four can be thought of as major characters, dramatically equal—four protagonists, then.

Though it ends with the suicide of one of the main characters, Chekhov made a point of calling it a "comedy."

Its architectonics or musical structure is easily discernible, more sure-handedly laid out than in *Ivanov*, yet not so finely balanced as this mode of composition will become in the three plays that will follow. Another artistic advance over *Ivanov* is that the earlier play's melodramatic disfigurations are mostly gone.

Some commentators on the play, including Vladimir Nabokov, have chosen to dwell on the things they think faulty. Ronald Hingley, Chekhov's biographer and translator, perversely considers it inferior to *Ivanov*.

In his pioneering but now rather out-of-date study, David Magarshack accounted for Chekhov's arrival at artistic maturity in *The Seagull* by drawing a distinction between his earlier "scientific" approach to writing and a new spirit of human concern, and an even more important distinction between his old method of "direct" action and a new "indirect" composition. How useful are these distinctions now? Do they go far enough, or too far?

I think the reigning spirit of *The Seagull* is anti-romanticism.

To write about any Chekhov play is to risk going off on digressions, the homeopathic reason for this, or the imitative fallacy involved, being his own digressive procedures, his continual deviations from an expected narrative line. Is the temptation to wander off on side trips especially strong when writing about *The Seagull*? One reason it may be is just its relationship to the previous and ensuing plays: this one is so full of ripening method, archetypal situation, that you want to use those things to illuminate the whole of Chekhov's theater. Not that *The Seagull* doesn't have its own substantiality, independence, and artistic specificity; but as a storehouse of things to come it continually presses you to think ahead.

Another reason for the mind's being led afield by Chekhov is the way his writing so often suggests so much more than it directly says. All good writing does this, of course, but in his case the unstated is especially rich. You want to hunt his implications down, his very reticence setting in motion the loosening of your own tongue.

I'll save the question of the title until near the end of this essay, since by then the text, after being explored and meditated upon, should have something to say about its name. I'll look now at the words Chekhov used to describe the play, "A Comedy in Four Acts." We can be sure that he knew exactly what he was doing, for he chose the subtitle with the same care he exercised on all the others. *Ivanov* is a "Play," *Uncle Vanya* is "Scenes from Country Life," *Three Sisters* is a "Drama," and *The Cherry Orchard* is another "Comedy."

All these terms or, in the case of *Vanya*, descriptive phrases, are to one degree or another tactical alerts. In effect, they tell us not to bring preconceptions about types of drama to these works; they ask us to be supple in the way we wield artistic categories and to be open in our anticipations. The extreme flatness and neutrality of "Scenes from Country Life," for example, have an ironical quality in light of the text, which is scarcely a pastoral idyll, but they also warn us not to expect or look for a "high" theatrical experience, one that will induce in us what we think of as classical pity and terror. On another level, the subtitles indicate the relationship of the plays to one another in Chekhov's mind: lighter, graver, more subject to misreading, less so, and so on.

The most notorious instance of his gentle advice being ignored was Stanislavski's staging of the 1904 premiere of *The Cherry Orchard* at the Moscow Art Theater. I'll take this up again, but for now it should be noted that Stanislavski was a most serious man; his own writings and the accounts of others tell us that wit and humor weren't his strong points. And so he directed Chekhov's last play as something of a tragedy, the Russian term for which translates as "heavy drama." Like a number of directors after him, and performers and critics for that matter, Stanislavski wasn't able to see that for all the losses some of its characters sustain, *The Cherry Orchard* isn't heavy at all but powerfully light, a heartening gesture of freedom. It isn't too much to think of it as rather like Chekhov's *Tempest*.

In much the same way, *The Seagull* is also a comedy, not in spite of the suicide and other painful events but, in a quietly original way that at the same time has classical precedents, in part because of them. To discuss that now would be to run far ahead of myself but to talk more generally about "comedy" as a designation for a work it might not seem to fit wouldn't be inappropriate. And so a digression.

The two towering examples that come immediately to mind are *La divina commedia* and *Le comedie humaine*. In both cases, the word "comedy" clearly isn't being used to denote a conventional genre or to describe the main substance of the works; both, after all, enclose more than enough suffering, death, evil, and other decidedly unfunny goings-on. Instead, it points to or controls a final, governing response. The word "comedy" suggests the answer to these questions: What is our state of mind or spirit after we finish these works? How are we to understand them, to "take" them, as we like to say?

With Dante the matter is comparatively clear. Because the movement of the great poem is from despair to rejoicing, hell to heaven, it ends happily, that much is obvious. Not so obvious, we might think, is why this outcome should earn for the whole work the term "comedy." It does because such is the morale, the lasting attitude, wrung from the entire arduous yet successful journey "upward," that Dante has toward his creation and we are meant to share.

For beyond its ordinary function of making us laugh or smile, comedy has a wider, deeper action, as Shakespeare's comedies make evident: to restore, to heal, to embolden. Just as there are "thoughts that lie too deep for tears," so there are those that lie beyond the relative simplicity of laughter. Comedy in Dante's universe is a lightness retroactively at work for those who qualify, the potentially saved (and, by analogy, for nonbelievers of good will, as Eliot pointed out); it's a relief from spiritual anxiety, a reminder of redemption, a restoration and a new existence of hope; it's God's difficult yet loving "joke."

Balzac uses the word in a different, much more problematic sense, deliberately and more than half-mockingly adapting his title from Dante yet in the end retaining something of the poet's meaning. The new title suggests a God-like perspective, with the novelist's eye replacing the divinity's omniscience. In this secular world, life is "comic" in a negative sense because it lacks the dignity of tragedy as well as the metaphysics to sustain a tragic view, and in a positive sense, which is to say one it *does* deserve, because it contains its own principle of redemption.

Forever defeating itself, like a haplessly suffering circus clown, Balzac's "comedy" roughly resembles what we call a "comedy of errors," rather more grave and consequential than is customary in such a genre, no doubt, but still full of endless deviations from or betrayals of the ideal, perpetual failures of understanding, slipups, cross-purposes, and gaffes—some of them, to be sure, fatal ones. But though it may be a comedy we sigh over, a "black" farce at times, and though some of its humor may be of the gallows variety, it isn't in the end conducive to despair.

The imaginative act has intervened. Simply to *see* this roiling series of mistakes, miscalculations, and failings, this burlesque of the ideal, to observe its inexhaustible variety—comedy is always much more multifarious than tragedy—and organize all that in the creating mind as a sort of failed *Divine Comedy*, is to bring, paradoxically enough, some of the relief Dante gives us. It's to offer hope through perception, a "cure" through the description of the disease. Even the darkest moments in Balzac, the particular novels or events that recoil most strongly from being called comic, take their places in the general easing of anxiety which occurs whenever experience is recovered from shapelessness and made less inexplicable.

Chekhov, it goes without saying, is much closer to Balzac than to Dante. Like the French writer, he hasn't any religious convictions that can make for comedy in a sublime sense, he isn't dealing in salvation. Like Balzac, he gives us nothing that resembles a conventionally "happy ending" either. But Chekhov has an even more wry and rueful appreciation of human frailty and folly, and he is far less disposed to draw moral conclusions—he isn't disposed that way at all—or to impose his own views. He doesn't try to substitute for God, as Balzac often seems to be doing, nor does he wish to extend his artistic dominion over *everything*. His comedies aren't part of any broad "canvas," but are instead the products of alternations in his moods or particular visions.

When Chekhov is engaged in writing a comedy, the situations he invents receive their identifying energy and shape from his sense that something can be done about them; they remain open, not yet determined. The comedic aspect of *The Seagull*, as of *The Cherry Orchard*, lies, then, in Chekhov's attitude toward the situations he describes, not in the literal series of events or despite any of them. This is so obviously true that I hesitate to make anything of it. Yet misunderstandings of such matters abound, especially in regard to Chekhov, whose "subject matter" is so often seen to dictate his manner, instead of the other way round.

Attitude shows itself, of course, not declaratively but in structure, design, and tone. One thing we see in *The Seagull* is that Chekhov constantly deflects matters away from being taken too seriously, which in this context means either tragically or in too absolute a way. This is so even in the plays he didn't call comedies, such as *Ivanov*. In the more "serious" works the openness remains, if not the physical way out.

The resulting "lightness" in the noncomedies is nothing like a diminution of seriousness, and in the comedies nothing like frivolity. In their different ways both kinds of drama offer us something like breathing room, space in which we can maneuver, take emotional or intellectual steps of our own, set matters in order, compare, *recognize*. All this is an act of freedom from what deconstructionists would call a programmed response. As a corollary of this, or its executive means, Chekhov's tone in *The Seagull* is either bantering or matter-of-fact, never somber. He'd enjoyed writing the play, he said, something rather rare for him, and the pleasure permeates the text.

In a much-quoted letter of 21 October 1895, Chekhov wrote to Alexie Suvorin that he was at work on a new long play, his first since *The Wood-Demon* of six years earlier. In the interim he had several times expressed his disgust with the condition of the theater in Russia—"We must strive with all our power to see to it that the stage passes out of the hands of the grocers and into literary hands, otherwise the theater is doomed"—yet he had also given voice to those by now familiar doubts as to his own talent for writing plays. But he told his friend and publisher: "I can't say I'm not enjoying writing it, though [*because* would have been more nearly true] I'm flagrantly disregarding the basic tenets of the stage. The comedy has three female roles, six male roles, four acts, a landscape (a view of a lake,) much conversation about literature, little action and five tons of love."

He had some way to go before he finished, but *The Seagull* would turn out to be almost exactly as he had described it, with the addition of a fourth, minor female character and rather more action than he had suggested.

Chekhov wasn't exaggerating the weight of love in *The Seagull*. It announces itself almost immediately and by the end of the first act a character will remark, "What a state they're in and what a lot of loving." Indeed, what a cross-hatching of amorous relationships and would-be ones, too! He wasn't overstating, either, the prominence of what he had called "conversation about literature." Actually, the conversation—and not just that but also monologues, interjections, spoken thoughts, and private murmurings—is about fiction and writing it, plays and writing them, the state of the theater, the nature and profession of acting and, most widely, the life of both art and the artist.

The Seagull, then, is a play, a comedy, largely "about" art and love, creation and the erotic. I put "about" in quotation marks to make what I think is an important point, the one Beckett was making when he said of Joyce that "he is not writing about something, he is writing something." This is to say, the subjects of imaginative literature, in which I include plays as texts (and also in performance, though that's another question) don't exist independently of the writing itself. They're not like prey waiting to be pounced upon by a verbally gifted hunter, or seedy rooms needing to be refurbished by a painter in words. In turn, writing isn't the expression or treatment of a preexisting reality but an act that discovers and gives life to a "subject" within itself.

Ibsen once said that "I have never written because I had, as they say, a 'good subject'" but out of "lived-through" experience. And Picasso, to turn to another art to which Beckett's observation is every bit as pertinent, said once, "Je ne cherche pas, je trouve." By which he certainly didn't mean that he found things to paint—just imagine him coming upon a woman with three noses or legs like giant sausages and crying "Aha!"—but aesthetic reality of a visual order in the making of the painting.

Following on this, *The Seagull* is about art and love not in the sense that they are its topics so much as that the entire play quite literally surrounds them, providing those abstractions with the dramatic context or field in which they can come to life, working themselves out as motifs, or maybe it would be more useful to think of them as something like "notional presences," ideas attached to bodies. Chekhov takes art and love *into* his writing, turning them from their disembodied state into dramatic energies. These are then deployed throughout the play, and in the process art and love necessarily assume new identities, since they are not being written about but written. This is what happens whenever we encounter something in an imaginative work and say, I never saw it that way before; you couldn't have because it wasn't *that way* before.

But this isn't all of it. What his characters say or think about love or art has to be revelatory of what they are, of their natures, not discrete attitudes or a series of opinions (though having more opinions than passion is itself a revelation of character)—which is to say that themes have to be active, incarnate, endowed with physiognomies, or else they plague us as inert thought.

Who are these characters in so many of whom love or art has lodged or taken over like an infection? An anatomy of the dramatis personae might be in order here.

Irina Arkadina is a famous or at least well-known actress, vain, voluble, a "foolish, mendacious, self-admiring egoist," Chekhov said about her, which might be just a little strong; she's concerned about her son, Constantin Treplev, yet constantly forgetful of him or actively hostile, and she's in love with her companion, Boris Trigorin. Constantin is in his early twenties, starting out as a playwright and writer of fiction; he's self-absorbed and self-pitying, with, one suspects, something of an Oedipal fixation on his mother, and he's romantically in love with Nina Zarechny.

Trigorin is a very famous writer, possibly modeled on someone Chekhov knew, absorbed in his craft but indifferent to his celebrity; an essentially selfish man, he'll leave Arkadina for a while when he falls in love with Nina. She's an aspiring actress, sensitive, warm, impulsive, someone we might in today's debased vocabulary call "vulnerable"; she's in love with Constantin at first, then succumbs temporarily to Trigorin.

These are the four principals. It's interesting to note that all are actively in love and all are practicing artists in one way or another.

A few degrees below them in significant presence are Peter Sorin and Eugene Dorn. Sorin is Arkadina's brother, a retired civil servant, self-deprecating, genial yet fussily melancholy over the onset of old age; he's somewhat reminiscent of Shabelsky in *Ivanov* and a characterological ancestor of Gayev in *The Cherry Orchard*. Dorn is one of the four doctors in Chekhov's major plays (only *The Cherry Orchard* lacks one); an intelligent, wryly skeptical man with a lyrical streak tempered by a mild philosophical bent, he might be considered the only "balanced" person in the play.

The four other characters occupy with varying bulk the remainder of the dramatic space. We can think of them as participants in subplots or lesser agencies for the working out of perception, but they're never simply functional, like the servants, guards, messengers, and the like, of classical drama. Ilya Shamrayev, Sorin's estate manager, is a brusque, officious, somewhat despotic man and the only character apart from Sorin who isn't either in love or the object of someone else's carnal, or at least amorous desire. His daughter Masha is an intelligent self-dramatizing young woman hopelessly in love with Constantin, and her mother, Polina, is an efficient, loyal family retainer lifted from a merely functional status by being unrequitedly in love with Dorn. And Simon Medvedenko, a schoolmaster both pedantic and long-suffering, pathetically desires Masha, who treats him contemptuously for his pains (though she'll later, with unchanged contempt, agree to marry him); he is a direct forerunner of Kulygin in *Three Sisters*.

The setting for the comedy they enact, Sorin's estate in the country, is similar to those for all of Chekhov's major plays with the apparent exception of *Three Sisters*, which has an urban milieu; still, it's linked to the other mise-en-scènes by the extreme provincial dullness of the town. These settings provide Chekhov with dramatic conditions, or conditions for a drama, that wholly suit his artistic intentions, and so irresistibly compel a digression at this point.

The places are isolated, at a distance from the hurly-burly and multiple distractions of big cities, from "culture," careers, formal amusements, professional entanglements, politics, ideas, the sway and clutch of complicated, often abstract associations. In his long story "The Duel" Chekhov has a character "stuck" in the Caucasus and ardently, if a bit journalistically, longing for the pleasures of Moscow and St. Petersburg. People in those places, he thinks, "discuss trade, new singers, Franco-Prussian accord. Everywhere life is vigorous, cultured, intelligent, brimming with energy." And then of course we will hear the Prozorov sisters' repeated "Moscow! To Moscow!"

In the deprived country settings the characters are pressed back on themselves and on each other, including those who—like Arkadina,

Trigorin and, at the end, Nina of *The Seagull*, Ranevskaya and some of her extended family of *The Cherry Orchard*, and the Prozorovs and Vershinin of *Sisters*—have known or will come to know what the larger world, the "great" world is like. In his two comedies Chekhov offers relief from the narrowness of provincial or rural life—this is one reason they're comedies—but even so the alternative is given to us offstage, talked about, offered as a possibility but not lived visibly on the stage.

On these isolated estates people gaze, speak, gesture, kiss, think, and weep in a severely limited atmosphere. They're enclosed in an enclave, tiny, burdensomely self-sufficient, stifling at times yet also, for the purposes of Chekhov's art, in a very special way "pure," reduced to essentials. They are far from the vast sprawling human country whose distant voices they hear, speaking of another, richer life. And they're where they are because Chekhov has put them there, by design, to exist in one kind of play rather than another, not, as those who see him fundamentally as a social observer think, because he looked around and found a fitting object in these "deprived" lives for his famous brooding, pitying, humane, and mournful glance.

In the way he *chooses* to circumscribe his characters' situations he is closer to Beckett than to any of his contemporaries, or to any other Russian writer for that matter; Gorky put many of his people in a romanticized poverty, Turgenev in an elegant rusticity. The restricted circumstances Beckett and Chekhov fashion for their plays resemble one another beneath their enormous physical differences, and the artistic purpose of this confinement is much the same for both.

In their plays—so much straitening, so much absence. In *Endgame* as in *Uncle Vanya*, in *Waiting for Godot* as in *Three Sisters*, the inescapable fact is that there's nothing much to *do*. Beckett's plays are of course far more radically denuded than Chekhov's, though certainly not on that account better, but the surprisingly dramatic result of the scarcity and want in both playwrights' invented lives, so unpropitious for drama, one would think, is nearly the same.

For what *is* done is closer to fundamental life than the seductions toward activity, toward choice and mobility as the very essence of meaningful existence, ever allow us to come in the conventional theater or to see in our own lives. Deprived of distractions, having to rely on their own primitive or sadly provincial ones—all that keeping "the ball rolling" or fussing with the bag in Beckett, all those card or lotto games or musical evenings in Chekhov—bereft of the consolations of staying *busy*, on the road neither to fulfillment, that fictive aim or shibboleth, nor to wisdom, nor even in most cases understanding: all of Beckett's characters and nearly all of Chekhov's are reduced to the essential tasks of getting through the days and nights, making their way, with what is left to them, through time. Once again, we remember that in the comedies more is left to them, but even so such a residue is on hold, so to speak, for the future, which in both dramatists, for highly significant reasons, has no status, is simply a fiction.

And then, or rather along with this they go off in that quintessential human way of holding back the darkness: they talk; they tell their lives; they ad lib their hopes, joys, and sorrows, creating their fates in language as they go, and our recognition of their fates. These outwardly minimal existences come to us with all the freshness, peculiar as the word may sound in this context, of the root, the way it is at bottom, Beckett's *comme c'est ça*.

And so the characters of *The Seagull* talk. Naturally, there are physical events too, but nearly all the decisive ones take place offstage. This is one of the things Chekhov meant when he spoke of consciously ignoring the fundamental tenets of the stage, and is at the center of David Magarshack's argument about Chekhov's emergent mastery. The subject is so dense and important that I'm tempted to go off on another digression to pursue it, but I'll content myself with simply saying here that among the theatrical principles (pieties, we might better call them) Chekhov was challenging was the notion that offstage is only for things that for reasons of propriety or mechanical difficulty can't be shown directly. In Greek and Roman drama, of course, important events took place offstage, as well as in Shakespeare and other classics, but for a long time offstage had been chiefly where the stagehands waited.

As he does in every one of his full-length plays after *Ivanov*, Chekhov quickly brings on all the persons of the drama. From *The Seagull* on, no play will fail to introduce everyone of any significance—which is to say nearly everyone, since almost no character, however "minor," lacks dramatic weight—within the first few minutes. The strategic point of this is that it works against the linear or accumulating movement of the usual play. Nobody will come onstage later, bringing important news or actively furthering developments and so extending a line of more or less strictly unfolding narrative. The quietly revolutionary effect of this is that the characters take their places almost like players in a game such as soccer, occupying a field and ready for what will happen.

The very first stage direction informs us that art, in the form of theater itself in this opening scene, is going to figure in *The Seagull*. Setting the scene, Chekhov writes of "a rough stage put up for an amateur performance" and of "workmen . . . hammering and coughing . . . behind the drawn curtain." Then in the first lines of dialogue "love" also makes its appearance, in intimate (if a little ludicrous) connection to art.

Medvedenko and Masha are onstage; he tells her that "Nina Zarechny will act in it [the play for which the crude stage has been set up] and Constantin Treplev wrote it. They're in love and this evening they'll be spiritually united in the effort to present a unified work of art." After this banality, he goes on to complain that unlike Nina and Constantin he and Masha aren't "soul-mates at all." Masha has a moment earlier indicated her own lovesickness in the play's wonderful second line, the dourly cryptic "I'm in mourning for my life," after Medvedenko's opening, "Why do you always wear black?"

After a few more exchanges they're soon joined by all the other characters, who lay out for us, offhandedly and in some respects unconsciously, most of their ruling qualities and idiosyncracies, as well as what binds them factually and emotionally to one another. Little signatures show themselves—Sorin's self-deprecating laugh and his finishing his remarks with "and so on" or "stands to reason," Dorn's bemused singing of snatches of songs—the kinds of things that so unaccountably irritated Nabokov. And we hear the first mention of the bird in the title when Nina says that she feels drawn to the lake as though she were a seagull.

They've gathered for the performance of Constantin's play. They're mostly in an amiable mood, except for Masha, who's almost never amiable, Constantin, who's nervous, and Arkadina, who's clearly disgruntled by her son's having dared to step onto her territory. "When does the *thing* [italics mine] start?" she asks, and then breaks out in a pointed declamation from Shakespeare—"O Hamlet, speak no more . . ."—to which Constantin replies with another speech from Hamlet that in the most literary way reveals his Oedipal rivalry with Trigorin (he's already revealed his envy of him as a writer): "Nay, but to live in the rank sweat of an enseamèd bed."

The inner play begins with a prologue by Constantin, who "loudly" orates: "O ye ancient, hallowed shades that float above this lake at night." The curtain parts to reveal Nina, in white, sitting on a rock. "Men, lions, eagles and partridges, horned deer, geese, spiders and silent fishes," she begins, launching into a long futuristic monologue that speaks of a time when everything in the world is dead except for some vague spirit that will do battle with the Devil and, victorious, will establish the "reign of cosmic will" and harmony.

The "experimental rubbish," as Arkadina so cruelly yet not without reason will call it, suggests the worst of German expressionist drama of a generation later, in its whole tone and in lines like "That World Spirit am I. I." Still, it does give some evidence of anarchic talent and urgent ambition, and this, rather than any reasoned scornfulness, lies behind Arkadina's gibes, so jealous is she of what she considers her own fiefdom. After she's interrupted Nina several times, Constantin abruptly stops the performance, saying bitterly, "I'm extremely sorry, I forgot that writing plays and acting are only for the chosen few."

In a generally most perceptive essay on *The Seagull*, Robert Louis Jackson makes an ingenious case for Constantin's play as highly significant in its own right. He offers a detailed reading of it in terms of a creation myth, a metaphor for the artist's journey and a disguised Oedipal confession, and then extends his findings beyond their source and into the main text. I owe a great deal to Jackson's other ideas and will have occasion to draw on them in this essay, but I think he makes too much of this one.

Whatever the literary motifs of Constantin's play, they seem to me less important in themselves than what, among other things, they tell us about Constantin, which, to be sure, Jackson partly acknowledges. Yet in his eagerness to use the little play to shed light on the larger one, he pushes his interpretation too far, overloading a relatively uncomplicated if subtle comedy with abstract ideas and in the process losing sight of a concrete function of the inner play, which, as I see it, is to set going talk about art and the artist. We can be sure that Chekhov didn't provide Constantin with any old overblown piece of writing because he wanted to discredit him, but he didn't give him such an arcane and ponderously philosophic one as Jackson thinks either.

The talk set in motion by the inner play, Chekhov's "conversation about literature," which as I said earlier is about other things too, begins even before the aborted performance. "Your play's hard to act," Nina tells Constantin as they wait for the others to take their places. "There are no living people in it." "Living people!" Constantin explodes. "We should show life neither as it is nor as it ought to be but as we see it in our dreams." Nina calmly ignores this, going on to say, "There's not much action, it's just a lot of speeches. I think a play really needs a love interest."

The exchange tells us a good deal about where they are in relation to their art at this point and obliquely suggests their eventual destinies in the comedy. Constantin's ideas are vague, soft, *inexperienced*, a young man's aesthetic, and they're peculiarly belligerent. He'll drop the "program" later on, but he'll do so for tactical reasons, not out of conviction, when he turns into a technician in the fiction he comes to write. Still, he won't overcome the absence of life from his work, and by continually trying to justify his writing on one basis or another, usually by attacking other people's, he reveals something dangerously defensive, polemical, and theoretical in his approach to art.

As for Nina, she's basically right in her criticism but she too betrays a weakness, provisional in her case; her remark about a play needing "love interest" indicates that she's not yet a serious artist but is in the preliminary phase of being stagestruck. We should notice that in a delicious piece of irony Chekhov has written her into a play with an abundance of love interest, only of a kind and with dramatic implications as far as they can be from what she means here.

Constantin's play provokes other responses besides Nina's and

Arkadina's, and each provides a little revelation of character. Trigorin is neutral, evasive in his "everyone writes what he likes as best he can," and Medvedenko adds to his reputation for boring pedantry with "No one has the right to separate Spirit from Matter, since Spirit itself may well be. . . ." Dorn's surprising approval—"I liked the play. It has something"—can be ascribed to his usual kindness but is better explained by his confession to Constantin after praising him that if "I'd ever experienced the uplift that an artist feels when he's creating I think I'd have taken wing and soared into the sky." And the play also inspires Sorin to admit to having in his youth dreamed of being a writer.

Understandably, the talk about art and the artist has as its chief participants Constantin, Arkadina, Trigorin, and, with especially great consequence at the end, Nina. They are the artists and each has something to elucidate, press for, or defend. In everything they say we can feel Chekhov's presence, beyond the obvious sense of his having written the dialogue; the points of view and attitudes he presents touch, often intimately, on his own concerns as a writer. He doesn't necessarily endorse any of them, he clearly disapproves of some, but he anchors the "debate" in animate personalities who have a stake in its outcome, and so keeps it from becoming abstract.

As we would expect, Constantin is most vociferous. Besides the conversation with Nina before his play begins, he also talks to Sorin about his mother and the theater, the two "topics" merging into one argument. "She adores the stage," he says, "serving humanity in the sacred cause of art, that's how she thinks of it. But the theater's in a rut nowadays. . . . [T]hese geniuses, these high priests of art . . . out of mediocre scenes and lines they try to drag a moral, some commonplace that doesn't tax the brain . . . a thousand variations on the same old theme."

To this point his views would certainly have been echoed by Chekhov (except for the note of envy they contain), as would his remark that "What we need's a new kind of theater." But when he adds, "New forms are what we need, and if we haven't got them we'd be . . . better off with nothing," an alarm goes off.

As we know, Chekhov never spoke of "new forms." He wanted changed morale, a theater of truthfulness and resiliency instead of dead mechanics, but he never consciously or avowedly aspired to technical change or pursued it as an end in itself, as Constantin seems to do. When Trigorin says of him that "he frets, fusses and crusades for new artistic forms," the verbs suggest that Constantin's quest for originality has something inorganic and inauthentic about it, simply because it's a mission too conscious by far.

At the end of the play, after he's achieved an empty success as a writer of fiction, Constantin will partly recognize his own condition. "I've talked so much about new techniques," he tells himself, "but now I feel I'm . . . getting in the old rut." He unhappily ponders Trigorin's "easy" methods for a while, quoting some images from one of Trigorin's stories that are actually from a Chekhov story, *Wolf*, comparing them to his own stressful, slick, and brittle style (qualities we identify from his own and others' comments), then says: "This agony. (Pause.) Yes, I'm more and more convinced that old or new techniques are neither here nor there. The thing is to write without thinking about technique—write from the heart, because then it all comes pouring out."

Chekhov isn't advocating, through Constantin, any naive or primitive aesthetic; he's not saying, "The hell with how you write, it's *what* you write that counts." But for him technique was always in the service of vision and experience, not the other way round, just as originality was a possible outcome, never a goal. Constantin's "agony" is spiritual, not the result of wrong methods. Dorn, who admires him, says near the end, "I'm only sorry he has no definite aims [the exact words Chekhov had earlier used about Constantin in his notes; for "aims" we can read "intentions beyond the ego"]. He produces an effect, that's all, and mere effects don't get you . . . far." Trigorin sums it up: "None of his characters is ever really alive." A most subtle point Chekhov is making about Constantin is that *ideas* don't guarantee anything.

Trigorin talks even more about writing than does Constantin but never aggressively and never as a matter of theory. Quite the contrary: in the play's longest speeches he tells Nina about the writer's, or artist's, life, countering her breathlessly romantic notions of what it must be like with prosaic, deflating comments. When she speaks of "fascinating, brilliant lives full of meaning" he replies, "Sorry, but this nice talk only reminds me of boiled sweets—something I never eat." When she insists that his life must be "marvelous" he says, "What's so nice about it?" and goes on to tell her that writing for him is compulsive, not inspired. "I'm always writing, never stop, can't help it. What's wonderful and brilliant about that?"

In her infatuation with him or at least as much with the life he seems to inhabit, Nina continues to press him. When he keeps denying that his vocation is glamorous she tells him, "You're simply spoiled by success." Trigorin's reply is crucial to an understanding of Chekhov's idea of the artist in *The Seagull*, as Nina's thoughts on the subject will also be at the end. "What success?" he asks. "I'm never satisfied myself. I dislike my own work. I drift around in a trance and often can't make sense of what I write."

The words may not represent Chekhov's feeling in every respect, but the self-critical position does, as we know from his repeated expressions of it. He once wrote in his notebook that "Dissatisfaction with oneself is one of the foundation stones of every true talent" and this, among other things, is what distinguishes Trigorin from Constantin, whose later self-depreciation is a matter of injured ego, not creative modesty. Moreover, Trigorin's scoffing at Nina's idea of success—acclaim by the world—echoes Chekhov's often-expressed and passionately held opinion that, defined this way, success is more than contemptible. Though he wasn't without a reasonable interest in his own reputation, he hated the sort of celebrity that produced followers, a cult. In 1898, at a low point in his morale, he wrote to Lydia Avilova, an erstwhile fiction writer who was in love with him, that "what disgusts me so much is not the writing itself as the literary entourage from which it is impossible to escape."

There are other connections between Trigorin and Chekhov. Trigorin tells Nina, for example, that early in his career as a playwright he was afraid of the public: "When I put on a new play, I always felt the dark-haired people in the audience were against me, while the fair-haired ones didn't care either way." We are immediately reminded of Chekhov's letter to Suvorin in which he says that before performances of *Ivanov* he was sure that "the dark-haired men" among the onlookers would be "hostile." None of this is to say that Trigorin is Chekhov's alter ego; there are important differences, but the connections are clear.

If Trigorin isn't an egotist about his art, he's not free from one occupational disease of the writer, which is to exploit others for one's art. "I try to catch . . . every word you and I say," he tells Nina, "and quickly lock [them] in my literary storehouse because they might come in handy." And indeed we see him at this work of plucking what he calls the living "flowers" for imaginative use. Into his ever-present notebook go jottings about Masha—"Takes snuff. Drinks vodka. Always wears black. Loved by schoolmaster"—and Nina too: "A plot for a short story," about her and a seagull, he says of one note she sees him making.

Dangerous as it is to interpolate from a writer's life to the work, it seems justified in this case. On several occasions, most notably concerning a short story of 1891, "The Butterfly," Chekhov was accused of having exploited for literary purposes some embarrassing facts about friends of his. He denied any conscious intention and there is no reason not to believe him, but the matter must have remained vaguely oppressive. We're put in mind of how Ibsen tried to expiate in his last plays his guilt for having "sacrificed" to his art the people closest to him. While Chekhov is nowhere near such moral anguish, he does, I think, render Trigorin in part as a cautionary figure and a delegate from his own conscience.

Arkadina doesn't talk so much about art as about the artist—herself. Chekhov called her an "egoist," and many touches contribute to a portrait of the actress as Narcissus. We've seen her attack her son for his own artistic ambitions; later she'll announce that she's never read his published stories, "never have time." In their famous quarrel, as she bandages his self-inflicted head wound, she calls him a "pretentious nobody" and he in turn calls her a "hack." Constantin's epithet is rather more accurate. Fame, éclat, position are what his mother wants. When she does speak about acting it's to call attention to her successes: "I had such a reception in Kharkov. . . . I'm still dizzy. . . . I was superbly turned out."

There's fine irony and splendidly deft characterization in her re-action to a Maupassant story they've been reading aloud at the beginning of act 2. Arkadina reads from *On the Water*: "Writers are very popular. So when a woman's marked one down for capture, she keeps on at him, flattering him, being nice to him and spoiling him." She breaks off reading to say, "Well, the French may be like that, but we're different"; then she reads some more lines to herself and tells Nina, "Oh well, the rest's dull and unconvincing."

She speaks highly of Trigorin's stories but we suspect she hasn't read them, having instead "captured" him and his name. She's a miser who gives three servants a ruble to split among themselves; she's a prima donna in almost every respect. But though she clearly incarnates Chekhov's deep dislike for the artist or practitioner consumed by self, something a little more positive about her escapes his authorial vigilance. She does love her brother and, in a besieged way, her son, and she encourages Nina to go on the stage. The point about these things is that she should never be played on a single strident note. She isn't a villain but the occupant of one end of a spectrum covering the variations of selves as they engage with art and love, the way Nina stands at the other end.

Nina. I wrote earlier of how she begins as stagestruck and of her infatuation with some presumedly thrilling artistic life. As an aspect of that, we see her also as "star-struck." When Shamrayev rudely tells Arkadina that no horses are available to take her to the station, Nina says to Polina: "Imagine saying no to a famous actress. . . . Her slightest wish, her merest whim . . . surely they're more important than your entire farm." The evolution, or education, that carries her far past these immature conditions of mind and spirit lies behind Chekhov's having written, "To me, Nina's part is everything in the play." I have to defer my consideration of how this "everything" accumulates and decisively asserts itself, until we have the rest of *The Seagull*'s substance in our grasp.

If we were to imagine a piece of music inspired by some aspect of *The Seagull* a likely one might be called "The Love Variations" or maybe, borrowing from Bach, "Chaconne for Violin Solo on an Amorous Theme." "Five tons of love," Chekhov jestingly said the play contained, but of course the real point isn't such undifferentiated heft but the diversity and intermeshings. In that last regard there are moments when we're reminded of Arthur Schnitzler's *Reigen* or, as it's better known to us, *La ronde*, written five years later out of a very different, far narrower sensibility and idea but somewhat resembling Chekhov's play in the way its characters link up in a chain of carnality or carnal aspiration, as well as romantic longing.

I'll begin with the lesser characters' longings, all of them, as it happens, unconsummated. I say "as it happens," but Chekhov never lets things simply happen; he is always and wholly the deliberate artist. Not to have your desires fulfilled is as instructive and dramatic as to attain satisfaction, especially in light of the fact that for the major characters satisfaction is always partial, temporary, or fugitive. What love *doesn't* bring or do is a central "action" of *The Seagull*, and how it affects other aspects of life, most pointedly the morale of artistic practice, is another and even more important one.

Medvedenko loves Masha, Masha loves Constantin, Polina loves Dorn. None, in the old-fashioned sense, is requited and much of the play's lower level or integumentary buzz and hum of conversations and musings is made up of their sense of injury or deprivation. Medvedenko is the first to declare his emotion, to which Masha's response is, "Your loving me is all very touching but I can't love you back and that's that." Then, in a fine example of how Chekhov, beginning with *The Seagull*, will often have his characters change the subject whenever it threatens to become too ponderous—or, at times, too disturbing—she adds, "Have some snuff." Later, in despair over Constantin's indifference to her, she consents to marry Medvedenko, rationalizing her decision to Trigorin: "To be helplessly in love, just waiting, waiting for years. . . . [B]ut when I'm married I shan't bother about love."

She's lying or deceiving herself. When she does marry Medvedenko she continues to treat him with brutal scorn and keeps the torch burning for Constantin, to the point where Polina embarrassingly pleads with him to give her daughter "just a few kind looks." For her part Polina "imploringly" says to Dorn, "Eugene, dear, let me come and live with you, darling." Dorn, who earlier had made the remark about the "lot of loving" going on, tells her, "I'm fifty-five, it's too late . . . to change my life." The most skeptical of all the characters, as well as the least "involved," Dorn moves to deflect and disarm the passions swirling around him with bits of balladry, half-mocking commentary on the love-charged atmosphere: "Oh tell me not your young life's ruined" and "Oh, speak to her, you flowers."

These three minor characters in love aspire to an "other" as an agency of deliverance: Medvedenko from his material and emotional impoverishment and the lack of self-esteem his sententiousness masks; Polina from her unhappy marriage to the cold-spirited Shamrayev; Masha from the emptiness of life without a man she thinks equal to the high estimate she's made of her own worth—Medvedenko clearly doesn't fill the bill. And motivations or dispositions like these are present in the major characters, too, only with greater complication and weightier consequences.

Arkadina needs Trigorin for her own amour propre and as a shield against the loneliness or, more deeply, solipsism her selfish, brittle way of life creates. In turn, Trigorin stays placidly with her, out of what he calls his "spineless" nature (one way he doesn't resemble Chekhov) until his writer's quest for new "material" and his need for emotional replenishment encounter Nina. She begins by being in love with Constantin, mildly, as a kind of early habit, we suspect, then falls for Trigorin, who promises a glamorous new life. And Constantin needs Nina for reasons of ego as well as for a muse, a source of inspiration.

For all the characters-in-love the common condition is *need*. This sometimes displays itself directly but more often through speech whose excessiveness and rhetorical zeal betray a disjunction between feeling and fact, emotion and its object. I said at the beginning that the prevailing spirit of *The Seagull* is one of "anti-romanticism." This negative quality is grounded precisely on repeated expressions of romantic desire itself, flowery outbursts of oratory about the wonders of the *other* and dirges on love's absence. The characters lay bare their hearts and in so doing reveal their dreamy or febrile overvaluation of love.

Listen to the twittering eloquence of the love birds, along with some harsher notes:

Constantin on Nina: "I can't live without her. The very sound of her footsteps is so beautiful . . . entrancing creature, my vision of delight."

Masha on Constantin, talking to Dorn: "I'm so unhappy. No one, no one knows how I suffer [lays her head on his breast, softly]. I love Constantin."

Trigorin on Nina: "Young love, enchanting and magical love that sweeps you off your feet into a make-believe world." And to her: "You're so lovely . . . your wonderful eyes, your tender smile . . . your look of angelic purity."

Nina to Trigorin: "If you should ever need my life, then come and take it," a line from a short story, ostensibly his but actually from Chekhov's *The Neighbors*, which Nina has had engraved on a medallion. And to herself: "It's all a dream."

Arkadina to Trigorin: "My marvelous, splendid man . . . my delight, my pride, my joy. . . . If you leave me for one hour I shan't survive, I shall go mad."

A few notes on these urgencies and avowals. One of Chekhov's purposes throughout his writing is to expose or, if that's too harsh, to bring out the ways we fashion our feelings out of culture, articulating them along literary—that is to say, borrowed—lines. Constantin's "I can't live without her" is just such an appropriation; the point is we *do* or ought to be able to live without her or him if necessary, and in the way *The Seagull* unfolds this will become part of a cautionary tale.

The line on the medallion Nina gives Trigorin, from Chekhov's story *The Neighbors*, was actually engraved on a medallion by Lydia Avlova; on the back were the words "Short Stories by A. Chekhov." Avlova evidently hoped to stir his passion but Chekhov wasn't to be moved by literary solicitations, not even of his own authorship.

Those two themes or motifs or subjects—better to go back to a term I coined earlier, "notional presences"—begin to converge as the play moves toward its close. In a brilliant stroke of dramatic imagination, Chekhov prepares the way for the final fusion of these presences—the confrontation at the end between Nina and Constantin—by having some central elements of the narrative occur offstage.

At the end of act 3, which closes on a "lengthy kiss" between Nina and Trigorin, a stage direction reads: "There is an interval of two years between Act Three and Act Four." The events of this period include Masha's marriage to Medvedenko, Constantin's unexpected literary success and, most important, Nina's affair with Trigorin and subsequent start of a career on the stage. All this news reaches us almost entirely through apparently casual conversations, especially, as it concerns Nina, one between Dorn and Constantin, who has kept up with her life, even "follow[ing] her about for a while."

The facts, as he knows them, are these: Nina had a baby, which died, Trigorin "tired of her" and went back to Arkadina, and the "disaster" of Nina's life, as Constantin sees it, extended to her acting in provincial theaters. He secretly saw some of her performances and tells Dorn that her acting was basically "crude and inept, with lots of ranting and hamming," though with a few high histrionic notes too—"she screamed superbly." Later he'd had some letters from her, "bright, affectionate" ones, but he had "sensed that she was deeply unhappy." She'd seemed to him "slightly unhinged" and had strangely signed her letters "Seagull."

Chekhov drew most of his material for Nina's life away from our gaze from a longish piece of fiction of his own called *A Boring Story*, written in 1889. In the story, a stagestruck young woman runs away with an actor, has a child who dies, is jilted by her lover, and then goes on the stage, though she has severe doubts about her talent. To this point her story is almost exactly Nina's, but the moral and intellectual consequences of these material details are wholly different for Katya of the fiction and Nina of the play.

The Seagull's climactic actions, some of the most passionately unfolding and swiftly revelatory in all of Chekhov, begin with Constantin in his room, meditating on writing, technique, his own feeling of sterility. The others are playing lotto in an adjoining room. Nina knocks on the French window and when Constantin brings her in she "lays her head on his breast and sobs quietly," reminding us of Masha's having done this earlier with Dorn.

But once again material actions resembling each other have entirely different aftermaths. From then on, in Nina's and Constantin's agitated, discordant, and ultimately "failed" conversation, everything having to do with art and love, talent and the ego, is brought together and we witness what is best described as the exposure and testing of the two characters' deepest—or rather, since Chekhov isn't interested in depth psychology—their most dramatically representative selves.

For Constantin, Nina's reappearance seems to be a miracle; she's come back to save him, he thinks. Earlier he had told his mother, "She doesn't love me and I can't write any more," but now his hope springs up. Nina is at first bewildered, almost incoherent at times, struggling to express the hard wisdom her recent life has taught her and about which he knows nothing, despite his possession of the "facts."

"I'm a seagull. No, that's wrong," she says several times, identifying herself with the bird as victim and with her youth at the lake, then quickly taking on a *real* description not a fictive one—"I'm an actress." And she says to him, still partly under the sway of their easy youthful romance and shared ambitions, "You're a writer now . . . and I'm an actress." Then, in a prologue to the rapid, violent change in attitude she will soon have to him, a movement away from the waywardness of memory and the pull of early desire, she tells him, "I loved you and dreamed of being famous. But now—." The "now" indicates that neither of these things is any longer true and the break launches her into a recital of some details of her physical life as an actress. She thus unwittingly baits a trap into which Constantin will immediately fall.

Ignoring her words and so revealing that his interest in her is only instrumental, a function of his need, Constantin pours out his misery and persisting desire, telling her that since she left him "life's been unbearable, sheer agony." Then, in the most fateful line of the play, he adds, "I call upon you, kiss the ground you have trodden on." To which Nina, "taken aback," replies, "Why does he say this— why, why?"

Nina's use of the impersonal "he" instead of "you" indicates her sudden understanding of Constantin's character, so that her "why's" aren't really questions but a recognition and an expression of regret. He has in effect hanged himself by the romanticism that coats her in such sentimental language and by his having pinned his sense of himself as a writer, his ego, to her former and potential love for him. Early in the play he had engaged in the "She loves me, she loves me not" game with the petals of a flower, and this seemingly innocuous action can be seen in retrospect as a foreshadowing of his fatal lack of emotional maturity.

What Nina regrets or fleetingly mourns is her loss of innocence in regard to Constantin, the death of her sense of their shared values and beliefs. She has already lost her larger innocence. In several long, beautifully modulated speeches she traces the course of her spiritual growth. Because of "the cares of love" and his "laugh[ing] at my dreams" in her life with Trigorin, she had become "petty and small-minded" and her acting had suffered. "But I'm different now." Through a process of maturation Chekhov doesn't describe, and doesn't have to, she has learned to esteem herself and "adore" her work and, most significant for *The Seagull*'s pervasive themes, has learned what it means to be an artist.

"I know now," she tells Constantin, "that in our work—no matter whether we're actors or writers—the great thing isn't fame or glory . . . what I used to dream of, but simply stamina. You must know how to bear your cross and have faith . . . [W]hen I think of my vocation I'm not afraid of life." In various ways Nina's idea of "stamina" will be active in every Chekhov play to come.

In profound contrast to Constantin's having allowed his romantic hunger for Nina to ruin his self-possession, she confesses to still loving Trigorin "passionately" yet without this weakening her resolve to forge her own life as an artist or in any way diminishing her determination to endure. When she leaves, she allows herself a moment of fond remembrance, quoting from Constantin's little play, something from their mutual past. Along the way she has exorcised the image of the seagull with which both Trigorin, for whom she and the bird are material for a story, and Constantin, stuck in barren literary imaginings, continue to identify her. Left to himself, Constantin offers one last revelation of his weakness and immaturity. If his mother were to learn of Nina's visit, he thinks, "[i]t might upset her." A few minutes later, from behind his closed door, we hear the shot.

"I'm flagrantly disregarding the basic tenets of the stage." In that famous high-spirited letter, Chekhov for one of the few times we know about spoke of, or at least alluded to, matters of technique in his work, the methods he was choosing to make his plays take their shape. Uncharacteristically, he had claimed originality for *Ivanov*, but that was in regard to its plot, which he had called "unprecedented" because it had broken with the long tradition of plays as moral struggles, pitched between heroes and villains. And though *Ivanov* exhibited a number of innovative dramaturgical steps, they were uncertain or incomplete and were surrounded by elements of a not-yet-fully superseded past; nor, in any case, did Chekhov make mention of them.

The most basic theatrical "tenet" he was ignoring in the composition of *The Seagull* was that of the nature of *action*, as this was conceived by the largely melodramatic or farcical imagination out of which proceeded nearly all the plays of the reigning French style and its Russian imitations. The principle he was spurning or sidling around had energized most classical drama, too, though much more subtly.

A play has to be materially active, it was thought, full of incidents or built around one or two really big ones, and what physically happens on the stage is of a different order from, and almost always more decisive than, what is said. Chekhov's implicit reply to this was that speech can make up a good part, perhaps even most, of what "happens" in a play, as much an action as any sword thrust or discovery of a lover in a closet or arrival of a letter with fateful news.

Eugene Scribe, the high priest of *les drames des boulevards*, those "well-made" plays of French popular theater, once wrote that "when my story is right, when I have the events of my play firmly in hand, I could have my janitor write it." With what magnificent shamelessness does this stand as the polar opposite of Chekhov's method, indeed of his entire sense of drama as an art. For him, events don't dictate the writing but very nearly the other way round. Speech *is* action, some-

thing taking place. Dialogue can therefore be much more than comment on physical activity, or an environment for it, an instigation
toward it or its verbal counterpart. Beginning with *The Seagull* things
said in Chekhov's theater constitute most of the drama. Material
occurrences have their own necessity and integrity, but in a shift
with enormous consequences for the future of the stage they mainly
serve to spring speech—the executive instrument of thought—into
life, behaving as language's outcomes more than its causes. Or events
accompany language as a sort of ballast, preventing words from flying off like balloons, the way they do in the sort of sterile dramas we
disconsolately call "talky," of which Constantin's little play in *The
Seagull* is an example.

That the chief physical eventfulness of *The Seagull*—Nina's flight
with Trigorin, her baby's death, and her early career as an actress;
Masha's marriage to Medvedenko; the shooting of the bird and Constantin's suicide—that all this takes place offstage has several powerful effects. It deeply undercuts if it doesn't entirely eliminate the
possibility of melodramatic excess; it "cools" the play down and so
allows reflectiveness to control sensation; and it therefore enables us
to experience the play more as a pattern of animate consciousness, a
set of moral and psychic rhythms and discoveries, than as a narrow,
emotionally overwrought tale.

This shift from the explicit to the implied or reported on, from
activity before our eyes to that which reaches us through language, is
the movement Magarshack so usefully if incompletely and program-
matically described as being from "direct" action to "indirect." For
all its basic accuracy, the formulation is too neat; it tends to blur the
relationship between physicality and speech and gives insufficient
weight to language's own directness, its being action in its own right.
To be able to account for the radical change in Chekhov's methods
Magarshack saw the process in too formulaic a way, but his fundamental argument, that at some point Chekhov stopped building his
plays around large physical scenes in favor of a dispersal of action and
the replacement of statement by suggestion, was a greatly original
perception and remains essentially sound.

Whatever its nature, the "indirect" has the great and mysterious
virtue of freeing us from the tyranny of a priori assumptions, the

ones on which sentimental drama, or any heavily plotted kind, is based. Melodrama, I once wrote, "may be defined as physical or emotional action for its own sake, action without moral or spiritual consequence or whose consequences of those kinds have atrophied and turned into cliché precisely by having been the staples of previous 'high' drama." Theater—this is as good a time as any to say it—is the most cannabalistic of the arts, forever chewing on its own history.

The a priori assumptions—amorous passion can be fatal, murder is detestable, a cuckold is ridiculous, and the like—move us in the direction of the already known; they create a stasis of imagination, its defeat, really, by sensation, habit, cliché. On the most trivial level, physicality tends to carry its own fixed meanings; to scratch one's head is to indicate bewilderment, to shake one's fist is to show anger. In regard to the theater, where the connections between inner and outer reality are of course paramount, these correspondences have always been present and were more than once codified, perhaps most notably by Goethe, who composed a manual for actors in which a great range of emotions and states of being were given their "correct" physical equivalents or objective correlatives.

We may be more sophisticated than that, yet so strong is our compulsion to read things this way, so thorough has been our training for it, that one secret of good acting, *pace* Goethe, is to make gestures that are unexpected, unpredictable, but that feel exactly right in the *aesthetic* context—to scratch one's head in anger, it might be, for the purposes of this argument, or to shake one's fist in bewilderment.

The larger point about this in relation to *The Seagull* is that had we witnessed any crucial parts of Nina's life between the acts, had it been given to us unmediated, we would have been swayed toward emotions too inelastic and circumscribed for the play's amplitude, too small, paradoxical as that might sound, because fixed and conventional. Pity for the infant's death, sympathy for the abandoned lover, perhaps contempt for Trigorin: such "natural" feelings would have flattened out the subtleties of Chekhov's scheme, confined the truest action—Nina's movement into spiritual and psychological maturity against a frieze of other characters more or less arrested within their situations and personalities—to the story of an ill-treated, doggedly ambitious young woman who somehow manages to survive.

As the play is constructed, Nina's inner change takes place away from our awareness; what we do see are the crystallization and articulation of her new self. We get the "facts" about her interim life first from Constantin, who wholly misinterprets them because he sees them conventionally, and then the truth from her. The contrast, which is at the same time the difference in their natures, is superbly dramatic, unfolding as a coup de theatre in the realm of consciousness such as an ordinary drama of highlighted physical events could not have given us.

Except for Anna's death, *Ivanov* had offered its substance to our direct gaze. And surely the most instructive demonstration of Chekhov's growth from that play to *The Seagull* is the suicides with which both dramas end. Ivanov shoots himself before our eyes, Constantin away from them. The obvious difference is that the latter suicide is at a distance, reaching us obliquely—the sound of the shot, Dorn's whispered words to Sorin—and that this greatly diminishes the emotional impact of the event. But this is an accession to the imagination, not a loss, for the assault on the senses of the suicide on-stage leaves no space for reflection, specifically about the significance of the act in itself and in relation to other things.

No space for reflection and not much material for it. Ivanov's shooting himself is essentially solipsistic, isolated from the rest of the drama or, more pertinently, from any large pattern of consciousness, as such melodramatic actions tend to be. We've interpreted the suicide, relying on the character's own words, as in part an attempt to recapture his "old self," through a last catastrophic but at least decisive act. It's also simply a way out of his untenable situation and a device by which Chekhov can end the play. Missing from it is any significant connection to other lives.

Suicide is always carried out in the moral or psychic neighborhood of other people, directed toward them ("See what you've made me do!") or implying something about them, so that taking one's own life invariably poses questions about those who don't take theirs, those who live. Camus called suicide "the only truly serious philosophical problem," and this dimension of thoughtfulness, of ontological query, is just what's lacking in Ivanov's shooting himself. By contrast, it's abundantly present in the circumstances and aftermath of Constantin's self-destruction.

His suicide exists at the imaginative center of *The Seagull*'s con-

cerns, which are chiefly the different ways people confront themselves in situations of love and vocation, or if they lack a calling,
like Sorin and Masha, whatever niche they do occupy. Especially
being tested is the relationship between love and talent, with Nina
and Constantin as the exemplary figures, while most of the other
characters circle at various distances from this thematic center.

When Constantin kills himself, it's squarely in the light of Nina's
stamina, her *going on*. Her strength has revealed to him his own
weakness in two connected ways. She has taught him in an instant
how pallidly romantic and compensatory is his desire for her and
he has learned (we sense rather than are told this) that he lacks
the courage—a clearheaded capacity to *continue* on through vicissi-
tudes—that she incarnates. Her visit and its words hover in the air
of the final scene, as the lotto game so casually goes on; behind the
closed door Constantin, brooding about what she has shown him,
"defeated" by her example, prepares his pathetic counterstatement.

This is why the play is a comedy, in one of the ways I defined the
genre earlier, why the suicide is neither tragic nor bathetic. For Constantin's death is the result neither of some fatal crack in existence
nor of an attempt to pass beyond limits; its "reality" is brilliantly
seen against a contrasting one, a choice of life that will be lived
bravely and with honor. Something essential has been saved out of
the entire human substance of the play, the principle of relief from
fatality that governs all comedy is now in place, so that the imaginative balance is toward what remains, not what has been lost. Constantin is the cautionary figure in this dramatic positioning of selves
and self-questioning, as Nina is its force of redemptive acceptance.

The mainsprings of its plot having been moved offstage, *The Seagull* presents a surface without any visible peaks, the landscape of a
remarkably flat terrain. But this flatness is of a physical order, not
an aesthetic or intellectual one. On those levels there is ceaseless activity, usually small, often apparently casual, an intricate meshing
of gesture, speech, and idea. And something else becomes apparent
when we have adjusted our sights to the newness of the dramaturgy.
For the first time in Chekhov we see the drama proceeding as though
its language and actions are gradually filling in a field, not moving
in any sort of conventional straight line, the usual unfolding of ex-

position, development, and denouement. The energy thus released, the force of locomotion turned into that of presence, is exactly the principle of "newness" in Chekhov's theater, Magarshack's idea of the "indirect" but more accurately formulated this way, I think.

Ivanov had begun this transformation but stumblingly and with an incompleteness that came from Chekhov's inability at that point fully to shake off the past, the seductions toward melodrama, the mechanical deference given to physical sensation. Resisting these, Chekhov could greatly extend, even free from their surrounding narrative pressures all those scenes without preamble or immediate aftermath, without *plotted logic*, that had constituted the rough technical originality of the earlier play.

In *The Seagull* characters move in and out of our sight and of each other's, in a constant traffic of direct encounters, glancing meetings, conferences, interruptions, breakings-up and reassemblings, all of it governed sometimes by mutual understanding and sometimes by its lack. A seemingly structureless drama, it's really all structure, if by that we mean, as we should, something inseparable from texture and pattern. The play isn't an edifice laid horizontally yet rearing its "meanings" skyward, but a meshing of revelations, withholdings, recognition, everything serving as clues to the whole.

The entire substance is somewhat thinner than it will become in Chekhov's next plays—its characters' destinies, Nina's most saliently, are a little too predicted beyond the play instead of being fates wholly within it—but the ground for the full flourishing of Chekhov's imagination is prepared. His vision will darken in *Uncle Vanya* and even more in *Three Sisters*, to lighten again in *The Cherry Orchard*, but here for the first time vision and method have largely fused.

The Late Beginner: Bernard Shaw

Becoming a Dramatist

Stanley Kauffmann

 wish I could write you a real play myself; unfortunately I have not the faculty." Thus Bernard Shaw wrote to an actress in February of 1888 when he was thirty-one. He was thirty-six before he changed his opinion of himself and first finished a play. "It is ironic," says Dan H. Laurence, editor of the *Collected Letters*, "that Shaw should not have completed a play until 1892, his thirty-seventh year, when all evidence points to his dramatic instinct having surfaced when he reached his teens." That irony prompts two questions that are not fully addressed by any of his biographers and are scarcely mentioned by some. Why did Shaw, the greatest English-language dramatist after Shakespeare, take so long to begin his theatrical career? Why did he begin it when he did?

Three forces in Shaw's life emerge as answers to these questions. First is the strong influence on him of Ibsen. Second is the different but pervasive influence of Wagner. Third is the invitation in 1892 to provide a play for the Independent Theatre, an invitation that confirmed in him the influences of Ibsen and Wagner, that gave him entry into the theater, and that was in itself the result of giant currents in nineteenth-century art. Let us explore.

When Shaw left Dublin for London in 1876 at the age of twenty, he had no specific literary ambition. He emigrated because he felt constricted in Dublin and because his mother, who had preceded him to London by three years, now had room for him in her house after one of Shaw's two sisters died. Insofar as he had any formulated ambition, it was to be a painter, persuaded in this notion by his reverence for Michelangelo. But a few drawing lessons in London convinced him that he was not quite up to the Michelangelo mark. He looked elsewhere.

Mostly he read, visited museums and galleries, attended theaters and concerts when he could afford them. A singing teacher named Vandeleur Lee, a friend of Shaw's mother (who was herself a singing teacher), invited him to ghostwrite a music-criticism column of Lee's in a small journal, without pay. Shaw leaped at the chance. Because of his mother's teaching and the atmosphere in which he had grown up, he felt equipped for the job. As he said later, "At the end of my schooling I knew nothing of what the school professed to teach; but I was a highly educated boy all the same. I could sing and whistle from end to end leading works by Handel, Haydn, Mozart, Beethoven, Rossini, Bellini, Donizetti, and Verdi." He began his ghosting for Lee with pleasure, but he quit after eleven months because of the way the journal's editors tampered with his work. This was only the first instance of his refusal, long before he had any professional status, to permit meddling with what he wrote.

He tried other kinds of journalism, without success. The first noteworthy Shaw writing, done early in 1878, is extraordinary in its form—a long letter called *A Practical System of Moral Education for Females.* (It was not published until 1956, under the title *My Dear Dorothea.*) Literary psychoanalysts can make what they will out of the fact that a young man of twenty-one, unmarried, not especially acquainted with children, chose to write an extensive letter of moral advice to an imaginary little girl. For others, the interest of the letter is intrinsic. The style is astonishingly poised: smooth, epigrammatic, cautionary but wryly so. "Hypocrisy is just like Selfishness. It is only bad when it is improperly used." The letter prefigures the *Maxims for Revolutionists* in the appendix to *Man and Superman*.

At about this time, in early 1878, he made his first attempt at a play. Derived from the New Testament, it was a blank-verse drama called at first *Household of Joseph*, then *Passion Play*. It is not of much substance, yet it has retrospective fascinations. The language is often gaudy—Jesus's entrance line is "Now to the purple grave of this wild day / Hies fast the flaming sun"—but there are pungencies. The play opens with Joseph saying to Mary, "I want my dinner." At one point Jesus says of Judas: "I never think that man a genius but / He straight-way shows himself a mountebank." This became a criticism often leveled at Shaw, sometimes by himself.

He left *Passion Play* unfinished. Later that year he made notes for a novel to be called *The Legg Papers*. These notes, too, he set aside. In the following year, 1879, he began and actually finished a novel called *Immaturity*, a title that has not escaped snickers. This was the first of five novels that he wrote during the next five years, all of which were rejected by many London and New York publishers and only two of which appeared reasonably soon after completion in journals. (*Immaturity* was not published until 1930.)

More relevant to this inquiry than the quality or subjects of these novels, although they have some rewards in both ways, is the fact that, after a brief flurry with a play and despite his unwavering passion for the theater, he turned to the writing of novels. This choice was influenced at least in part by his friendship with a novelist named Elinor Huddart, who studied music with his mother and who evidently encouraged him to try fiction as the proper outlet for a gifted person. ("Everybody wrote novels then," he said in 1905.) But very probably a stronger reason, a negative reason, turned him from plays to novels.

What was the quality of the London theater in those years? How could it have attracted a seriously ambitious writer? Aside from a great amount of overproduced Shakespeare, bowdlerized and trimmed to fit the whims of stars, the theater dealt mostly with melodrama and farce. As a whole, that theater was full of energy, and it was highly nourishing to the middle-class audience that was growing in numbers and power. But it was not a theater that could appeal to an intellectually aspiring young author. The furthest that the theater of those days went toward intellect was in the plays of T. W. Robertson, and, as George Rowell says, "Robertson could not evolve a play of ideas because his own ideas were largely superficial."

Paradoxically—not the first or last paradox in Shaw—he liked some of Robertson's plays. He also liked many of the melodramas and farces, and he reflected that liking in his own earlier plays, when he came to them, both in structural terms and as a source of character types for him to refine. Still, Shaw's response to the theater around him might be compared with the response of a modern serious writer to popular films: enjoyment, even possibly some structural influence, but no wish to be involved in them as a writer.

Something else distanced him from playwriting—his growing political passion, which would have been taboo in the theater. In 1879 he joined the Zetetical Society, a group, says William Irvine, "of advanced young middle-class intellectuals dedicated to the worship of Mill, Malthus, Darwin, Spencer, and lesser deities." (1879 was the year in which Shaw, having abandoned his first play, began his first novel—ostensibly a more fittingly serious occupation.)

Three years later he wandered into a meeting where an American named Henry George was speaking on land nationalization. "He struck me dumb," Shaw wrote in his old age, "and shunted me from barren agnostic controversy to economics." Two years later, in 1884, he joined the newly formed Fabian Society, became a socialist and a speaker. At the time he joined the Zetetical Society he had not done any public speaking, but he soon became involved in the society's debates. Thus experienced when he joined the Fabians, he launched into an (unpaid) career as a public speaker, indoors and outdoors. "This went on for about twelve years," he wrote later, "during which I sermonized on Socialism at least three times a fortnight average."

The theater had little to offer him in comparison with the intellectual/political forum that socialism provided; and the theater could not encourage the serious literary career that novel-writing promised. He could even blend his two occupations. Some of his political and social ideas could be, and were, used in his novels. Even though his fiction was not making much of a mark, he could feel that he was not pouring effort and thought completely down the drain, as he might have felt by writing serious plays.

Then, in 1885, William Archer entered his life. Archer, exactly Shaw's age, was already an established theater critic. The two men met at someone's house and became friends, and eventually Archer proposed collaboration on a play. Archer later recalled: "I was to provide [Shaw] with one of the numerous plots I kept in stock, and he was to provide the dialogue." Shaw agreed. But, said Archer, "After about six weeks he said to me, 'Look here, I've written half the first act of that comedy, and I've already used up all your plot. Now I want more to go on with.'"

Archer of course replied that his plot was an organic whole and could not arbitrarily be expanded. Shaw, who was already using the shorthand that he employed for much of his writing throughout his life, had to explain to Archer what he had written. Archer said subsequently: "I saw that, far from having used up my plot, he had not even touched it. There the matter rested for months and years. Mr. Shaw would now and then hold out vague threats of finishing 'our play,' but I felt no serious alarm." Shaw, with Archer's help, had become busy as a literary and music critic, and it was seven years before he finished the play, which he called *Widowers' Houses*. Long before that, and surely without foreseeing the extent of the effect, Archer had enlisted him in the cause of Ibsen.

Archer had family connections with Norway and had grown up bilingual in English and Norwegian. He was able to read Ibsen long before most others in Britain. He had made a translation of *Pillars of Society* in 1873 and had followed it with other translations. These translations, though there were others even then, were the ones that established Ibsen in the English-speaking world. Archer carried them forward as Ibsen continued to create. (Ibsen wrote to him in 1889: "I shall always feel that I owe you a great debt of gratitude for all that you have done, and are still doing, to introduce my works into England. . . .")

Shaw, already a political radical, forlornly hoping for fresh air to blow through the musty Victorian theater, was ready for the Ibsen inoculation. Probably he had heard of Ibsen before he met Archer. He may not have known of the first London production of Ibsen, a single matinee of *Pillars of Society* in December of 1880, but he must have noticed, at about the time he was getting to know Archer, that a magazine that was serializing a novel of his was also serializing a translation of *Ghosts*. In any case Archer, an Ibsen apostle, surely heated Shaw on the subject.

Again a paradox: Shaw at first disclaimed Ibsen's influence, maintaining that he had anticipated the latter's ideas. *A Doll's House*, he wrote later, "as a morally original study of marriage did not stagger me as it staggered Europe. I had made a morally original study of marriage myself. . . ." He cited his second novel, *The Irrational Knot*, written in 1880. A married woman goes off with her lover. After the affair ends, she encounters her husband, who offers to take her back even though she is pregnant. She declines. Her husband says: "Very well: you have liberty . . . and you are right to try whether it will not make you happier than wedlock has done." It certainly has a pre-Ibsen Ibsenite ring.

Nonetheless, the heterodox material in this novel, and in other Shaw novels, only confirms Ibsen's subsequent influence—by the very fact that, up to this point, Shaw had put such material in novels, not plays. After his immersion in Ibsen, he turned, though not immediately, to plays. He wrote afterward: "I concerned myself very little about Ibsen until, later on, William Archer translated *Peer Gynt* to me *viva voce*, when the magic of the great poet opened my eyes in a flash to the importance of the social philosopher."

"Later on" was 1888. In August of that year Shaw discussed with a Norwegian friend a plan for a joint translation of *Peer Gynt*, the friend to provide the English and Shaw "to put it in shape." That plan did not materialize; still, it proves Shaw's enthusiasm. The many entries about Ibsen that lace his diaries in the late 1880s up to 1892 manifest further the growth of his passion. "When Ibsen came from Norway," he said in 1927, "with his characters who thought and discussed as well as acted, the theatrical heavens rolled up like a scroll."

Early in 1889 he considered launching yet another novel, his sixth, but he put it aside. He wrote to a friend:

Some time ago I tried novelizing again, and wrote a chapter and a half, but I could not stand the form: it is too clumsy and unreal. Sometimes in spare moments I write dialogues. . . . When I have a few of these dialogues worked up and interlocked, then a drama will be the result—a moral, instructive, suggestive comedy of modern society.

Sydney Olivier, a fellow Fabian and a friend, wrote of this time in later years:

> I was surprised one day when [Shaw] showed me that he had been trying his hand at a new sort of stuff, some of which he showed me . . . and which I realized was a dramatic dialogue. . . . I was surprised, because the quality of British play-wrighting, and the deadly artificiality and narrow conventions of native contemporary British drama were at that time so repellent to me that I could not imagine any man of the intelligence of Shaw . . . expressing himself in the medium.

Olivier did not then know how Ibsen had affected Shaw. It was this effect, evidently, that had made the novel seem "clumsy and unreal" to him and that had shown him it was possible to cut through "the deadly artificiality and narrow conventions" of the theater roundabout.

The dialogues he was writing were portions of a contemporary drawing-room comedy called *The Cassone*, which he never finished. It was yet another three years before he finished a play—the play he had started with Archer in 1885. (Archer himself called his synopsis "twaddling cup-and-saucer comedy." Shaw took the twaddle, offered him by the very evangel of Ibsen, and shaped it more to Ibsenite ends.)

Through those last three years before he entered into his playwriting career, he was mostly engaged with music criticism, at which he had become preeminent in London, and with socialist work. But Ibsen was tugging at him more and more insistently. In 1891 he published a short book called *The Quintessence of Ibsenism*, which began as a lecture he gave to the Fabian Society. In 1892, when he returned to the centrality of his writing, it was as a dramatist. For Ibsen had shown him that, in the timid kittenish theater world of his day, it was possible to be a lion.

Richard Wagner's influence on Shaw, on his progress toward playwriting, is less directly demonstrable. It is more subtle than catalytic. True, *Widowers' Houses*, when it began as an Archer collaboration, was originally called *Rheingold*; the first act takes place on the banks of the Rhine; the plot is concerned with tainted gold. Much later in his life, Shaw wrote a work of Nibelung dimension, *Back to Methuselah*. But, in a sense, these are lesser matters. Wagner's chief influence on Shaw is in large liberation, in mythopoesis. In 1920 he called Wagner "Europe's last great tragic poet." Shaw, in essence, is a great comic poet, and his achievements owe much to Wagner's radical enlargement of the theater's figurative capacities.

From childhood, as noted, music had been a great part of Shaw's experience and imaginings. In his adolescence a Dublin friend named Chichester Bell led him to Wagner. Until then, Shaw had heard only the *Tannhäuser* march played by a military band.

> It was Bell who made me take Wagner seriously. . . . When I found that Bell regarded Wagner as a great composer, I bought a vocal score of *Lohengrin*, the only sample to be had at the Dublin music shops. The first few bars completely converted me.

The conversion flowered into a passion that eventually, in 1898, resulted in an analogue to *The Quintessence of Ibsenism*, a study of *The Ring of the Nibelung* called *The Perfect Wagnerite*.

Like the Ibsen book, it is one of the first significant works on its subject in English and is politically particularized in its view. (For this reason, just as the Ibsen book should be read in conjunction with Shaw's other writings on the subject, the Wagner book should be read along with Shaw's other writings on Wagner.) Shaw's view is based on the fact that the poems of *The Ring* were written at about the time that Wagner was involved in revolutionary politics, and Shaw certainly sees *The Ring* as an anticapitalist work. But there is more. Besides the "ready interpretation of the work's power as music" noted in the *New Grove Dictionary*, there is an even greater theme.

Edward Rothstein has written about this "powerfully argued" book: "Socialism is not actually the driving theme of the Wagner book. . . . Shaw read *The Ring* as an evolutionary drama. . . . *The Ring*, he asserts, provides 'faith' for a 'disciple' who believes in life's evolutionary power." Rothstein's comment underscores the amplifying influence that Wagner had on Shaw's views, his movement toward what became a dominant belief—in the Life Force, which itself evolved into Creative Evolution. This last is best defined by the Serpent in *Back to Methuselah*: "You imagine what you desire; you will what you imagine; and at last you create what you will. . . . In one word, to conceive. That is the word that means both the beginning in imagination and the end in creation." But this latter-day philosophy of Shaw's had its beginnings in *The Perfect Wagnerite*:

> The only faith which any reasonable disciple can gain from *The Ring* is not in . . . love, but in life itself as a tireless power which is continually driving onward and upward. . . . When your Siegfrieds melt down the old weapons into new ones . . . the end of the world is no nearer than it was before. If human nature . . . is really degenerating, then human society will decay. . . . On the other hand, if the energy of life is still carrying human nature to higher and higher levels, then the more young people shock their elders and deride and discard their pet institutions the better for the hopes of the world.

The magnitude of Wagner's moral mythology, plus the crowning fact that he had envisioned a theater in which to dramatize it, inspired Shaw to his own nonmusical drama, the drama he could create. After considering Wagner, he said: "There is, flatly, no future now for any drama without music except the drama of thought." This was his charter.

Eric Bentley has put it precisely. Dramaturgically Shaw followed Ibsen, but "receptively Shaw was probably more moved by Wagner."

Still, the inspiration of both Ibsen and Wagner might have had no immediate result had it not been for the founding of an avant-garde theater society in London. Clearly Shaw had been wearying of writing novels, especially as his interest in writing plays had been stimulated by his two mentors. In 1892 he took steps. His diary entry for 29 July 1892 reads: "Began to set papers in order, and came across the comedy which I began in 1885 and left aside after finishing two acts." In the weeks following, he mentions the work he is doing on the play.

Stanley Weintraub, the excellent editor of the diaries, says that the entry quoted above sets "to rest any theories that he dug it up and finished it because he had any specific revolutionary directions for the theater in mind; rather, finding it again was the impetus." But Shaw himself said: "Exhuming this as aforesaid seven years later, I saw that the very qualities which had made it impossible for ordinary commercial purposes in 1885 might be exactly those needed by the Independent Theatre in 1892." So, although he may have begun work on it before the actual invitation, it was the existence of a possible home for the play that spurred him—for the first time in his life—to finish a play. When the invitation came, he was ready.

That invitation came from a man named J. T. Grein. He was a Dutch businessman who had emigrated to London for business reasons but who had been a theater enthusiast in Holland and who furthered that enthusiasm in London. In 1891 he launched a society called the Independent Theatre, whose intent was to produce plays of merit that the West End managers would shun. The opening bill was Ibsen's *Ghosts*, a play that already had a police record, and it was followed by other foreign plays, except for an Elizabethan revival.

Shaw knew Grein, and one day in the autumn of 1892 the two men went for a walk, during which Grein said that he was disappointed because he had received no new plays from new English playwrights. Shaw said that he was a new English playwright and added teasingly that he had written a new play which Grein would not dare to produce. Grein thereupon accepted the play on the spot, unread. A few days later Shaw sent the play, now called *Widowers' Houses*, to Grein, who produced it in December.

A few days after the premiere Grein was invited by a London newspaper to explain the policy of the Independent Theatre. After stating that his interest was in "plays which have a literary and artistic rather than a commercial value," he said that the complaint that he was partial to foreign plays was untrue; he had simply not been offered many English plays of the desirable quality.

> Latterly, as our authors see that the Independent Theatre is a lasting and not an ephemeral affair, support has come from men who have hitherto kept aloof from the stage for want of an opportunity to obtain a hearing, for want of encouragement. . . . On Friday I came forward with the first play of Mr. G. B. Shaw, whom I consider one of the most brilliant men of the day, and whose play, which I admire, was worth producing, even if it had tended only to convince the author in what way he grapples with the craft of play-writing and what he has yet to learn. I think that . . . it is a step in the right direction to win such men as George Bernard Shaw for the drama.

Grein's theater, admirable and seminal though it certainly was, was not Grein's original idea. He had modeled it on a theater that had been created a few years earlier in Paris and that had already produced progeny in Amsterdam and Berlin. In 1887 André Antoine had founded the Théâtre Libre in Paris, a small, fiercely independent group dedicated to a principle that is now commonplace but that, at the time, was revolutionary. Antoine had started a theater for the production of new plays.

Obviously all the theaters of Europe and America had produced new plays before then. But for the major houses, new plays were an occasional novelty salted in with the generally standard repertoire, and in the popular theater of melodrama and farce, though new plays were more frequent, they were not predominant. To put it otherwise, there was not a theater in the Western world that would have missed a season if it had found no new play to produce.

The theater of the day existed for its actors. By and large, audiences attended to see X or Y or Z in this role or that—usually a familiar role. But Antoine sensed that the wind was changing, not primarily because audiences were tired of seeing old favorites in old plays but because writers were changing. The previous manufacture of vehicles—verse tragedies or melodramas and farces—all carpentered to established patterns, was giving way, at least among some gifted writers, to a centering on the play itself as the reason for production. A generation of writers was coming into being who felt that the actor should serve the dramatist instead of the other way around, that what the writer had to say and show ought now to be the reason why the audience came.

Partly this change was an effect, if something of an aftereffect, of the romantic movement; plays began to represent authors' experiences and ideas more than they filled conventional theater needs. Partly it was because of political/social ferment, especially in Europe, especially since 1848, that brought a questioning among thoughtful people of all acceptances, including cultural ones. Partly it was because of the influence of Ibsen, whose own work had roots in the causes just cited and whose plays became a kind of banner that signaled an advance in the theater of many countries. (The Théâtre Libre produced *Ghosts* in 1890. Shaw said, speaking of the changes in Europe, "The New Theatre would never have come into existence but for the plays of Ibsen.") Partly it was because of the growth, especially in France, of realism and its blunter sister, naturalism. (Zola was a friend of and a contributor to the Théâtre Libre.)

Antoine later came to dislike being labeled a naturalist and could point to much in his career that was otherwise. But naturalism was the initial hallmark of his work, a species of work that would have had no interest for an established theater, however wonderfully accomplished. Naturalism was Antoine's raison d'être, an emblem of the new theater in which the playwright took the stage because there was more to do on it than afford actors, however great, opportunities for acting.

From Antoine to Grein to Shaw, who may at the time hardly have heard of Antoine, the line runs directly. The shape of the European theater was changing because, quintessentially, the shape of Europe was changing. The nineteenth century was moving toward what we can see became the so-called modern sensibility, a climate of question and innovation, of independence, of a proud doubting and loneliness. Grein, charged by Antoine's example and Ibsen's achievement, responded; and through his agency, he brought forth the dramatist who, for the English-speaking world, was to take up the adventure.

We don't usually think of Shaw as a naturalistic dramatist, nor did he long remain one; his expeditions were otherwise. But it's remarkable that his first play was also, as Maurice Valency has said, "the first play by an English author that approached the tone of naturalism." (No other Shaw play has a scene more physically violent or sexually suggestive than the one between Blanche and the parlor maid in act 2 of *Widowers' Houses*.) Of course Shaw was not tipping his hat to Antoine. He was stepping into a theater situation that had been initiated by Antoine, and, once in, he was able to make his own way.

What we see, then, in Shaw's progress to the theater, is a confluence of tremendous forces that predicted, insisted on, the twentieth century. Ibsen had persuaded a writer, long in love with the theater as an art, that this art could serve idea. Wagner had warmed that writer with his magic fire. Grein, importing continental advances to Britain, provided the locus.

Shaw came into the English-language theater just when it needed a great writer to make the most of swelling cultural change. In proof, the title of this essay is an error. Shaw did not begin late in the theater. He showed his dramatic instinct by the very way he began. He timed his entrance perfectly.

Fascist Discourse and Pirandellian Theater

Mary Ann Frese Witt

he extent and nature of Luigi Pirandello's commit-
ment to fascism is still a matter of debate. Gas-
pare Giudice's 1963 biography remains the primary
source of information regarding Pirandello's actual
involvement with the party. Most critics, if they
deal with the matter at all, tend to accept Giudice's contention that whereas Pirandello was an
enthusiastic if unusual follower of Mussolini in the 1920s, he became
disenchanted with the regime in the 1930s. Whereas Giudice, and
many others, maintain that there is no connection whatsoever between Pirandello's literary work and his professed ideology—indeed
that his art is antifascist—critics such as Gianfranco Vené and Robert
Dombroski argue for a strong fascist presence in Pirandello's writing, although most of their attention has centered on the novels.[1]
If Pirandello's allegiance to the party were a matter of mere oppor-
tunism or a passing fancy having little or no effect on his work, its
interest at this distance would be primarily anecdotal. In the light of

recent research concerning the links between fascism and European modernism, however, it seems important to attempt to understand Pirandello in that light.[2] In order to approach the question of the ways in which his theater may reflect fascist aesthetics and ideology, it is necessary first to situate Pirandello's own ideological statements and contemporaneous criticism of his work in the context of fascist discourse of the period.

It has been argued, by Antonio Gramsci as well as by later commentators, that fascism had neither a coherent ideology nor an artistic style, and that this lack was proof that it did not represent a new stage in civilization. Indeed, to have a sense of the various fascist ideological tendencies one must, as Pier Giorgio Zunino's L'ideologia del fascismo shows, read the journals of the period. The document most often reproduced as the manifesto of fascist ideology, Mussolini's and Gentile's "The Doctrine of Fascism" in L'enciclopedia italiana, was written as a rather hasty response to those who claimed that fascism had no ideology of its own. One can nonetheless find in this document a typical statement of the notion of one major theme of fascist ideology: that of the "crisis" of liberal democratic society. If the nineteenth century, in the wake of the French Revolution, saw the predominance of abstract, rational doctrines such as Marxism and liberalism, these have outlived their usefulness and are no longer adequate to the twentieth century. Fascism, the argument goes, offers a "faith" and an "activism" or continuous creation in opposition to materialistic goals and abstract concepts such as "liberty" or "citizen." "Fascism is against the easy life [la vita comoda] and it rejects the equation well-being = happiness, that would change men into animals."[3] The true liberty of the individual will be found not in isolation, as in the liberal state, but in a new identity fused with the goals of the corporate state. (Thus Mussolini can claim that fascism is anti-individualistic and totalitarian while also saying that under it life returns to the individual.)

Reading fascist treatises and articles from the early days into the 1930s, Zunino finds a sense of "bewilderment" and "disquietude"— "all is in movement"—as well as the expectation of the coming birth of a new order. Liberalism and socialism appear as empty shells ("due gusci vuoti"), dead forms without life. Their error was to try to change human beings by merely changing institutions, whereas fascism demands an "interior transformation." In contrast to the abstract doctrines of the nineteenth century, fascism proposes intuition, improvisation, and continuous creation.[4]

Mussolini, it is well-known, was fond of envisioning himself as an artist and the state as a work of art. To Emil Ludwig he confided, "Everything depends on dominating the mass like an artist," comparing himself to a sculptor whose medium is men. The importance of theatrics for Mussolini is such that he wanted to "make a masterpiece of" and "dramatize" his own life. Zunino speaks of the cult of appearances and the play of forms in fascist political strategy as well as the "scenic splendor" of fascist rites. Silvio d'Amico found Mussolini's speeches in Piazza Venezia the perfect example of mass theater.[5] Although Pirandello's theater (with the possible exceptions of *The Festival of Our Lord of the Ship* and the "myths") hardly fits into the regime's ideal of the mass spectacle, the interplay of theatricality and reality, or the substitution of "creative" improvisational theater for the "dead" forms of social reality, seems like a Pirandellian sort of political discourse. Mussolini's understanding of Pirandello was undoubtedly not very deep and his statement to Ludwig on Pirandello's theater ("Pirandello, in essence, without wanting to, makes fascist theater: the world is as we want it to be, it is our creation") seems merely an echo of Gentile's concept of the spirit as pure act, but it may well have been taken to heart by Pirandello.[6] The Nobel Prize winner's 1934 declaration to his translator Benjamin Crémieux on why he could be considered a precursor of fascism would seem to indicate so.[7]

The "without wanting to" (*senza volerlo*) in Mussolini's statement highlights another important theme in fascist discourse on art. If the general fascist climate in the 1920s—judging from music, theater, book, and art reviews in journals such as *Il tevere*—did in fact encourage a certain amount of artistic freedom and innovation, important factions (most notably Bottai in *Critica fascista*) continued even during the 1930s to publish statements that, unlike the art of the communists or the Nazis, fascist art should not be designed as propaganda. True art produced under the regime, the argument went, would simply turn out to be truly fascist. Although various groups such as the futurists and *Novecento* tried to impose their art as *the* art of the regime—and it is clear that in architecture, for example, a fascist style emerged—the theory (if not the practice) of artistic liberty leading to fascist expression runs throughout fascist writing on art. An early article on Mussolini and art quotes Il Duce as saying that art "is re-entering the sphere of individuals and the state has only one duty: that of not sabotaging it . . . of encouraging artistic points of view." In a series of articles on art under fascism (the results of which are summarized in the 15 February 1927 issue), some of the writers in *Critica fascista* develop the argument that if artists are allowed to create freely, whatever great art they produce will necessarily be fascist.[8]

In the 1930s, when this argument is restated, the assumption still seems to be that the "true" fascist art is yet to come, but that it will be produced "naturally," as a result of the Revolution. In his *Fascismo e letteratura* (1936), Luigi Chiarini, along with the usual Romantic ideas as adopted by fascism on art as an antirational, spiritual "living force," stresses that artists must not make propaganda but that they should "feel" the political climate. Since art is born from profound spirits, no rules for its creation can be given, but fascist art will necessarily revolt against the universal abstractions of realism and naturalism; it will be both revolutionary and a return to the great Italian tradition. Although an expression of fascist values does not guarantee the quality of a work of art, every real work of art written in this period of "spiritual liberty" will necessarily be fascist(!). Present artists, looking for new forms of expression, are preparing the way, but a genuine fascist literature and culture will come only when artists have completely assimilated a fascist "faith."

Specifically in regard to theater, d'Amico, writing in *La scena italiana* in 1934, also contends that present dramatists are preparing the way for a truly fascist art and calls for writers who will express the "time to build" and the "virile construction of laws," but who will not make propaganda theater like Bolsheviks. In the same journal, under the title "How the Young View the Problem of Theater," a certain "Anton" reiterates the line that it would be a mistake for fascists to make propaganda theater. Fascist art will be born naturally, spiritually, through inspiration, rather than by being imposed from without. "Let us live as fascists [*fascisticamente*], and in our consciousness and thus in our artistic sensibility, *no matter what we write* there will be room for nothing but inspirations adhering to our time and affirming our ideals."[9] In an interview published 20 October 1933, also in *La scena italiana*, Pirandello had expressed essentially the same idea. The artist is necessarily of his own time, unconsciously influenced by it. "A poet can sing the fascist Revolution. . . . But he must not do it on purpose. . . . If on the other hand he has the soul of a poet and he lives the Revolution lyrically and looks only at the necessity of his own inspiration, he can easily be the poet of the fascist Revolution." The notion of an almost mystical rapport between the individual, apolitical creative process and fascist "faith"—entirely in keeping with a current of contemporary ideology—was one that Pirandello apparently maintained throughout the duration of his involvement with the movement.

The first critic to link Pirandello with fascism on a philosophical plane was Adriano Tilgher, who became an active antifascist. Writing in 1921, Tilgher expounds Gentile's position that for fascism the state is not an existing entity, but is continuously created by those who will it. Fascism is therefore an "absolute activism" stemming from relativism. He adds: "This point of view—a new proof of the absolute unity of every culture—finds its present expression in the art of Luigi Pirandello, the poet . . . of absolute relativism."[10] Along with Bergson, according to Tilgher, Pirandello demonstrates the uncertainty of our "constructions" of ourselves and of others, finding the only certainty, again like fascism, in *la vita vissuta*.

It is well-known that Tilgher's contention that the essence of Pirandello's work lay in its fluctuation between "life" and "form" had a major impact on Pirandello's critical discourse as well as on his fictional writing. It is therefore not unreasonable to assume that Tilgher's parallel between Pirandellian and fascist relativism may have strengthened Pirandello's sense of himself as the poet of the revolution—the Virgil, as he would imply later, to Mussolini's Caesar.[11] In any case, after Mussolini first received Pirandello at the

Palazzo Chigi on 22 October 1923, the writer's statements attempt to demonstrate a philosophical affinity between himself and Il Duce: "Mussolini knows, as few do, that reality is only in the power of man to create it and that it is created only by the activity of the spirit." He also noted that Mussolini had wished him luck in his American tour, and that Il Duce's favorite Pirandello plays were *Six Characters in Search of an Author* and *Henry IV*.

In the 28 October 1923 issue of *L'idea nazionale*, devoted to the first anniversary of the march on Rome, Pirandello paid homage to Mussolini, using Tilgher's life/form terminology. "Mussolini cannot but be blessed by someone like me who has always felt this inherent tragedy of life, which in order to hold together needs a form." Life dies if it congeals itself into a form, yet it must continue to create new forms. On the political plane, Mussolini understands "this double and tragic necessity of form and movement."

Pirandello must have believed fervently enough to carry his message abroad, for *L'idea nazionale* reports that he had explained Mussolini and fascism to Americans during his tour. The contact with American democracy also reaffirmed his antidemocratic tendencies. His views sound strangely similar to those of Ezra Pound. "I am antidemocratic *par excellence*. The mass itself needs someone to form it, it has material needs and aspirations that don't go beyond practical necessities. Well being for the sake of well being, wealth for wealth's sake have neither significance nor value." He reaffirms his great esteem for Mussolini, who "confers reality on things." [12]

On 10 June 1924 the socialist deputy Giacomo Matteotti was assassinated by the fascists; while many were leaving the party in protest, Pirandello joined, affirming in his letter to the hard-line fascist journal *Impero* that it was time to declare a "faith" previously "nurtured and served in silence." Telesio Interlandi, editor of the *Impero*, and friend of Pirandello, claimed a few months later that Pirandello was being persecuted abroad because of his fascism. In a November 1924 article on antifascism in general, he cites as an example a performance of the one-act play *The Imbecile*, cancelled at the last moment at a theater in Paris. The reason, according to Interlandi, was that Mr. Herriot, prime minister and "leader of the cartel of the left," was in the audience and people feared that he might be displeased by the bad treatment of the leftist protagonist and of the "sacred patrimony of Democracy." (This gives Interlandi the occasion to make ironic remarks on the practice of *liberté* in a so-called great democracy.) According to Renée Lelièvre, Charles Maurras also judged *The Imbecile* to be a fascist play and critical of Herriot.[13]

On 25 September 1924 a polemic over Pirandello's adherence to the fascist party began in the opposition paper *Il mondo*. The details, recounted by Giudice, are not worth repeating here, but the gist of the accusation was that Pirandello was a "vulgar man," an opportunist who had joined the party in the hope of becoming senator. Pirandello's strong rebuttal of this charge is entirely in keeping with prevailing fascist discourse, characterizing adherence to the movement as a spiritual "faith" transcending mere "politics." Just as he prefaced his antidemocratic/profascist statements with the declaration "I am apolitical: I feel like nothing but a man on earth," he announced to the Triestine daily *Il piccolo* on 21 October 1924 that he had nothing to do with "politics" but that he joined the fascist party "in the hope of aiding fascism in its work of renewal and reconstruction." Pirandello evidently believed that he could be of more use to the goals of the movement in the artistic rather than in the political sphere. Perhaps also in the spirit of emphasizing contemplative over active fascism, Pirandello did not attend the fascist "Convegno di Cultura" held in Bologna in March 1925, but sent a letter affirming his "full solidarity," best achieved, he said, by staying home and working.

The practical advantage that Pirandello sought from Mussolini was of course the realization of his long-held dream of instituting an Italian State Theater, for which he received much encouragement but experienced much delay. The government contributed heavily to the "teatro d'arte," inaugurated in 1925, but did not give its approval for a state theater until ten years later. On 3 April 1925, the *Tevere* reports on the opening of the teatro d'arte with *The Festival of Our Lord of the Ship*, praising Pirandello's art of the masses ("a popular religious festival") and comparing the play to Greek tragedy. Pirandello publicly thanked the government for its support and was received by Il Duce in his box. In keeping with one of fascism's more constant artistic tenets, Pirandello continued to be interested in the possibility of creating "religious" theater or "myths" for a mass audience.

When the teatro d'arte folded and the State Theater did not materialize, Pirandello and his troupe began extensive travels abroad. The amount of time he spent abroad in the late 1920s and early 1930s has been cited as evidence of his growing disaffection with Mussolini, but in his press statements Pirandello emphasized that his productions abroad were to serve the cause of "Italianate propaganda" and that he gave lectures "to illustrate the artistic, literary, and civic movement in the new Italy." In the course of an interview printed in both the *Tevere* and *L'idea nazionale*, Pirandello says of the success of his tournée in London and Paris that the most important result was that "Italy appears considered under a new light that ennobles and exalts it." Art, he adds, is "the best national propaganda." [14]

During a tour in South America at the end of 1927, Pirandello became more directly involved in the art/propaganda question. An article in *La stampa* reports that an antifascist journal in Argentina had accused Pirandello of being a worthless artist sent by his government for the sole purpose of spreading fascist propaganda. Pirandello is quoted as saying that he asked the director of the journal to retract this calumny because his tour was "purely artistic." Yet some Italians, he added, "vilely" interpreted this statement as antifascist while antifascist demonstrations against him continued! In support of his credentials, Pirandello recalls his entry into the party. "I had asked for the honor of the party card right at the time when such a request carried a certain dose of that courage which was lacking in so many for whom it is now easy and convenient to trumpet themselves fascists of purest faith." [15]

In his preface to *Novelle per un anno*, Corrado Alvaro reports that during this tour Pirandello was quoted as having said that "abroad there are no fascists or antifascists but we are all Italians," and that upon his return he was summoned by the Party Secretary Augusto Turati to explain certain press clippings assembled by Enrico Corradini. According to Alvaro, Pirandello then tore up his party card, threw his badge on the ground, and walked out, so that the party officials had to run after him to apologize. Although the anecdote may show, as Giudice claims, that Pirandello had enemies within the party, it also indicates in the light of the information cited above that Pirandello felt sure enough of his position to allow himself a tantrum and that the anger he expressed was at being accused of antifascism when he felt that his "faith" was as "pure" as that of his accusors.

For Giudice, as for critics who have followed him, the period of Pirandello's real commitment to fascism ended in the mid-1920s, and this incident marks the beginning of his disaffection with the regime. Actions by the fascist government, such as the suppression of freedoms and the foundation of OVRA (the secret police), according to Giudice, must have begun to disturb Pirandello's moral consciousness. One would like to believe so. There is, however, no evidence of protest or of antifascist statements on Pirandello's part. It is of course true that the press, under strict control during this period, would hardly have been likely to print such statements. However, what seems most likely is that Pirandello remained, like many writers of the time, in a sense truly apolitical. Preoccupied with his writing and with the success of his theater at home and abroad, he continued to espouse fascism with little concern for its practical effects while cooperating fully with the regime on artistic matters.

When Mussolini founded the Accademia d'Italia in 1929, Pirandello became one of the charter members. It is true that Pirandello shocked the other members by giving an anti-D'Annunzio speech, but this seems to have been motivated by personal and artistic, rather than political reasons, and again shows that he felt sure enough of his position within the party to say what he thought. In the early 1930s, when he spent a great deal of time abroad and had become less fashionable in Italy, there is less coverage of him in the press, although articles on his productions abroad as propaganda for Italy continue to appear. The next important incident, one that has been frequently cited as evidence for Pirandello's worsening relations with the fascist party, demands some clarification. This concerns the opera by Pirandello and the composer Malipiero, *The Changeling*, reportedly banned in Germany in March 1934 and subsequently performed to mixed reactions in Rome. One would think that if either the text or the music had been perceived as in any way antifascist, the fascist press would have panned the work or at least made some negative comment. What we find, however, is an entirely respectful, at times obsequious treatment of Pirandello, favorable reviews of the Roman performance, and surprise or shock expressed at the German banning.

The Changeling was performed with great success at Braunschweig where Hitler, as Pirandello himself pointed out in a 20 March 1934 interview in *La scena italiana*, attended the show. An article in *Il giornale d'Italia* cites a glowing review from the *Berliner Zeitung*, which claimed that the work demonstrates how the "Italy of Mussolini is today a free forum for cultural progress." The first production in Darmstadt was also a success and thus, according to the press, everyone was surprised when the Minister of Culture was said to have banned the work for the reason that it was "subversive and contrary to the directives of the popular German state." *Il tevere* claims to have telegraphed Goebbels and to have received the following response: "The work by Pirandello and Malipiero was not banned in Darmstadt but only the second production, because of technical difficulties, was postponed for a week. Thus the alleged ban is non-existent." The article in *Il giornale d'Italia* claims that the "technical difficulties" meant in fact that some of the actresses were too scantily dressed. Pirandello, however, was not satisfied with this explanation. The same article quotes him as surmising that the Germans had been unhappy with one of the important meanings of the play. "The prince prefers to the Nordic fog, which kills, the southern sun which heals and promotes life. That's all!" This is a view that conforms to contemporary Italian fascist attitudes of "Mediterranean" superiority to the Nazi barbarians.

Pirandello elaborates on this theme in an interview with Luigi Chiarini in *Quadrivio* (18 March 1934). He accuses the Germans of being motivated by racism because they had seen in the play an exaltation of southern over northern countries, or a glorification of Mediterranean values. Chiarini also expresses surprise at the ban, saying that in his view the work is essentially an "exaltation of maternal love and of the poetry of simple and natural life," to which Pirandello responds "precisely." Their conversation then turns to Mussolini who, Pirandello says, has given us all pride and joy in being Italian. Pirandello then makes the following statement: "Today in Italy we have one great truth: the one that Il Duce has built with his most powerful and dynamic genius. But how many struggles . . . how much energy it has cost! Great truths are obtained by a similar price; for this reason they are beautiful, we admire them and we believe in them most strongly."

In an almost simultaneous interview in *Lavoro fascista* Pirandello, again reflecting fascist discourse of the period, says that his fable has a moral. "It is a moral to be identified in faith, in the strength of spirit against the fragility of matter." The review of the Roman performance in *Lavoro fascista* is most laudatory. Only the last paragraph mentions that the third act left the public divided. Other papers were more mixed in their reviews and more explicit about the division that occurred in the third act. The reviewer for *La tribuna* on 27 March 1934 found that Pirandello's philosophical arguments were not well expressed in music, although he claimed that applause prevailed over dissension and that "cultivated people without preconceptions" were capable of understanding the work. According to him, Pirandello had summed up its meaning as "Everything may be or may not be true; it's enough to believe it." The *Messagero* and *La stampa* also have primarily favorable reviews, with comments on Pirandello's success in Germany. All of the papers report that although a vociferous group disrupted the performance during the third act, the applauders prevailed in the end. Mussolini, however, was apparently incensed by a scene in a brothel, contrary to "morality and family."[16]

As an academy member, Pirandello continued to perform official duties for the regime. When a state prize for drama, "Il Premio Mussolini," was awarded to Rosso di San Secondo, Pirandello gave a speech in which he alluded to "the renewal of heroic values in the new Italy." In October 1934, he presided over the international Volta conference on the theater, having first presented the conference themes to Il Duce and received his blessing. One of the conference themes, on the institution of the State Theater, was surely designed to convince Mussolini of its desirability. Speeches on the second theme, "the spectacle in the moral life of peoples," center on primarily two contentions: the importance of mass, sometimes called "religious," theater (while not neglecting "intimate" theater), and a critique of narrow "propaganda" theater along with a reaffirmation of the idea that great art will necessarily reflect its own time and place, thereby becoming the best national propaganda.

Bontempelli, Marinetti, Copeau, and d'Amico all speak of the theater's essential "religiosity" and of the importance of mass communication through theater, as in antiquity. Pirandello claims that he attempted to direct D'Annunzio's *La figlia di Jorio* (the official conference production) in this spirit. D'Amico reaffirms his belief that the best example of true mass theater is Mussolini speaking to the crowd from his balcony. D'Amico also speaks to the necessity of the state's involvement in theater. Since "liberal states" such as the United States and England don't have such involvement, their theater doesn't reflect a national soul.[17]

Pirandello's opening speech appears to have set the tone for the development of the theater-propaganda theme. The artist, he states once again, necessarily reflects his own time but to do so on purpose means to make politics and not art. Artistic creation cannot be rationally planned; rather it is a mystery like the mystery of natural birth. Nevertheless, art can also be "the instrument of a noble political or civil action." Similarly, Yeats, speaking on the Abbey Theatre, says "the deepest propaganda is, and will always remain, art." And Marinetti claims that the political climate should not produce "art with a message" but that politics necessarily manifests itself in art, especially now that "fascist energy is imposing itself on the world." Noting the danger of using theater for propaganda as the Soviet and the Nazi theaters did, d'Amico recalls that Pirandello once said of propaganda in art: "Yes, but one must not do it on purpose." If a message is not imposed from outside but born from within an artistic work, the true artist will necessarily be the voice of the new ideals. "What propaganda truer than a work of art?" In a similar vein, Goffredo Bellonci also criticizes the narrow propaganda theater of the Soviets and the Germans, affirming that the new artistic forms born from the fascist revolution will become "spiritual forms."

Pirandello's closing statement to Mussolini, stressing Il Duce's love of the theater, no doubt reflected his still fervent hope for support of a national theater. The speech Pirandello delivered in Mussolini's presence at the Teatro Argentina on 29 October 1935 uses extended theatrical metaphors to praise the "Poet," the "true man of the theater," and the "providential Hero" who "acts in the Theater of the Centuries both as author and protagonist" in general, and the Ethiopian campaign, "a spectacle of real and great beauty," in particular.[18]

Giudice offers a 1962 reminiscence by Gian Gaspare Napolitano as evidence that no official celebration was held after Pirandello received the Nobel Prize and thus that the fascists were lukewarm toward the honor. The fascist press, however, tells another story. On 11 November 1934 *Quadrivio* announces Pirandello's prize as new proof that "our literature, today animated and sustained by fascism, exercises a very great effect everywhere" and the journal devotes almost its entire 18 November issue to laudatory essays on Pirandello. The front pages and cultural sections of journals such as *Il tevere*, *La tribuna*, and *L'Italia letteraria* also sound the theme of Pirandello as a monument of glory for Italy. The fascists could hardly let this national treasure remain unexploited.

Giudice claims that the speech at the Teatro Argentina was the last indication of Pirandello's allegiance to fascism. Yet an article by Giovanni Cavicchioli entitled "Introduzione a Pirandello," in *Termini*, a monthly journal published in Fiume, October 1936, cites what was probably the last interview Pirandello gave, and one in which some of his strongest fascist language appears. In defining the nature of his theater, Pirandello seems to incorporate some of Mussolini's best-known slogans, such as "noi siamo contro la vita comoda" ("we are against the easy life") and "vivi pericolosamente" ("live dangerously"), along with other fascist catch phrases:

> Mine is a serious theater. . . . It demands the entire participation
> of the moral entity, man. It is not an *easy* [*comodo*] theater. . . .
> A difficult theater, let us say a *dangerous* [*pericoloso*] theater. . . .
> In *times of action and revolution* this theater is a theater of revo-
> lution and of capital executions. In this sense I consider it a
> theater of my time. Destruction requires *reconstruction*. It makes
> a tabula rasa so that *new values* will appear. For this reason it
> calls for and collects man's *deepest vital forces*.[19]

Pirandello further comments on the "religious" nature of his theater, calling *Lazarus* a *mistero moderno* and his most religious play. He expresses contentment that Catholics see this play as orthodox and that none of his plays have been banned by the Church. He repeats the theme that propaganda should not be imposed on art, praising artistic "spiritual freedom" and also calling for a true "Mediterranean art."

The fascist government may have been, as Giudice and others argue, unhappy with Pirandello's wish not to have a pompous state funeral. In the months following his death, however, the fascist press is again

filled with articles on Pirandello, some of them commenting senti-
mentally on his last wishes. Vitaliano Brancati praises Pirandello's
simple funeral and his wish to return to the land of his origins as a
demonstration of simplicity and force of life. Gentile speaks of "his
disappearance, as he wished it, silent, desolate, with neither funeral
nor mourners" and of Pirandello's profound humanity. The editor of
Critica fascista, Giuseppe Bottai, in an article entitled "Pirandello,
uomo e poeta," eulogizes Pirandello's "faith" and his last desire to
return to the land of his fathers. Massimo Bontempelli's well-known
essay, "Pirandello, o del candore," was also written as a eulogy. For
Bontempelli, Pirandello's art may be negative in that it expresses the
European postwar crisis of consciousness, but it is also an opening
onto the new age: "the preparation for cataclismic regeneration" and
"the new desert on which we must construct the new epoch."[20]

The view of Pirandello's work as an essentially negative critique of
postwar and parliamentary Italy but therefore an essential precursor
of the affirmative, virile art of the fascist era (usually portrayed as
still to come) is a constant in fascist criticism. Fascist discourse criti-
cizing democracy indeed sounds at times almost Pirandellian. Writing in the 21 August 1924 *L'impero*, Domenico Bagnasso, in an article
entitled "Fascism before Its Own Destiny," opines that "democracy
is the most colossal and shameless political deception . . . nothing
but the mask of plutocracy." By showing that life is a "farce in which
we all play parts," according to d'Amico, Pirandello's theatricality
exposes this masked or "constructed" society in which man (in Mussolini's terms) is replaced by the artificial "citizen."[21] For Gentile,
Pirandello's philosophy, a "vertiginous relativism . . . that throws
man into an infinite and fearful silence," is "true but insufficient"
in that it exposes the hypocrisy of the old, false values, but has not
constructed anything on the new ones.

Some critics, however, see an incipient positive "faith" within
Pirandello's very negativity. In a review of *Signora Morli, One and
Two*, Riccardo Bacchelli reasons that since the protagonist finds her
truth through her maternal instinct, the play's social critique finishes in a positive synthesis for the individual: "The negation of all
constructed truths does not wish to be negation but re-fusion in a superior and new truth." With the "myth" plays, especially *Lazarus* and

The New Colony, the theme of the hope of regeneration through faith, maternal instinct, or the irrational as opposed to rational "constructions" is further developed in the criticism and by Pirandello himself. In the fascist-Catholic view of Pirandello represented by d'Amico, Pirandello is not a pessimist; instead, he takes us into the abyss in order to perceive the hope of redemption. Pietro Mignosi also argues that Pirandello's relativism is a "homeopathic cure" for man in need of God and that *The New Colony* portrays a society with Christian values.[22]

It is Ascanio Zapponi, "lictor" for the theater or official fascist theater critic, who develops most intelligently the thesis of a Pirandello destroyer/creator. In a short treatise entitled "La Funzione del teatro nella propaganda politica," Zapponi restates the Volta conference contention that the theater should not overtly make propaganda but should nevertheless reflect the contemporary political climate. Using Pirandello as his only example, he argues that Italy's most important dramatist understood and portrayed the political reality of the crisis in Europe after the war. Pirandello's "unmasking" of rationalism and parliamentary systems reveals a society which "opposes the instinct and the natural demands of men to the conventional needs of citizens." Furthermore, Pirandello is a writer of the Revolution in that he reveals the death of the old forms and the birth of new laws. Zapponi elaborates this rather cryptic statement in an essay entitled "Pirandello rivoluzionario." By exposing the "constructions" of an outmoded, abstract democratic society and returning to the figure of the mother as an "irreducible construction," Pirandello offers a solution to the falsity of the "geometric world." Final dramatic actions, such as the laughter of the stepdaughter in *Six Characters* and Henry IV's attempt to kill Belcredi, demonstrate the emergence of a new, instinctive human being: "Will against the law; man against the citizen; the corporation against the social contract."[23]

What emerges from the history of Pirandello's involvement with fascism and of fascist critical comment on him is something of a two-way street. Just as Tilgher's claim that Pirandello's major theme—the perpetual interplay between "life" and "form"—influenced the development of his theater as well as his statements on aesthetics, so contemporaneous fascist criticism seems to have influenced Pirandello's concept of his work while his statements on fascism encouraged this vein of criticism. The themes in fascist discourse discussed above—the "crisis" of outmoded liberalism and socialism, the cult of the irrational, the use of aesthetic and, in particular, theatrical terminology in ideological statements, and the notion that propaganda in art cannot be rationally imposed but that it will spontaneously emerge—all penetrate Pirandello's own pronouncements as well as the writing of fascist critics on his work. Viewed in the light of this discourse, the separation that Pirandello maintained between "art" and "politics" does not indicate, as Giudice and others have claimed, that Pirandello espoused a "pure" art free of political contamination and, consequently, that his art and his politics had nothing to do with each other but, on the contrary, that his statements on aesthetics were well in tune with at least a certain vein of fascist ideology. Although Pirandello evidenced no support for the virulent and violent aspects of fascism and was no doubt attracted more by the doctrine of destroying old values than by the building of the new regime, he appears to have maintained his "faith" to the end. Even his claims to be apolitical are, in the context of the times, political. His own statements and those prevalent in fascist discourse on the necessary separation between true fascist art and propaganda suggest that one should not expect to find much political or ideological content in his works. It is nevertheless true, as Dombroski, Vené, and Alonge have shown, that some "direct" apology for fascism can be found in Pirandello's novels. In the theater, the relationship is much less evident and more difficult to define, but nonetheless consistent with fascist ideological and aesthetic positions.

Tilgher's early parallel between Pirandellian relativism and fascist "absolute activism" provides one point of departure for an approach to Pirandello's theater in the light of fascist aesthetics and ideology. Pirandello's experiments with theatrical form as well as his philosophical relativism are certainly consistent with the 1920s fascist call for revolt against "bourgeois" canons of realism and rationalism and the promotion of the irrational, constant creation, and improvisation. But does this theater, as fascist criticism claimed, portray the dissolution of bourgeois-liberal values and social forms? Does its theatrical subversion of form and observable reality constitute what we might call Pirandellian deconstruction? On the "affirmative" side, does it seem to call for totalitarian authority as the remedy for chaos? To what extent does it postulate utopias consonant with fascist ideology?

Pirandello's critique of a society based on what he saw as the abstract, worn-out formulae of traditional democratic liberalism, as well as of socialism, is devastating and inexorable. It goes hand in hand with his exposure of the subject as illusory: "We believe that we are one," says the Father in *Six Characters in Search of an Author*, "but we are many." [24] If the "I" is forever changing, or constantly to be created, how can it be accounted for in a society based on rule of law in which the vitality of the human being is replaced by the abstract notion of the "citizen"? Pirandello's theater in a sense elaborates on the passage in his 1904 novel *The Late Mattia Pascal*, in which one of the characters expounds the theory that democracy is nothing but "the most odious tyranny, tyranny masked as liberty." [25] The numerous maskings and the playing of roles in roles in Pirandello's highly theatrical theater suggest both the hypocrisy endemic to modern society and the constant need of the individual to create a self. It is not the wearing of a mask or the playing of a part that is in itself hypocritical, since the theatricality of social life seems to be a given, but rather the illusion or pretense that the social mask is somehow a true face. Thus the one who most consciously plays his part (like the "artist" who leads the masses through instinct, illusion, and improvisation) is more in touch with individual reality than the parliamentary legislator who claims to serve an abstract "justice." This type of theatrical critique of decadent and dying social forms is perhaps most powerful in *Henry IV*.

Written and produced in 1922, the year of the march on Rome and two years before Pirandello officially joined the fascist party, *Henry IV* brings to the stage not the historical drama that the title would indicate but rather a self-consciously theatrical "play" with history. The setting is in a modern villa that has been turned into a stage-set medieval castle. The fact that Pirandello eliminated the words "with meticulous historical reconstruction" from an earlier version of the initial stage directions suggests an intention to accentuate the theatrical over the historical.[26] The first scene, in which the "counselors" inform a new arrival that he must play his role in the eleventh-century court of Henry IV of Germany and not, as he had believed, in the sixteenth-century court of Henry IV of France, further emphasizes the playful nature of this pseudo-historical reconstruction. When the unnamed protagonist makes his appearance to the twentieth-century visitors dressed in appropriate costumes, he appears to be mad enough to believe that he really *is* Henry IV, but at the same time seems to be playing. His hair, dyed blond in front but gray in back, allows him, as he points out, to live in two temporal periods at once: as a young man of twenty-six when he humbled himself before the Pope at Canossa and as a mature man mourning the recent death of his mother. The death of his "historical" mother is also conflated with the recent death of his "real" sister, mourned by his nephew.

The superimposition of temporal periods is in fact the stuff of which the play is made. The forty-year-old Marquess Matilde Spina is confronted with a portrait of herself at twenty dressed as Mathilda of Tuscany at Canossa, a portrait of which her twenty-year-old daughter Frida will prove to be the living copy. Events from the eleventh century, from around 1920, and around 1900 conflate with and separate from each other so that time seems to stand still, or rather to become spatial. What we have is the very opposite of historical drama: rather than development over and through time toward crisis and resolution, *Henry IV* postulates a refusal of temporality in a sealed static world where progress is by its very nature excluded. What Henry calls "the pleasure of history . . . that is so great" is the negation of history as becoming.[27] It is rather a pictorial view of history (the masqueraders, including Henry, derived their costumes from a magazine picture) or a reenactment of what the Father in *Six Characters* calls "the eternal moment." The play's last words, Henry's "per sempre" (forever) deny even the future possibility of progression.

The emperor Henry IV took refuge in affirming absolute imperial power at a time when it was threatened by the demands of the papacy; Pirandello's "Henry IV" takes refuge in a utopian medieval recreation as if refusing both historical change and the twentieth century itself. Zapponi's view of the Middle Ages perhaps defines Henry's desire: "The Middle Ages: that was the time of force; legitimist to the point of being absurd, out of the fear it had of that mighty force that threatened at every instant to overthrow every law. . . . Man was bound to the law without hypocrisy."[28] In this (peculiar) view of medieval society, laws would seem to emanate from the person of the ruler rather than from rational agreement, and to serve as a haven against anarchy. Henry in fact creates his own "mad" universe, forcing all his visitors to play the game according to his rules. His self-conscious, totalizing theatricality paradoxically appears to the audience more "real" and less hypocritical than the normal social games played by the other characters who mirror contemporary society.

The principal dramatic action of the play concerns the desire of the twentieth-century characters to bring "Henry" out of his madness and back into the "real" world. The major peripeteia occurs when the protagonist reveals to his "counselors" that he is "not mad," or at least that he is aware of his play-acting. But it is because he lives self-consciously in a theatrical construction that he is able to expose the nonself-conscious "masks" (the marquess's makeup and hair coloring, the doctor's professional airs) and "costumes" (the white tie and tails they don for their club) of the aristocrats and the "alienist" who come to attempt to cure him. It is not only the life of the upper classes that seems to him stagnant and dead but also that of the common people, represented by the young men he has hired to be his "counselors." "Your way of thinking and feeling," he says to them, is "that of the common herd—miserable, feeble, uncertain. . . . And those others take advantage of it and try to make you think and feel as they do. . . . After all, what are they able to impose on you? Words, words, which can be interpreted in any manner. That's the way so-called public opinion is formed."[29]

The referent for "those others" is indefinite in this context, but the image of purveyors of words imposing their formulae on the credulous "common herd" parallels Mussolini's image of the socialists as "shepherds of the flock."[30] "Henry IV's" lucid-mad atemporal retreat figures his disgust with a society of talkers and pretenders along with his nostalgia for a world of legitimacy and organic wholeness. The impossibility of recreating the past is also acknowledged, but the consciously theatrical substitute allows the protagonist to criticize the hypocritical theatricality of the "real world." The impossibility of "Henry's" return suggests another romantic-modernist theme also adopted by the fascists: life in modern society suffocates the extraordinary individual.

The critique of modernity in *Henry IV* is then a negative one. As an atemporal, nonprogressing drama of refusal and frustrated utopian desire, the play portrays a vacuum without a suggestion of how the vacuum will be filled. The leader of the counselors, "Landolfo," explains that (in the manner of Pirandello's six characters) he and his colleagues are "like six puppets hanging on the wall, waiting for someone to take them and move them this way or that and to make them say a few words."[31] Similarly, the visitors to "Henry IV," wearing their medieval costumes, are unsure of how to play their parts, of what words to say. It is true that they are in a sense under Henry's direction, as they must take their cues from him, but his script is improvised and "mad," his fake castle an exposure of and a refuge from social collapse, not a solution to it. The vacuum is basically the same as that in *Six Characters in Search of an Author*: the absence of an author(ity) capable of bestowing meaning and unity on gestures and words. In the sense that it does not suggest how the vacuum will be filled or indeed if it will be filled, the ideological content of *Henry IV* may be said to be pre- rather than profascist. Although Zapponi zealously reads Henry's final lunge toward Frida and his stabbing of Belcredi as the signs of a new, vital, "revolutionary" man ready to kill, they seem rather self-destructive gestures, confirmations that the protagonist is unable to live in the twentieth century. The results of these actions—his decision to remain "forever" in the domain of the atemporal and the fake utopian—appear scenically as a death in life, perhaps marked by the awaiting of "authority."

If *Henry IV* is a drama whose title announces it as historical but which refuses history, the one-act *The Imbecile* produced in the same year seems initially to be a political play but ends by affirming the "imbecility" of politics. The scene is in the office of Leopoldo Paroni, head of the Republican party and director of the newspaper *Vedetta repubblicana*. Paroni's sole desire is to have the socialist deputy Guido Mazzarini assassinated. When he learns that one of his colleagues, a certain Pulino, has committed suicide, he declares him to be an "imbecile" because he threw his life away instead of first assassinating Mazzarini. He, Paroni, would have paid for the trip to Rome! Luca Fazio, a twenty-six-year old who appears to be extremely ill, closes himself in a room with Paroni and tells him that Mazzarini paid for his trip from Rome so that he would assassinate him, Paroni, before killing himself. Paroni at first takes this to be a joke, which in a sense it is, but at gunpoint from Fazio writes a declaration that *he* (Paroni) is the true imbecile. For Fazio, Paroni is a "buffoon" and "a little red man" whom he sees from "far away."[32] The spectator or reader surmises that Fazio is not in Mazzarini's service but instead disdains the political squabbling of all "little red men," be they socialists or republicans. The fact that it is a young man (of the same age as "Henry IV" at the time of his fall) who is deathly ill and who has resolved to commit suicide suggests that a political system dominated by republicans and socialists allows neither hope nor future. Thus the play negates "politics" (which for Pirandello, as often for the fascists, designates parliamentary politics) and again portrays a social and spiritual vacuum. "Politics" is associated with the meaningless squabbles and empty words of the left, suggesting but not explicitly stating that the vacuum can be filled only by a movement transcending politics as usual. The fake political play, like the fake historical one, postulates a theatrical and devastating critique of modernity.

If Pirandello's theater generally conforms to his credo of not making propaganda on purpose or not imposing messages on art, some of his later plays tend to valorize a major theme in fascist discourse—the adulation of motherhood, or the mystique of the *madre/madonna*. In Pirandello's writing, as in early fascism, one witnesses a curious combination of a revolutionary, modernist indictment of bourgeois institutions such as marriage and the family with an attachment to the most conservative values.[33] Pirandello's intense love of his mother along with his suspicion of his father are well-known. Giudice suggests that one of the sources of his espousal of fascism may be his anarchic adolescent rebellion against his father in conjunction with his adoration of his mother, leading paradoxically to a final acceptance of the need for authority. In any case, it is clear that in Pirandello's theater, as in fascist ideology, the only "true" role of woman is that of mother.[34]

"The mother is an irreducible construction," says Baldovino in *The*

Pleasure of Honesty: a phrase which Zapponi glosses to argue that on this "instinctive" as opposed to "intellectual" basis, in conformity with fascist ideology, one can begin to construct. Baldovino makes this remark just after delivering a most Pirandellian speech on the "construction" of one's personality in various situations. If our "constructions," as Baldovino maintains, are masks that hide our most intimate feelings—what we are for ourselves as opposed to what we are for others—then it appears that maternity is the one construction in which social role and intimate feelings coincide, a role so all-consuming that it eclipses all others. Paternity, as Baldovino himself will show by pretending to be the father of another man's child, can be intellectually constructed, whereas maternity need only be instinctively accepted. *The Pleasure of Honesty* ends "happily," with a triumph of maternity. Baldovino says to his wife: "With maternity, the lover [in you] had to die. Now you are nothing but a mother."[35] The biological father, as often in Pirandello's theater, can be dispensed with.

More than in any other play, motherhood is upstaged in *The Life I Gave You*, with its almost entirely female cast and its ostensibly female concerns. Yet the entire action is dominated by a male, donna Anna's dead son. She attempts to preserve his life first by keeping his room as it was before he left home and then by keeping with her Lucia, the woman who will bear his child, so that "the life she gave" will be given back to her. This desire is frustrated when Lucia's own mother arrives on the scene to convince her daughter to return home to her other children. As she comes to realize the fact that Lucia, not she, will be the mother, donna Anna concludes that her life will now be a kind of death. Her role has changed from that of *madre* to that of *mater dolorosa*, and she foresees a similar destiny for Lucia: "Go daughter, go into your life . . . poor broken flesh like mine.—This is what death is." The mother's lot is to "break her body" (as Pirandello says elsewhere), giving life only to move toward a status of death in life when her children no longer belong to her. The women praying to the Virgin at the opening of the play ("Mater Christi, Mater Divinae Gratiae, Mater purissima") announce the primacy of the mother-son relationship and its resolution as *mater dolorosa* in the play.[36] Fathers are hardly mentioned. As is frequently the case in both Pirandello's

comedies and serious dramas, the man's role is to believe or to pretend he is the father, to play Saint Joseph. In this case that role will
fall to Lucia's husband.

The figure of *mater dolorosa*, sometimes a "widow" of both husband and son, was certainly a familiar one on the European scene
in the years following World War I. In the interest of glorifying sacrifice to the *patria* and what seems to have been a fanatic fervor to
increase the Italian birthrate, Mussolini attempted to raise to a level
of almost mystical veneration the images of both the young mother
and the sacrificing mother. In 1923, the year in which *The Life I Gave
You* was written, the first congress of fascist women was held. As recounted by Maria Macciocchi, both Mussolini's discourse and that of
the fascist women themselves portray Il Duce as not only the Super
Male, Husband, and Lover of all women, but also in some mystical
sense the father of their children. In the words of the Marchesa di
Casagrande's address to Il Duce: "The mothers raised the children,
but you inspired their birth; you placed in their soul not a torch but a
living fire. . . . They are your soldiers, the purest flowers of the Italian
spring. . . . Out of our love . . . under the auspices of Il Duce, we have
convened here from all the lands that have heard the roar of the lion
of Saint Mark, to sow the seed from which will sprout the flowers
of the new spring."[37] Sacrifice and reproduction: the roles assigned to
women in *The Life I Gave You* are here glorified through bombastic
rhetoric and erotico-mystical devotion to Il Duce. Macciocchi theo-
rizes that what fascist discourse really implies is the castration of all
Italian males except for Il Duce—he alone will be Husband to the
women and Father of the sons of the new Italy. Certainly the "giorno
della fede" ("the day of the wedding rings / of faith"), 22 December
1935, when Mussolini asked Italian women to give him their wedding
bands to help support his Abyssinian campaign, must have had something of the aura of a mystical mass marriage. (Pirandello contributed
his Nobel Prize gold medal to the campaign.) As in Pirandello's theater, the "irreducible construction" of motherhood is glorified, but
the biological fathers are replaced by a father figure.

The idealization of maternity conflates with a vision of utopia in
one of the plays that Pirandello called a "myth," *The New Colony*
(1925). As Susan Bassnett-McGuire has pointed out, the play bears

a certain superficial resemblance to Brechtian drama, complete with good-at-heart criminals and a capitalist villain (Padron Nocio) who corrupts some of them.[38] The differences, however, are revealing, for it is not class conflict but rather the obliteration of class that is valorized; not struggle but utopian desire and instinct that conduct the drama. A prostitute named La Spera (suggesting "hope") leads a band of smugglers and thieves to an island, a former penal colony, where they intend to found a new society. Her lover and the father of her child, Currao, establishes himself as their leader, partly because he "possesses" the only woman on the island. As she plans to change her life, milk begins to flow from La Spera's breast; once on the island she is transformed from whore to angel of mercy, giving of herself to care for (but not to sexually satisfy) all of the men. An old man, Tobba, is the keeper of the agrarian dream that promises happiness through work and the simple life, but the men begin to quarrel and the dream remains unrealized. When Padron Nocio arrives on the island with women, drink, and other reminders of the corrupt city, the divisions intensify. Currao wants to put away La Spera and marry a pure young girl, the daughter of Padron Nocio, but he wants his infant son. La Spera argues: "If he really loved him, he would understand that my son must stay with his mother, because only I can give him *true* love. . . . These are not pacts that can be made. What? Make contracts on my blood? On my flesh?"[39] La Spera threatens that if Currao attempts to take the child by force, an earthquake will occur and indeed this natural deus ex machina resolves the drama. Currao reaches for the baby, La Spera grasps him in a "mother's desperate embrace," the earth trembles, the island and its inhabitants sink into the sea, and La Spera remains alone on a rock, nursing her child upon the waters. The "fallen woman" has become not only madonna but Mother Earth.

La Spera's anti-legalistic outcry is an emotionally heightened echo of previous discussions. During the utopian phase of the initial settlement on the island, Currao attempts to convince one of the men who says he came to the island to "stay outside of the law" that although they reject the law of others, imposed from outside, they will create their own through their work, a law that will belong to each of them. Later, Currao tells Padron Nocio that by coming to the island, "you have put yourself outside of your law, and you have at the same time destroyed ours."[40] By marrying Padron Nocio's daughter, and by dealing with him to share power on the island, Currao has in effect renounced the attempt to create a kind of ideal corporation and has capitulated to the old order of power, wealth, and externally imposed law. It might be possible to read this as a critique of the fascists' growing ties with capitalist institutions in contrast to their earlier "purer" ideals, but it would be unusual for Pirandello to make such specific reference in a play. Utopian desire remains only in the maternal figure of La Spera, the "irreducible construction" on which the attempt to create a society founded on "blood," "flesh," and agrarian work, uncorrupted by the old economic and legal order, may begin again. One might conclude that the actual father has proved inadequate but that the ideal father figure has not yet arrived.

Mother Earth figures in conjunction with utopian desires appear in other "myth" plays, such as *Lazarus, The Giants of the Mountain,* and *The Changeling,* the latter of which makes use of a popular superstition (the "women" who come to change babies) to create a fairy-tale opera culminating in the reunion of mother and son.[41] At the same time, the script celebrates return to the native soil and the healing power of the sun. The changeling "prince," who returns from his kingdom in the foggy north to his true mother in the sunny south, gives a Pirandellian argument for why it doesn't matter who becomes king. "Believe me, it doesn't matter if it's this or that person: it's the crown that matters! . . . Nothing is true, and everything can be true; it's enough to believe it for a moment." As opposed to this type of political "truth," the prince finds another sort of truth by recognizing primordial feeling. "Now I know my truth. I was a little boy here, with this mother, born in this sun; poor, but what of it? With this mother love, and this sky and this sea is health and the joy to live 'my' true life for myself!" The opera ends with what seems to be an ecstatic Oedipal reunion as the mother exclaims, "My son! My son!"[42]

Pirandello's theater from beginning to end "plays" with the elusiveness of truth or reality, the theatricality of life and the superiority of theater in a severe critique of the hypocritical illusions and the false certainties of modernity. In a world devoid of truth, however, the one visceral certainty seems to be the love between mother and child (usually son), a relationship more and more celebrated in the later plays. In the sense that they do not attempt to construct a positive model for a new society, or for a Duce, and that they never really become "popular" or "religious" theater designed to stir the masses, even Pirandello's "myths" are not propagandistic. In line with the doctrine that maintained that true fascist art would not contain consciously created propaganda, Pirandello aestheticizes history and politics through the relativism, the utopian desires, the primacy accorded to the irrational, and the atemporality characteristic of his theater. If his fundamental skepticism does not allow him to imagine a society that would fulfill the desire for utopia, he nevertheless suggests that it may be possible to construct one by returning to the cult of woman as mother/madonna and by awaiting a new authority. Although complex rather than dogmatic, and more destructive and nihilistic than "revolutionary" in the fascist sense, Pirandello's theater, in accordance with his professed "faith," belongs at least in part to the canon of fascist modernism.

Notes

I wish to thank the Research Committee of the School of Humanities and Social Sciences at North Carolina State University for supporting my research for this essay. I am deeply grateful to Alexander DeGrand and to Robert Dombroski for reading drafts of the manuscript and making several helpful suggestions. All translations from the Italian in this essay are my own.

1 See Gaspare Giudice, "Fascism," in *Pirandello: A Biography*, trans. A. Hamilton (London, 1975), 143–65; Gianfranco Vené, *Pirandello fascista: La coscienza borghese tra ribellione e rivoluzione* (Venice, 1981); and Robert Dombroski, *La totalità dell'artificio: Ideologia e forma nel romanzo di Pirandello* (Padova, 1978).

2 The classic Marxist statement on the relationship of modernism and fascism is that of Georg Lukács, *Realism in Our Time*, trans. J. and N. Mander (New York, 1964). See also Matei Calinescu, "Modernism and Ideology," and Russell Berman, "Modernism, Fascism, and the Institution of Literature," in *Modernism: Challenges and Perspectives*, ed. Monique Chefdor, Ricardo Quinones, and Albert Wachtel (Urbana, 1986), 79–83, 94–102; Fredric Jameson, *Fables of Aggression: Wyndham Lewis, the Modernist as Fascist* (Berkeley, 1979); Robert Casillo, *The Genealogy of Demons: Anti-Semitism, Fascism, and the Myths of Ezra Pound* (Evanston, 1988); Alice Kaplan, *Reproductions of Banality: Fascism, Literature, and French Intellectual Life* (Minneapolis, 1986); and Robert Dombroski, *L'esistenza*

ubbidiente: Letterati italiani sotto il fascismo (Naples, 1984), as well as the special issue of the *Stanford Italian Review* 7 (1990), "Fascism and Culture."

3 Benito Mussolini, "La dottrina del fascismo," in *L'enciclopedia italiana* (Florence, 1937), 29.

4 Pier Giorgio Zunino, *L'ideologia del fascismo: Miti, credenze e valori nella stabilizzazione del regime* (Bologna, 1985), 140–42. The fascist press is full of such statements. Here are two examples:

> . . . [I]t is the principal merit of fascism to be anti-doctrine and anti-philosophy by definition! . . . [W]e are elaborating day by day . . . in the breath of life a thought which is continuous creation because it is instantly transmuted into action. (*Impero*, 14 August 1924)

> The state . . . derives its strength and authority from the inner spirit of individuals. . . . [I]t is never completely made, but it is a continuous making. (*Il giornale d'Italia*, 9 March 1934)

Giovanni Gentile also stresses that fascism is never an "ideology" or a "closed system," but a "doctrine in action" and a "spiritual attitude." See Giovanni Gentile, *Fascismo e cultura* (Milan, 1928).

5 Emil Ludwig, *Colloqui con Mussolini* (Milan, 1932), 125, 219; Zunino, *L'ideologia del fascismo*, 37, 70; Silvio d'Amico, "Nuove tendenze nel dramma italiano," in *La scena italiana*, November 1934.

6 Ludwig, *Colloqui*, 205–6.

7 ". . . I think that each of us can construct his life, *not once and for all, but day after day*. . . . In the measure in which fascism has been the refusal of all preconceived doctrine, the will to adapt to reality, to modify one's action as that reality modifies itself, I think that one can say that I have been one of the precursors" (Luigi Pirandello, "Am I a Destroyer?" in *Le journal de Paris*, 31 December 1934, 1). The emphasis is Pirandello's, the translation mine.

8 See "Mussolini, Friend of Art," in *Idea nazionale*, 4 April 1923; see also Jeffrey Schnapp and Barbara Spackman, "Selections from the Great Debate on Fascism and Culture: *Critica Fascista*, 1926–27," *Stanford Italian Review* 7 (1990).

9 See d'Amico, "Nuove tendenze nel dramma italiano," 3; and "Anton's" piece in the same journal (March 1934). The emphasis is "Anton's."

10 Adriano Tilgher, *Relativisti contemporanei* (Rome, 1921), 66.

11 In *Le journal de Paris* (31 December 1935), speaking of himself and Mussolini, Pirandello argues that both activists and interpreters are necessary to society. He adds, "Caesars and Octavians must exist in order for there to be Virgils."

12 Interview with Giuseppe Villaroel in *Il giornale d'Italia*, 8 May 1924.

13 Renée Lelièvre, *Le théâtre dramatique italien en France, 1855–1940* (La Roche-sur-Yon, 1959), 424.

14 See *L' idea nazionale*, 31 July 1925, and *Il tevere*, 19 December 1925.

15 "Pirandello e la sua 'tournée americana,'" *La stampa*, 13 December 1927.

16   See Giuseppe C. DiScipio, "Pirandello and Politics: La Nuova Colonia," *The Italian Journal* 3 (1989): 32. DiScipio's conclusion that the opera got Pirandello into serious trouble with the regime seems, however, unwarranted, as does his reading of the earlier "Nuova colonia" as an antifascist play.

17   See the articles in *Quadrivio*, 7 October 1934, and in *Tribuna*, 10 October 1934.

18   See *Quadrivio*, 3 November 1935.

19   Italics mine.

20   Massimo Bontempelli, "Pirandello, o del candore," in *La nuova antologia*, 1 February 1937, 274, 281.

21   See *La scena italiana*, November 1936. In "La dottrina del fascismo," Mussolini asserts that when an abstract concept of liberty replaced a "spiritual" or "vital" one in the liberal state, "Man no longer recognized himself in the citizen" (20).

22   See Silvio D'Amico, "Ideologia di Pirandello," *Comoedia*, 20 November 1927, 7–9, 43–44; and Pietro Mignosi, "Pirandello e il mondo cattolico," *Quadrivio*, 24 March 1935.

23   Ascanio Zapponi, "La funzione del teatro nella propaganda politica," in *Gruppi universitari fascisti* (Naples, 1936), 37–39.

24   *Opere di Luigi Pirandello* (Milan, 1981–85), 4: 72. All references are to this, the Mondadori edition—volume number followed by page number.

25   Luigi Pirandello, *Tutti i Romanzi* (Milan, 1973), 1: 536.

26   *Un manoscritto inedito dell Enrico IV di Luigi Pirandello*, ed. Livia Pasquizi Ferro (Rome, 1983), xvii.

27   *Opere di Pirandello*, 4: 355.

28   Ascanio Zapponi, "Pirandello rivoluzionario," *Scenario*, March 1936, 107.

29   *Opere di Pirandello*, 4: 194.

30   Benito Mussolini, "Pastori del gregge," *Popolo d'Italia*, 1 May 1919, 3.

31   *Opere di Pirandello*, 4: 301.

32   Ibid., 5: 663.

33   See Barbara Spackman's interesting analysis of this apparent dichotomy in Maria Marinetti, "The Fascist Rhetoric of Virility," in *Stanford Italian Review* 7 (1990): 81–102.

34   See Giudice, *Pirandello*, 33. For a more complete discussion of women in Pirandello's theater, see my "Woman or Mother?: Feminine Conditions in Pirandello's Theater," in *A Companion to Pirandello Studies*, ed. John Louis di Gaetano (Westport, Conn., 1991), 57–72.

35   *Opere di Pirandello*, 4: 644.

36   Ibid., 4: 498, 451.

37   Maria Macciocchi, *La "donna nera": Consenso femminile e fascismo* (Milan, 1977), 41–42.

38   See Susan Bassnett-McGuire, *Luigi Pirandello* (New York, 1983), 148.

39   *Opere di Pirandello*, 5: 1153.

40   Ibid., 5: 1102, 1131.

41   See Roberto Alonge, *Struttura e ideologia nel teatro italiano fra '500 e '900* (Torino,

1978), 200–233. Alonge discusses mother figures at some length and what he calls "the problematic of Mother Earth" in the late plays, arguing that Pirandello's vision coincides with the fascist dream of a return to a precapitalist, agrarian society.

42 *Opere di Pirandello,* 5: 1301–2, 1304.

Shepard's Split

David Wyatt

am Shepard does not write dramas of recognition. His characters renounce insight and resist growth; they seem, instead, the scene for their author's projection of violent, contradictory, inchoate emotions. Shepard's language remains acutely aware of this, but it is an awareness in which the characters scarcely participate. Few of the characters believe in any existence apart from a role, and one purpose of the plays is to explore this. Yet it also seems a limit by which the characters are bound, a repetitive irony through which the playwright asserts his superiority over his players. The conception of life is essentially dramatic, as Richard Gilman argued about Shepard in 1981:

> [W]e either take our places in a drama and discover ourselves
> as we act, or we remain unknown (as some indeed choose to
> do). In the reciprocal glances of the actors we all are, in our
> cues to dialogue, the perpetual agons and denouements that we

participate in with others, identities are found, discarded, altered but above all *seen*. Not to be able to act, to be turned away from the audition, is the true painful condition of anonymity. But to try to act too much, to wish to star, the culmination and hypertrophy of the common desire, is a ripeness for disaster.

This seems so brilliantly right as nearly to forestall the need for future criticism. If it speaks to the basic thematic tension in the work, it also reveals a stance *toward* tension, Shepard's stubborn—almost willful—ambivalence. Ambivalence has been less his subject than his mode: his imagination craves what it spurns. "I think we're split in a much more devastating way than psychology can ever reveal," he has said. This torn mind has given his work its thrilling and irritating air of irresolution; he seems to like being split. "To be right in the middle of a conflict—right exactly in the middle—and let it play itself out where you can see . . . well, that's where things begin to get exciting. You can't avoid contradictions." Only in the most recent work for the stage does he begin to move beyond this habitual ambivalence toward a vision of resolution, of a world offering the possibilities of change and even choice.

Shepard's plays explore the troubled relation between our fear of performance and our lust for attention. They do so by taking the careful measure of the spaces between us; there is nothing casual about the physical positions of the bodies on his stage. The blocking explicit in his stage directions and implicit in his scene dynamics advances a complex argument about the possibilities for character and action in his world. Exits and entrances reveal themselves as perilous moments of definition or self-loss. Characters seek without knowing it an instant of distinction or notice. Shepard's management of "where we stand" in respect to others reveals his conception of life as an unending and often unwilling competition for space and love.

Shepard's most celebrated play, which won the Pulitzer Prize in 1979, takes its power as much from how the actors move as from what they say. The subject of *Buried Child* could be called "the stark dignity of entrance." The phrase is from the William Carlos Williams poem in which he imagines the way a new shoot shoulders the earth crumbs and pushes up into the light. *Buried Child* ends with Halie's great speech about how shoots and people come into the world:

> Good hard rain. Takes everything straight down deep to the roots. The rest takes care of itself. You can't force a thing to grow. You can't interfere with it. It's all hidden. It's all unseen. You just gotta wait til it pops up out of the ground. Tiny little shoot. Tiny little white shoot. All hairy and fragile. Strong though. Strong enough to break the earth even. It's a miracle, Dodge. I've never seen a crop like this in my whole life. Maybe it's the sun. Maybe that's it. Maybe it's the sun.

If Shepard ends the play with this appeal to a sustaining natural order, it is because the cultural space of the family has so utterly botched the task of nurturance. What makes us grow, draws us out? The play foregrounds such questions by focusing on the birth of each character into the space of the stage. The moment of truth is the one of coming on to the set.

A set summary of *Buried Child* might read like this:

> Lights come up on a living room, with stairs upward to the left and a screen porch to the right. Wife Halie begins speaking upstairs, unseen, and husband Dodge talks back from his seat on the couch at center stage. Dodge yells for son Tilden and Tilden *"enters from stage left, his arms loaded with fresh corn."* Halie finally enters slowly, down the stairs, and *"continues talking."* She does so after introducing by report another character we will never see, dead son Ansel. Near the end of act 1, son Bradley drags himself in on his wooden leg. He slips, enters from the screen porch *"laboriously,"* shaves and bloodies his father's scalp. Act 2 begins with Shelly's offstage laughter. She and her boyfriend, long-lost grandson Vince, enter the house unnoticed. The final entrance is effected by Tilden as he again carries something on, the bundle of the buried child, the last character to be granted entrance.

If kinds of entrance bespeak types of character, we get this reading of the play: Halie is the perpetually absent mother, a voice that speaks without loving or noticing. Dodge is the present but absent father, the paternal force who never leaves the stage and whose death occasions no notice. Memory-ridden Tilden carries the family burdens. Ansel exists only as rumor, the fantasy child who replaces the one his mother actually conceived and buried. Bradley's noise and violence measure his actual impotence. Stranger Shelly sneaks on and off, and so will fend off this uncanny family by finding it temporarily "familiar." Vince must revise his unremarked first entrance with a second, forcing the recognition—only Halie briefly grants it—his initial homecoming fails to evoke. The buried child appears in the play's last scene—its father presents it to its mother—so as to bring an end to the repressions set in motion in the first scene.

The major interruption in the play is Vince's second entrance; as act 3 winds down he cuts his own door through the screen and climbs, knife in mouth, into the central space. By doing so he also cuts short the recognition scene, Dodge's articulation of the story of the buried child. But interruption may be too strong a word. No one picks up the dropped stitch of Dodge's narration; attention simply shifts to Vince. An interruption can best occur during a continuing and focused act of attention, and this is what Shepard's plays do not provide. Instead, the inattentiveness of character quickly schools the audience to expect a series of arresting distractions. I once attended a production of *Buried Child* in a theater in the round, a space with fewer than two hundred seats. At the end of act 1, as Bradley began to shave Dodge's head, a man in the front row fell into a seizure, his breath short, his head tipped back. The audience soon noticed him, called for the lights. The lights came up and the house manager announced a ten-minute pause. A policewoman strolled in; the man's wife stroked his head. The house went dark; the lights came up on act 2. Nothing felt lost—only added. Asked to accommodate an unlooked-for interruption, the play did so as it had its other entrances, by revealing that its very structure was built out of whatever next thing managed to make us watch it.

"Me to play": Hamm's first line in Beckett's *Endgame* might well be the motto for Shepard's people. They insist on playing, on keeping the performance alive, without any solid faith or even interest in being comprehended or known. Attention without recognition; this is what they unhappily, desperately want. In *Buried Child*, "recognize" proves the operative verb. The verb gets attached to Vince, the un-remembered son and grandson, but it extends to everyone, from the Halie who *"doesn't really notice the two men"* in her living room to the death of Dodge, *"completely unnoticed,"* against the TV. "I recog-nize the yard," Vince says. "Yeah but do you recognize the people?" Shelly replies. Tilden's answer to the question "Do you recognize him" refuses Vince any fatherly recognition: "I had a son once but I buried him." Shelly persists in forcing the issue with Dodge, but he turns it into a comic interrogation:

DODGE: (*watching T.V.*) Recognize who?
SHELLY: Vince.
DODGE: What's to recognize?

To learn, see, know again—this is the burden of the verb. Shelly insists on keeping alive the fiction of recognition in a world in which no original cognition occurred. Recognition is the promise of drama, the experience Aristotle thought distinguished it from other literary genres. Shepard's conception of drama is so pure that his characters have been reduced to the desire to perform in spite of the absence of an action to be imitated. The outcome is no outcome, no *anagnorisis* or *cognitio*. The recognition that would lead to catharsis and hence to the end of drama and the need for drama—this is what Shepard's plays do not give.

While watching a Shepard play we are not present, then, to a world of character isolated by a deed. Things happen; there is plenty of noise and motion on the set. The scenery is relentlessly domestic or mundane; we are not allowed the escape hatch of thinking the action merely an allegory or a dream. Props play an abundant part. The major elements onstage at the end of *Buried Child* are less the actors than a wooden leg, a blanket, a rose bouquet. It is as if in the moment of discovering the expressive possibilities of the physical space of the stage this playwright had lost faith in the conventions of drama. The surviving given is the impulse to perform. Shepard's theater thus becomes not a space for the imitation of an action but one for acting out.

The space beyond roles, beyond the imperative "to act," is the un-

known space within the self, the frightening realm of the "personal."
This is the space Shepard has recently begun to explore. Jake uses the
word "personal" in *A Lie of the Mind* (1985) to describe the part of
himself he would never tell. It is a space he can conceive, yet one
he refuses, consciously, to inhabit. He does this by refusing to remember. Through a recovery of Jake's lie of the mind, Shepard goes
beyond the staging of behavior into his first sustained analysis of the
motives for why we stage it. This inquiry into his characters' reasons
for acting is made possible by his own deepening understanding of his
reasons for writing.

Shepard's longest play, *A Lie of the Mind*, takes four hours to produce onstage. Its three acts trace the collision of two families linked
by marriage. Each family has four members. Lorraine absentmind-
edly mothers sons Jake and Frankie and daughter Sally. The father is
mysteriously dead. Meg and Baylor maintain a Montana ranch where
their son Mike still lives, and to which their daughter Beth returns
to convalesce from one of her husband Jake's near-fatal beatings. The
action follows the two brothers, Jake and Frankie, as they work their
way back toward Beth and into a forgotten past. At the play's end, the
major characters have assembled around Beth, and, as they slowly
exit, she is left in the arms of her brother-in-law, Frankie.

Repression is the lie of the mind, and Shepard's play turns upon the
words "forget" and "remember." The story features two crimes Jake
could keep in mind: his beating of his wife Beth, and his "murder" of
his father. The first crime is as much "in" Jake's mind as the second
is out of it. "You remember the night he died too, don't ya?" his sister
asks Jake about his father. Jake answers: "That's the part I forgot."
It is possible to wonder whether Jake abuses Beth because he killed
his father, thereby submerging the taboo role of parricide into that of
wife beater. (In his "Notes on Scenes" for *A Lie of the Mind*, Shepard
himself asks the leading question: "What's the connection between
Jake's break up with Beth & his quest for his dead father?"). Forgetting—hiding a part of the mind from the whole—is what people do
in this play, how they get by, live onward. Both mothers forget that
their children have married. Baylor triumphs over anger and ennui
by remembering how to fold a flag. "HOW COULD I KNOW SOMETHIN'

THAT I DON'T KNOW?" This is Jake's rhetorical question, and Shepard's emerging definition of the human. To know what we don't know, to be perpetually threatened by the irruption of memory—this is the painfully anxious state that energizes performance and drives people deeper into their roles.

Except Beth. Through an irony so violent that it may be intolerable, she has had forgetting knocked out of her head. Jake has beaten her into a permanent state of remembering, a mind, perhaps, without an unconscious. She is returned to the eloquence of primary process; her work now is to "never forget." And she knows it, or at least says it. "This is me. This is me now. The way I am. Now. This. All. Different. I—I live inside this. Remember. Remembering. You. You—were one. I know you. I know—love. I know what love is. I can never forget. That. Never." Beth lives "in" the permanent presence of her once and future feelings—in a state of terrifying mental health. It is a freedom we might also call madness, one no doubt purchased at too great a price.

Beth's oneness with her mental state defines by contrast the nature and necessity of performance in her play and in Shepard's work as a whole. Beyond pretending, she can speak now about its pleasures. "Pretend. Because it fills me. Pretending fills. Not empty. Other. Ordinary. Is no good. Empty. Ordinary is empty." Frankie responds to this with "You liked acting, huh?" and reminds us that the action of the play is set in motion by the response to a play. Jake claims that he beat up Beth because she had fallen in love with an actor she was "in love" with in a play: "I know what that acting shit is all about," he tells Frankie.

FRANKIE: What?
JAKE: They start doin' all the same stuff the person does!
FRANKIE: What person?
JAKE: The person! The—whad'ya call it? The—
FRANKIE: Character?
JAKE: Yeah. The character. That's right. They start acting that way in real life. Just like the character.

So, according to Jake, Beth goes crazy before he makes her lose her mind. This is madness for Shepard: to believe and become one's part. Yet it is also the way of life; it is nearly impossible to locate a "person" in his plays who does not mistake himself for a "character," who does not reduce and perfect himself in a role. Shepard's people mount performances that presume a massive act of forgetting; they become lost in what they "pretend" to be.

So is self-hate at the bottom of it all, and is the action of the mind a sort of guilty hiding? Yes, in part. Shepard's plays about families and their psyches operate to expose a secret, a buried child. Not the one out in the backyard, but the one within, the angry and therefore guilty and therefore repressed survivor of early loss. The plays are remarkable not in their grasp of this human pastime but in their sense of the vigor and variety of performances that lying minds can conjure up.

Shepard's play about lying turns upon an act of physical abuse, a chillingly beatifying exercise of male power, and yet its basic fantasy is of a confusion of family and even gender roles. Sally takes Jake's place in bed; Mike claims Frankie and Jake are "the same person"; Frankie even stands in for a deer. Baylor maintains that "a deer is a deer and a person is a person," but he's just shot the one for the other. Identity can so easily be mistaken because it is so haplessly confined to the role words—"brother" "daughter" "wife" "son"—ticked off by Frankie in act 3, scene 2. But the one division Shepard most diligently explores is that between woman and man.

Beth imagines something one hasn't seen before in Shepard, a "woman-man." She does so in her pretending with Frankie, the man whose wounded thigh has left him in her care:

BETH: Pretend to be. Like you. Between us we can make a life. You could be the woman. You be.

FRANKIE: What was the play you were in? Do you remember?

BETH: (*Moving toward* FRANKIE) You could pretend to be in love with me. With my shirt. You love my shirt. This shirt is a man to you. You are my beautiful woman. You lie down.

Beth tries to push Frankie down on the sofa; he resists, and tells her he's come on Jake's behalf:

BETH: Your other one. You have his same voice. Maybe you could be him. Pretend. Maybe. Just him. Just like him. But soft. With me. Gentle. Like a woman-man.

(BETH *starts moving slowly toward* FRANKIE. FRANKIE *stands awk-
wardly, supporting himself by the sofa, on his bad leg.*)

FRANKIE: I need to find some transportation outa here! I need to
find my car! I can't hang around here, Beth.

BETH: (*Moving toward* FRANKIE) You could be better. Better
man. Maybe. Without hate. You could be my sweet
man. You could. Pretend to be. Try. My sweetest man.

This is an astonishing scene from a writer so concerned to shoulder
the burden of American manhood, for better or for worse. *A Lie of
the Mind* can shock in the way Hemingway's *The Garden of Eden* did,
an unlooked-for outcry against the cost of the performance of being
male. Yet both careers leave many signs of uneasiness along the way.
Here, Shepard projects a fantasy, in the voice of a battered woman,
that ought to become central to his future work. (It will not become
so by simply clearing the decks of testosterone and then asking, as he
does so endlessly in *Far North*, "Where's all the men?") But it is also
a fantasy so embattled that he conjures here as its nemesis one of his
most scary self-characters, Beth's brother Mike.

Mike inhabits the stage as the insane playwright, staging a revenge
that requires Jake to memorize his lines. He compels performance
and respects only roles. He lives within the myth of a solidarity (a
family) that can be "betrayed." "I'm the only one who's loyal to this
family!" he screams, and one hopes that, after Mike, Shepard himself
will let his own loyalty lapse. His plays present the family, in Robert
Stone's phrase, as "an instrument of grief," and yet he remains on
record as stubbornly attached to it:

> Family—in the truest sense of people related by blood, know-
> ing they are in a relationship with one another from birth to
> death—that's unbelievably awesome. . . . There's no way you
> can deny it. If a person denies it, he only ends up like Faust,
> you know?
>
> No matter what your family situation is—whether it's wonder-
> ful or chaotic—you have to accept it as part of the process of life.
> You can't jump out of it and say, "I'm free. I'm an individual."
> If the family exists in some kind of hell, that means you have to
> live in hell. Family is the soil you're born into. You gotta use it.
> You got to get through it. You can't run away from it.

Whatever Shepard's future take on the family, he has exposed in *A Lie of the Mind* the limits of a structure in which men "protect" women, brothers avenge sisters. Here Beth speaks to her brother Mike:

> BETH: (*Stiffens, stands back*) No! You make—you make a war. You make a war. You make an enemy. In me. In me! An enemy. You. You. You think me. You think you know. You think. You have a big idea.

Mike is a male who forces entry; he has no respect for Beth's "in." He thus becomes the double of what he sets out to punish, abusing what he is "tryin' to protect." Yet if the brother-avenger is merely an extension of the husband-abuser, it remains the case that Beth has been put into the position to be avenged and hurt and inspired by a man. Jake's act has "killed" her, as he says, but it has also created her, shifted her into a new vision and language. Upon this unresolved irony the play terribly turns, and so continues to betray Shepard's ambivalence about the fruits of male power.

The manuscript versions of *A Lie of the Mind* suggest that Shepard has become committed to revision of his work as well as to the revisions of lives within it. If early on Shepard thought that revision was "cheating," by the 1980s he had become fully committed to its possibilities. *True West* (1980) was revised thirteen times. The papers on deposit at the University of Virginia contain at least five manuscript versions of *A Lie of the Mind*, from the "Notes on Ideas for Plays" he sketched on 10 May 1984 to the final script from November 1985, one in which the pencilled cuts and revisions make their way into the typed text of the play. Two complementary motions of mind are revealed by these versions: one away from the "expository," and one toward the fusion of the themes of repression, revenge, and manhood. An examination of these manuscripts shows a writer hard at work changing both his stance and style.

Shepard's working drafts make much more room for a discursive imagination than does his finished work. In June 1984 he jotted down a list of "intrinsic necessities of the play." Foremost was "the need to allow the thing to tell its own story without bothering it with asking its meaning every step of the way." He didn't want the play to ask obvious questions: "What scenes are too expository right now?" Yet it seemed useful to ask about meaning at the start. A handwritten list of characters reduces them to themes:

Repentance—(Jake)
Transformation—(Beth)
Insanity—(Meg, Lorraine)
Betrayal—(Lorraine)
Revenge—(Sally, Mike)
Time, Tradition—(Baylor)
Love—(Lyle)
Fear—(Lou-Ann)

Lyle and Lou-Ann would get discarded; Frankie, the pivot man, is missing here. The earliest list of characters included Frankie, but not as Jake's brother. It is dated 10 May 1984:

The Man
The Woman
The Friend of the Man
The Brother of the Woman

Translated into the play's final terms, this list would read: Jake, Beth, Frankie, Mike. Here character gets reduced to gender or relational roles. Shepard begins with the function each character will essentially express. A third list can be found among Shepard's notes for the play:

Imaginary Roles
HEART SICK
REAL LIFE
Imitation
Play Acting
The War in Heaven
Pretending to Die
FRACTURED
Broken
On the Borderline
A LIE OF THE MIND
PROTECTION
Believing a Lie

These proposed titles are handwritten on a piece of white typing paper. Shepard made the right choice; none of those discarded pose themselves as a kind of riddle that governs the play without explicating it.

If *A Lie of the Mind* explores the logic of the unconscious, Shepard chose not to make that easily plain. In act 1, scene 3, Jake insists upon Beth's hanky-panky as an actress: "I knew what she was up to even if she didn't." Frankie responds: "So, you mean you're accusing her of somethin' she wasn't even aware of?" In the "First Version" of the play (dated May–August 1984), the reply read this way: "You mean this was all unconscious on her part?" Strike the analytical term when everyday words will do. A more substantial revision involves the original act 1, scene 9, a scene eventually removed from the play. Why did Shepard cut it? First, because it contains the discarded character Lou-Ann. Lou-Ann is an actress who was to have replaced Beth when she is forced by Jake to drop out of her play. Second, the scene is relentlessly thematizing: in Shepard's words, "too expository." In it, Lou-Ann does a monologue from the part she has inherited from Beth, and what she talks about is something called "a lie of the mind." The play within the play here becomes too obviously an exemplum of the whole, and Shepard decides, unlike Hamlet, not to have his "mousetrap" snap so sententiously shut.

A final example suggests how Shepard allowed the play, in his words, "to tell its own story." In act 2, scene 3, Shepard reaches for the most radical emotion of the play, Beth's attempt to convert Frankie into her "woman-man." In what he labels the "True Second Version" (dated 5 November 1984), Beth tries to get Frankie to remember "making love to me." He cannot, because she has imagined it. She then says: "Nobody needs to have brain damage to wipe things out. You just chop it off. You just take someone in your arms and if it doesn't work you chop it off. You cancel the whole thing out like it never happened." These lines are crossed out by Shepard's pen. If repression is a kind of self-castration, as these rejected lines suggest, it was a case Shepard chose to make through staging and action rather than through strict exposition.

Shepard sought to protect his themes from his own literal intelligence; he did not stint, however, from amplifying them through the careful elision and revision of scenes. Three major scenes—they are the three on which my reading has focused—had to be invented or substantially altered after he had completed the first version of the play. These scenes were to become:

Act/Scene	Date
1.7 Jake and Lorraine: "How was it he died?"	24 August 1984
2.1 Beth, Mike, Baylor, Meg: "You make a war."	5 November 1984
2.3 Frankie and Beth: "Like a woman-man."	November 1985

The order in which these scenes compelled his attention suggests that Shepard had to work his way through many versions to his deepest and most original material.

The Jake we see onstage represses nearly everything about his father's death. "How was it he died?" he asks his mother. He does remember one thing, about the ashes. "Where's that box?" The focus here is on the fetishized remains. The end of the scene, where, in the original stage production, Harvey Keitel blows lightly into the box and sends his father's ashes up into a beam of light, has been called by Frank Rich the "play's most overwhelming theatrical moment." All that can be remembered is that remains remain. In the original version of the scene, the reach of memory does not stop with the ashes (Mrs. Willis will become mother Lorraine):

JAKE:	Where's he?
MRS. WILLIS:	He's gone. He's been a long time gone.
JAKE:	Dead? I remember him. [handwritten]
MRS. WILLIS:	Yeah.
J:	He's dead. [handwritten]
MRS. WILLIS:	Yes, he is. [handwritten]

Jake's active remembering here—his volunteering of the word "dead," a word Shepard typed and then crossed out—does not prove compatible with the emerging pattern of his lying mind. So Shepard adds the business with the ashes, and the talk about the father's unremembered death. The theme of repression is protected and amplified through these changes.

Beth gets to say two wonderful things to her brother and her brother-in-law: "You make a war" and "Like a woman-man." The first makes a point about what men do for and to women; the second, about what they could become with them. These central sayings are part of dialogues that did not exist in Shepard's "First Version." It was in Charleston, West Virginia, in early November 1984, that Shepard wrote the scene in which Beth confronts Mike and tells him that his "love" makes a war. And it was not until November of the next year that Shepard pencilled these lines into the "Final Script": "With me. Gentle. Like a woman-man." He worked away on act 2, scene 3, even as the play went into production, as five pages of green-lined paper torn from a notebook attest. In the archaeology of Shepard's imagination the most radical material proves the most deeply buried, or difficult to retrieve. His discovery that the male avenger could become the androgynous lover was truly that, an emerging fiction he wrote his way toward over the eighteen months he worked on *A Lie of the Mind.* Shepard's growing willingness to revise suggests that self-editing may someday replace self-assertion in his work as the exemplary human performance.

Shepard's continual reimagining of *A Lie of the Mind* leads him into a complex of insights about the relations between performance and male power. And he locates these insights within the voice and experience of a woman. Everyone complains that up until Beth, his women characters aren't given much to do. They inhabit the stage as objects or audiences. Shepard has said that "the real mystery in American life lies between men, not between men and women." Shepard seems to be tiring not only of the mystery "between men"— *True West*'s struggle of the brothers—but also of the entire ethic of performance, of the desperate "vying" such a mystique expresses and entails. But to give up performing—to cease the lie of the mind— is also to risk being unmanned. This is the dangerous territory into which he has now strayed, as he evolves from the poet into the critic of American manhood.

David Leverenz has written that if "women writers portray manhood as patriarchy, male writers from Melville to Sam Shepard, David Mamet, and David Rabe portray manhood as a rivalry for dominance." A woman's experience of men differs from a man's experience of being a man, and while the latter certainly carries its cultural privileges, it is not without its pains and burdens. Why recent American theater has been centered around these men and their preoccupation with being male is a question perhaps worth exploring. It is a theater dominated by hurt or angry sons. Try as we will to incorporate Beckett, we seem to end up recapitulating O'Neill.

Shepard's stance toward experience is an openly "male" one, confrontational, aggressive, penetrating. Entering "into" something is a recurrent figure of his speech. "So rather than avoid the issue, why not take a dive into it?" He asks this in response to a question about his supposed "macho" image:

> Just because machismo exists, doesn't mean that it shouldn't exist. There's this attitude today that certain antagonistic forces have to be ignored or completely shut out rather than entered into in order to explore and get to the heart of them. All you have to do is enter one rodeo event to find out what that's all about . . . and you find out fast—in about eight seconds! So rather than avoid the issue, why not take a dive into it? I'm not saying whether it's good or bad—I think that the moralistic approach to these notions is stupid. It's not a "moral" issue, it's an issue of existence. Machismo may be an evil force . . . but what in fact is it?

The imagery of ordeal may be no more persuasive here than the work done by prepositions like "in" and verbs like "enter." Shepard brilliantly begs the interviewer's question by answering in a language that presupposes that the world is a place requiring a certain kind of courage, one willing to get to the heart of things. It's a courage possessed by persons seasoned through many falls, persons—and here is the circularity of the argument—who usually happen to be men.

But there is another Shepard, one that antedates the uneasy machismo of *A Lie of the Mind*, one that even in his oldest surviving play longs for a different stance and style. This counterpressure issues in what I call the dream of liquidity.

The first image from the earliest play Shepard chooses to reprint is of spilled milk. "(*The* GIRL *drops her glass and spills the milk.*)" It is the same milk Gatsby's father spills from the glass he is handed at his son's funeral, the same "incomparable milk of wonder" Gatsby forsakes when he kisses Daisy and enters fallen time. The dream of the imperial self—of being an eternal suckling—tumbles out of the glass at the novel's end, and so marks an end. Shepard begins with this moment. From the start the self is spilled, scattered, lost to wholeness or a sense of origin. Yet spilling and being spilled also appeal in early Shepard: they afford escape from the hardness of identity, the need to "practice" and perform. The closing monologue of *The Rock Garden* captures Shepard's ambivalence about overflow:

> (*A long pause*)
>
> BOY: When I come it's like a river. It's all over the bed and the sheets and everything. You know? I mean a short vagina gives me security. I can't help it. I like to feel like I'm really turning a girl on. It's a much better screw is what it amounts to. I mean if a girl has a really small vagina it's really better to go in from behind. You know? I mean she can sit with her legs together and you can sit facing her. You know? But that's different. It's a different kind of thing. You can do it standing, you know? Just by backing her up, you know? You just stand and she goes down and down until she's almost sitting on your dick. You know what I mean? She'll come a hundred times and you just stand there holding on to it. That way you don't even have to undress. You know? I mean she may not want to undress is all. I like to undress myself but some girls just don't want to. I like going down on girls, too. You know what I mean? She gives me some head and then I give her some. Just sort of a give-and-take thing. You know? The thing with a big vagina is that there isn't as much contact. There isn't as much friction. I mean you can move around inside her. There's different ways of ejaculation. I mean the leading up to it can be different. You can rotate motions. Actually girls really like fingers almost as well as a penis. You know? If you move your fingers fast enough they'd rather have it that way almost. I learned to use my thumb, you know? You can get your thumb in much farther, actually. I

mean the thumb can go almost eight inches whereas a finger goes only five or six. You know? I don't know. I really like to come almost out and then go all the way into the womb. You know, very slowly. Just come down to the end and all the way back and in and hold it. You know what I mean?

Here a Shepard speaker first steps into wild verbal space. The verbal transgression matches the sexual one; the boy's saying is above all a disturbance of speech, a protest against and relief from the talking past each other of the play. Shepard has said that "*The Rock Garden* is about leaving my mom and dad.*" Just as little in family life prepares us for the shocking discoveries in sex, so nothing in the play has signaled the boy's latent verbal power. The fantasy here is of control ("holding on") and the challenge, as ever in Shepard, is to "go in." But what arrests and amazes the boy is his own capacity for meltdown, the self "like a river." In the very act of proving his manhood he dissolves it, confounding the categories of loss and gain.

Men in early Shepard often turn to juice. "Juice" is a big word in *Hawk Moon* (1981), Shepard's most violent meditation on the liquification syndrome. *Chicago* (1965) imagines "a mound of greasy bodies rolling in sperm." *Icarus's Mother* (1965) turns upon a pee on the beach. In the unfinished "Machismo Sagas" (1978), Frankie fantasizes about being able to "vomit like a man." *Red Cross* (1967) ends with a white world stained red, the blood that streams down Jim's forehead. *La Turista* (1973) has Kent reduced to a "stream of fluid" by dysentery. Here Shepard goes beyond liquification to "abjection." This is Leonard Wilcox's judgment on *Red Cross*. He reads the suddenly bloodied face as a castration "upwardly displaced," the agony of a man caught between the maternal and patriarchal orders. If Jim is Shepard's sacrifice to such pressures, Kent seems to have passed beyond them. In the second act of *La Turista* his affliction gets refigured into a "thing of beauty" as he passes into a vision of a completely unsolid and unsullied self.

Shepard shows that for a straight man the experience of sex requires entrance into another and an alien body, and that achieved union with that body requires a transformation of his own. Solid flesh melts. Hamlet puns this into a kind of suicide, and frequently Shepard's meltdowns mingle ecstasy with extinction. *Hawk Moon* delivers up a catalog of exhausted males: "An orgasm would be nice but not all the love making preparation." This book poises stick shifts and guns and guitars against salt water, semen, blood, milk, urine, gasoline, sweat. The violence against women ("bleeding pussy") expresses the persistent fear of and desire for the loss of self in a woman's body: "I keep waking up in whoever's / Body I was with last." Shepard's anger at sex flows from the sheer fact of sex differences ("Boy or girl?" he asks), from a universe in which "The Sex of Fishes" could even be an issue. These unlike bodies compel some into an act of fusion as momentary as it is unforgettable. Sex risks the perpetual fulfillment and frustration of the human desire to be, as expressed in the last line of *Curse of the Starving Class* (1978), "like one whole thing." And on the insufficient dynamics of this act the culture has built an entire further set of expectations and demands. Better to be beyond desire and its consequences, the despairing *Hawk Moon* suggests, better to be a "Stone man."

Shepard's sexual material, like Hemingway's, expresses anxiety rather than bravado, a felt need for alternatives, not a smug posturing from within an embraced stance. They both see and see through early the imperative of performance. As the act that requires of the man the assertion and the loss of control, sex ought to provide a model for performance itself. But of course for Shepard's characters it does not. It is precisely the "give-and-take" of which the boy speaks in *The Rock Garden* (the 1970 *Operation Sidewinder* inverts the phrase: "[I]t's all about take and give") that is absent from these performances, especially the mutuality of verbal exchange.

Dialogue becomes like liquidity, then, a desired and feared thing in Shepard, a state which, if achieved, could signal a scary break-through to a new way of being. "You gotta talk or you'll die," Tilden says in *Buried Child*. No one fails to talk in these plays, or at least to make noise. They are "Dyin' for attention," in the words of *The Tooth of Crime* (1972). These characters speak like actors, bypassing the intimacy of conversation for the insistence of monologue. Speech is directed outward, forensic, not to be heard but overheard. Talking forces with little to say press for a piece of turf onstage. The most poi-gnant of questions may be Salem's, in *La Turista*: "Are you listening?" The typography of the play's final pages gives an answer: two columns of print each assigned to one speaker. The lines are meant to be spoken simultaneously; here the "back" does not wait for the "forth."

These are style matches, and victory depends less on physical strength than the invention and mastery of a unique language. In *The Tooth of Crime* the duel unfolds between two visions of the status and power of words. For Hoss, language expresses; for Crow, it constitutes. Hoss displays a psyche; Crow inhabits a discourse. The values of sincerity and authenticity vie with those of arbitrariness and recombination. The price of victory is utter loneliness; Crow "wins" and becomes stellified, a star revolving in unpeopled space.

But these contesting plays—and *True West* is the other strong example—actually eschew victory for standoff. At the end one man has beaten or talked down another, but the real situation is parity, a kind of endless struggle of the brothers. *True West* gets divided into nine scenes, with each scene in turn divided into mood units by "pause." The lack of strong act or scene divisions or even of a simple rising action testifies to repetitive rather than climactic outcomes. The appearance of the mother near the end of *True West* confirms this. This may be the most astonishing entrance in Shepard's work. It is as if Lee and Austin have been fighting in order to grab a little of her notice, and this is what she cannot give. Her focus relentlessly elsewhere, she is the ever-present Shepard absent mother, the one for whom there is no here. Shepard's plays explore the uncanny continual return of the prodigal parent:

> (AUSTIN *makes more notes,* LEE *walks around, pours beer on his arms and rubs it over his chest feeling good about the new progress, as he does this* MOM *enters unobtrusively down left with her luggage, she stops and stares at the scene . . .*)

It will take five utterances from the sons before Mom finally speaks: "I'm back." If the moment of coming onstage is epiphanic for a Shepard character, none enter with a greater sense of diffidence than these perpetually missing persons, the women whose bland, insistent, unnoticing voices seem beyond the register of dramatic change or effect. "I don't recognize any of you": the voice is Shelly's, in *Buried Child*, but she speaks for most of Shepard's characters and virtually all of his parents, especially the female ones. These are anti-Oedipal dramas which deny that the self can be found—recognized—at home. So many of his plays dramatize the avoidance of love because for Shepard, as Joseph Chaiken has written, "the human experience of love" risks "the difficulty of expressing tenderness, and the dread of being replaced." People keep exiting and entering in the hope that they will be uniquely loved, but at the beginning of things stands a woman who refuses to be an audience for her child.

To forget; to be male; to be loved, or, at least, noticed: the drive toward performance is perhaps Shepard's most overdetermined, one pressed upon him by all the complexities of his being. And although this last incentive seems to me the most comprehensive, performance for Shepard is finally an excess, a gratuitous human impulse beyond explanation or the need for it. That we perform is his redundant truth; why we do so, he, this least analytical of dramatists, usually doesn't wonder. As Shepard says of Bob Dylan: "The point isn't to figure him out but to take him in."

Increasingly, then, the interest in the career lies less in the will to perform than in its consequences. Shepard's reluctant celebrity is one of the more curious stances of our time. He dislikes interviews, and grants them. He prizes privacy and models for a photo spread in *Vanity Fair*. He has written brilliant plays but expends his time on mostly mediocre movies. Sam Shepard aspires to the very status his best work imagines to be death to the spirit. He wants to be a star.

In the small brown notebook where he sketched out ideas for *A Lie of the Mind* can be found an early draft of the song Shepard wrote with Dylan for *Knocked Out Loaded*. "Brownsville Girl" ends with a lament for a time "long before the stars were torn down." The song centers around Gregory Peck in *The Gunfighter*, a movie that images the price of celebrity as continual and failed vigilance against the murderous admiration of fans. After Peck gets ambushed by a rising young punk, the dying curse he passes on is that his murderer shall never escape the notice of those who will, in turn, try to supplant him. So Shepard teams up with the biggest star he can imagine in order to write about the cost of being one.

Is stardom simply one more cultural option that must be gone "into"? There seems more than a touch of bravado in Shepard's expense of spirit in a waste of fame. As he says, "So rather than avoid the issue, why not take a dive into it?" Anonymity is an anxiety for our time, one producing a craving for notice at once stimulated and resolvable through the media. As Frank Lentricchia has written about Don DeLillo's media-driven characters, especially Lee Harvey Oswald, "to be real in America is to be in the position of the 'I' who would be 'he' or 'she,'" to abandon our obscure first-person lives and to enter the realm of the "third-person singular," where we can speak of the self as an object of common attention, not the subject of our private fantasies. To make oneself something unique, to overcome the fury over likeness, to be irreplaceable—this dream drifts back over us as a collective wish, one Shepard has gone into with a reluctance almost self-sacrificing.

Between movies and drama Shepard now not only divides his time, but his imaginative needs. The pattern reveals an amazing fusion of talents; American life contains no precedent for an artist who is playwright, screenwriter, director—and actor. This more than double career allows Shepard to explore what it feels like—rather than means—to project an image.

It is as an actor that Shepard has become famous, and it was as an actor that he perhaps most dramatically confronted his ambivalence about performing. On 29 April 1971, Shepard's *Cowboy Mouth* had its American premiere. Shepard played the lead opposite Patti Smith. The next day Shepard disappeared, and Smith had to apologize to the audience for the no-show. "I attempted to play a part once," he explained a few years later. "Opening night was the only time I did it. I was in a state and ran off to New England, which wasn't very responsible. I like experimenting with acting, but I don't like the performance part of it. That's where it seems to get deadly." Since 1971, Shepard has performed in thirteen movies.

Things were tense the night he took off. *Cowboy Mouth* was presented as an afterpiece to *Back Bog Beast Bait*. *Bait* starred O-lan Johnson, Shepard's wife. Smith was his new girlfriend; he had been living with her at the Chelsea Hotel. The play rationalizes the predicament. Slim believes himself kidnapped away from his wife and child into a life of rock & roll stardom. "I ain't no star! Not me!

Not me, boy! Not me!" These are Slim's words, spoken that one and only night by Shepard. Just what was he running from, as he fled to New England? Perhaps not so much the split between but the awesome fusion of art and life, the terrifying convergence of the twain. Who is the character, and who the author here? And what of the double compulsion acted out by both—to mount and renounce a performance? The one split Shepard cannot maintain is the one he seems most deeply to desire, the split between the on- and offstage worlds. It has proven even tougher to maintain the split between the on- and offscreen worlds.

The work in film Shepard has done since his first screenplay (nineteen movies from the 1967 *Me and My Brother* to the 1991 *Defenseless*) can be read as a meditation on the difference between life on a stage and life on a screen. First and last, in America movies make you famous. Plays don't. When Shepard does his Gary Cooper imitation in *The Right Stuff* (1983) and rises phoenix-like from the burning plane, one of the ground crew sees a speck in the distance and asks, "Is that a man?" The other replies, "Yeah, you damn right it is." In this moment Shepard strides into focus and also into stardom, an actor who has earned, as the script acknowledges in these lines, his culture's most minimal and therefore highest term of praise. "Man." In a further twist of fame, he also insures through this performance Chuck Yeager's ability to finance his golden years by hawking engine lubricants on TV.

Since Shepard has been most successful in movies as an actor, his sense of the difference between movies and plays comes down to what it's like to be "in" them. The key variables are continuity and dimension. Movies lack much of either. They are made in lurches, short takes. The movie actor never acts, on one evening, his entire role. Moreover, while movies are acted in actual space, they are projected onto a two-dimensional plane, one the actor and audience cannot enter. The scale of a movie screen is inversely proportional to its accessibility, its vulnerability to intrusion or surprise. Shepard wrote the script for the brilliant *Paris, Texas* (1984). At the movie's end, a man in search of a woman finally finds her, and she is hidden behind a mirror. The climax in the movie reenacts the experience of a movie; when Harry Dean Stanton gets to Natassia Kinski, it is an encounter simply with a screen. Movies provide, for the audience, the illusion of space (dimension) and time (continuity) without affording for the actor the experience of either. Yet they continue to share with plays the emphasis on speaking bodies that are seen. They thus allow the actor—Shepard—to keep on projecting an image without having to risk the open-endedness of an actual historical occasion, or a performance in "three dimensions."

The 1982 *Motel Chronicles* contains Shepard's most extended inquiry into the ironies of working for the screen. The movie actor in Texas tries "to keep his mind on his business. What the scene they were shooting was about. Where it fit into the continuity." He can find no fit, and so drives away, out of the movie but into the character he was slated to play. Later a screenwriter remarks that "I've abandoned my film." "What happened?" a voice asks. "I lost the continuity." The continuity that a movie must evince proves shockingly fugitive in life, as the spliced-up structure of Shepard's book implies. One of its male voices simply intones, "The most intimate things were very broken off." There is a link here between formal structure and psychological concerns; one can see it in the typed manuscript versions of *Motel Chronicles*. Originally titled "Transfiction" or "Transfixion," the book was begun in 1978 and composed over some three years. By replacing the "c" with the "x," Shepard links fiction-making and suffering—writing becomes a kind of crucifixion. By finally abandoning both titles, he backs off from the melodrama in the claim. But he does not back off from the personal. *Motel Chronicles* begins and ends with memories of the mother; the speaker's birth; a mother's final illness. The last section on his mother-in-law's stroke was added late—on "9/29/80." The opening about Shepard's mother was added on the first day of that month. So the book moved toward the classic fictional openings and closings—birth and death, origins and ends. Yet these memories provide not continuity but merely arbitrary starting and stopping points. The most powerful impression of the mother comes in a fantasy of seeing her body after the speaker's birth: "I watched her body. I knew I'd come from her body but I wasn't sure how. I knew I was away from her body now. Separate." This is a discontinuity that cannot be edited into shape. Movies are not "as dumb as life," because they project a seamless continuity in which parts of the story are not broken off.

But the price of continuity is impotence, the powerlessness of an audience to share, enter, or alter the movie's space. Space is what plays provide. Kevin J. O'Connor says of Shepard that "most of his plays were meant to take place on a proscenium—he writes for that— or a space in front of you. He sees things coming on from the side or going off from the side—that's part of the world he's creating." Shepard's stage directions are detailed and architectural: he maps out the walls, doors, rooms. But despite his affection for the dimensional world, Shepard's plays also express a desire to escape its mortal limits. They thus advance a subtle rationalization for his own professional shift from stage to screen, outlining as they do so a pathology rather than a poetics of space.

The pathology is distinctively American. "I take SPACE to be the central fact to man born in America from Folsom cave to now." So Charles Olson begins his 1947 *Call Me Ishmael*. "I spell it large," he says, "because it comes large here. Large, and without mercy." (*Paris, Texas* opens with a "lone man" crossing a "fissured, empty, almost lunar landscape—seen from a bird's-eye view.") Large, Olson seems to be saying, like Moby-Dick. Olson's American stands toward space as Ahab does toward the whale. "We must go over space, or we wither." There is not a little phallic ambition in Olson's call for a continual westering, as if Manifest Destiny were a massive repression of castration anxiety. D. H. Lawrence would have agreed, and had already supplied the word "phallic." But he was less sanguine about the prospects for fulfillment in space, in America's "true west." As he says in *Studies in Classic American Literature*: "Absolutely the safest thing to get your emotional reactions over is NATURE." It is a big claim, like Olson's, and each writer capitalizes his key word. SPACE. NATURE. Like Mike in *A Lie of the Mind*, they "have a big idea." Big words. And today, Shepard seems to be telling us, nearly dead words.

Olson's book celebrates the discovery of a new American space: the Pacific. Lawrence's details the sentimentalization of a continent. We persist in both activities. America now lives in the era of the Pacific Rim, and there is no dearth of pieties about the renovating powers of the increasingly abused natural world. But to the immediate data of consciousness, the continuing colonization of space and valorization of nature are mere sideshows, distractions of history. To live in America as the century ends is to have withdrawn from the realm of the outside. We suffer from a greenhouse effect that owes more to the voracious will to enclosure imagined in Raymond Chandler's *The Big Sleep* than to excess carbon dioxide. We suffer, Shepard's work argues, from a sort of national agoraphobia—a fear of space.

In the southern California where Shepard grew up, the spaces inhabited had names like these: playground, downtown, driveway, front yard. The words imply a scene of relation and proportion between institutions in a built world of schools, roads, stores, and free-standing homes. Beyond all that lay the found world, what can be called the landscape. For many of us these words and spaces have become unrecognizable. We inhabit another order of terms focused on an interior world; in the True West of today, we can hear the sound of the crickets in the hills, but nobody leaves the house. If the primal American scene has heretofore been a body in a landscape—Wallace Stevens's "empty spirit / In vacant space"—then in the 1990s it has become a pair of eyes staring at a screen.

The new words are VCR, television, computer, FAX machine. People seem reluctant to leave them behind, to go outside, into space. I am married to a woman who owns a repertory movie theater. People have stopped coming; attendance was down in 1989 by seven thousand. Perhaps it's an aversion to going out at night into "cities under seige" in order to sit with strangers in a large, dark space. Our audience apparently prefers to stay at home and manage the screening of experience on a reduced scale. (In 1990 70 percent of American homes owned one VCR; 25 percent owned two.) The bunker mentality has triumphed, and we live less in space than in representations of space. What we increasingly have in common is not the physical landscape around our homes, but, in Michael Herr's words, a "glamour space" projected onto a screen. This is where we live, and move, and have our being.

Since *The Tooth of Crime*, Shepard's plays have argued that the price of the celebrity we most value—stardom on a screen—is *dislocation*, the erasure of specific identity in local space. Because such stardom relieves us of an even greater anxiety—"Dying," as Tympani says in *Angel City*—it is a price we are perhaps willing to pay. The play in which Tympani appears gives this paradox its most elegant expression. The action of the 1976 *Angel City* follows a crazed Culver

City production company as it tries to make a hit disaster movie. At one point, script-doctor Rabbit and musician Tympani enjoy this exchange. Rabbit asks, "What is the most terrifying thing in the world?" Tympani replies: "(*blankly*) A space." Space scares because it is the medium of vulnerability, even mortality:

RABBIT: So now you're just taking up space?
TYMPANI: I'm facing my death.

The human choice presents itself here as between facing death in space or achieving a dimensionless immortality on-screen. Rabbit states the case for the power of film:

> The vision of a celluloid tape with a series of moving images telling a story to millions. Millions anywhere. Millions seen and unseen. Millions seeing the same story without ever knowing each other. Without even having to be together. Effecting their dreams and actions. Replacing their books. Replacing religion, politics, art, conversation. Replacing their minds.

If Rabbit tries to control this process, and its effects, Miss Scoons is content simply to be its victim:

> I look at the screen and I am the screen. I'm not me. I don't know who I am. I look at the movie and I am the movie. I am the star. I am the star in the movie. For days I am the star and I'm not me. I'm me being the star. I look at my life when I come down. I look and I hate my life when I come down. I hate my life not being a movie. I hate my life not being a star. I hate being myself in my life which isn't a movie and never will be.

The recognition that Shepard's plays honestly refuse to provide is not even a promise of the movies. The self is lost while watching a movie, merged into the infinite "I am" of the star. The cycle of watching and coming down produces in the viewer an endlessly aroused and frustrated fantasy of imperial being.

Angel City sets out to show, despite its rhetoric to the contrary, that a screen is the most terrifying thing in the world. The play begins on a "*Basically bare stage. Upstage center is a large suspended blue neon rectangle with empty space in the middle. The rectangle is lit from time to time. . . . Upstage, directly behind the rectangle, is a narrow platform. . . . When the actors enter on this platform they have been framed by the rectangle."* This framing rectangle is the play's key protagonist, a kind of ever-present movie screen that treats the characters, as they enter, to a momentary apotheosis as a star. There is the illusion of being "captured in celluloid." It is a pleasant illusion, until it becomes fully literalized in the play's action. The company has been trying to introduce something "totally new"— something "three-dimensional"—into the medium of film. But the reverse happens. At the end, producer Wheeler gets trapped in the movie of his own imagining; one of the most terrifying moments in Shepard is when Wheeler's staff becomes an audience that watches him but refuses to wave back. They know that people on the screen cannot see people watching it. The terror here is that everyone collaborates in treating the stage as if it were a screen, as if it were not three-dimensional, as if Wheeler had passed from the space of drama's struggle to the nonspace of projected form. But this is what Shepard's characters typically do. They refuse the option of action and dialogue in a fully dimensioned space and play their parts as if they were audiences to—at best actors in—a movie. If "the plays," as Shepard said in 1977, "were a kind of chronicle I was keeping on myself," then his movies are perhaps a fable he is composing about us. Movies are for Shepard in his plays and prose a metaphor for American life as so often it is lived, and it is this urge toward withdrawal into the amplified, the dimensionless, and the continuity-ridden that he has set out, from the beginning, to place before us on the stage.

The conflicts that drive Shepard's career are not resolved—they are staged. By stepping with such willing reluctance into the felt tensions of American life, he continues to perfect his role as one of his country's leading cultural agonists. He takes things on, goes into them, acts them out. Experience must be overcome. The decision to write has been, he says, "a process of overcoming a tremendous morning despair. It's been diminishing over the years. But I still feel a trace of this thing that I can't really track down." The best way out is always through, and the end is not understanding, or reconciliation. The end is to keep the forces that make the play *at play*. Shepard remains willingly conflicted, generously divided. As he says of the Old Man and his feeling for the lovers in *Fool for Love*: "From his point of view, there's a danger of wholeness. Once they become whole, it shatters his entire existence, which depends on being split. . . . But there are a lot of different ways of looking at it."

Between L.A. and New York:

An Interview with Roberta Levitow

Mame Hunt

hen Jody McAuliffe asked me to do an interview piece, the first and most obvious candidate was my longtime colleague and friend, Roberta Levitow. I called Roberta with the idea. She laughed. What was the interview to be about? She wasn't sure she wanted to discuss "burnout," a popular topic in theater circles these days, given all our discourage-ment over the threats to the NEA, and so on. She's not sure that what she's feeling is burnout, exactly, and it's a harsh term. Levitow, a pri-vate person in some ways, is not usually one to publicly discuss such things. We would focus on larger topics. But when would we do it and how? Me and my trusty microcassette, over coffee, fitting around the shooting schedule of her film, *How Else Am I Supposed To Know I'm Still Alive?* which she was preparing for a February 13 shoot-date. The film is the fulfillment of her participation in the American Film Institute's Directing Workshop for Women, and marks her entry into

film directing. When I listed the other contributors and subjects of the *SAQ* special issue, she laughed again. "And why are we talking?" "I don't know. Maybe you're the token girl." "Well, I'm glad to be in such company, any way I can get there."

Roberta Levitow was born and raised in a suburb of Los Angeles. Her father was in the movie industry, as the animator of Mr. Magoo, among other projects, and later as a director of animated films. She started out in theater at Stanford as an actress. Like most ambitious, energetic theater students in California in the early 1970s, she spent time at the Pacific Conservatory for the Performing Arts, where Artistic Director Donovan Marley was the first to give her a shove into directing. Moving to Seattle to direct, she took over the Skid Road Theater there, later going to Seattle Rep as an NEA Directing Fellow. Most of her work then, as now, meant working on new plays, since it seemed, she once said, that the new play reading circuit was where they'd let you direct when they didn't want to set you loose on the subscribers. In those years of being locked into that reading circuit, she developed the skills and resources that would later make her one of the country's leading directors of new work. Years of free-lancing brought her to settle in L.A. as Casting Director for the first season of the Los Angeles Theatre Center (LATC). This was in 1985, and I was the Literary Manager there.

Roberta and I worked in the same building for over a year without actually working together. In the spring of 1986, in the course of one of his restructurings, Bill Bushnell ("Bush") moved Roberta into the literary department. Problem was, how was she supposed to fit? She had no desire to become a literary manager, and so we devised the position of Director of Special Projects. Bush approved the plan. Over the next two years, Roberta and I designed and produced two New Works Projects, an annual festival of new play development readings, as well as countless other readings of plays under consideration for production at LATC. Roberta supervised the early years of the Latino Lab, a major program of LATC. In 1987, Bushnell assigned her to direct the premiere of Darrah Cloud's *The Stick Wife*, for which I served as dramaturge; Hartford Stage then invited her to direct the play there a few months after its Los Angeles opening. The following season, she directed a successful world premiere of Marlane Meyer's *Etta Jenks*, which was a coproduction of LATC and The Women's Project and Productions in New York. In March of 1988, after *Etta* and the second New Works Project (which included a stunningly successful reading of Meyer's *Kingfish*, directed by David Schweizer), Roberta returned to free-lance directing. I soon left LATC as well to become Literary Manager of the Berkeley Repertory Theatre. Roberta's work since has included the world premiere productions of Meyer's *Geography of Luck* (South Coast Repertory), Migdalia Cruz's *Miriam's Flowers* (Playwrights Horizons), José Rivera's *Each Day Dies with Sleep* (a coproduction of Berkeley Rep and Circle Rep), Donald Margulies's *The Model Apartment* (LATC), Gary Leon Hill's *Back to the Blanket* (Denver Center Theater Company), and Constance Congdon's *Tales of the Lost Formicans* (Actors Theatre of Louisville), which toured to Helsinki, Finland, as part of the 1989 International Theatre Institute Festival. She is now an Associate Artist of the Mark Taper Forum and occasionally teaches new play directing and other theater courses at UCLA. In 1990, she was awarded the prestigious Alan Schneider Directing Fellowship.

One of the things that Roberta and I have in common is what we have come to call the Crusade. The Crusade is an accumulation of political passions and commitments. Taken to heart, these commitments make it possible to work in the not-for-profit theater, where the hours are long and the pay is low. Certain tenets of the Crusade were part of the artistic mission statement of the LATC while we were there. It found its expression not only in the choice of plays for production, but in the creation of one of the foremost homes for Latino theater artists in the country, early and rigorous multicultural casting, aggressive affirmative action programs at all levels of the institution, administrative as well as artistic, and a commitment to make our home in one of the roughest areas of downtown Los Angeles. Bush used to call us cultural terrorists. The Theatre Center was located on Spring Street on the edge of Skid Row. No Castle on the Hill for us; we couldn't neglect the disenfranchised, because they were right outside our doors every day. Spring Street was fuel for the Crusade.

As the issues of multiculturalism have become part of a nationwide debate, the Crusade has taken on new proportions for all those who were part of it. Those who opened the building on Spring Street in 1985 have gone on to other jobs, but many of us continue to carry the questions, curiosities, and issues of multiculturalism with us, working toward a time when multiculturalism will simply be. Until then, however, activating multiculturalism is difficult, and it is fraught with challenging and probing questions of self-criticism. Roberta recently wrote a letter to the editor of *American Theatre* magazine, in which she responded to the activism of the Theater Communications Group (TCG) biannual conference and the insights "shared by Athol Fugard about being a white spokesman for the black man's cause in South Africa: his humility at being welcomed into the heart and mind of a person who is the 'Other,' and his arrogance at wanting to be judged for the quality of his imagination and not the color of his skin. Don't we all have that right to humility and arrogance? I don't just mean white people having the right of entrance into other cultures, although, yes, that too. But more important, the right of artists of color and artists from other cultures to teach us through their humility and arrogance, through the quality of their imaginations. Perhaps this is our necessary dialogue. Mutual acceptance follows introduction, acquaintance, and then—at last—real appreciation. It is an ongoing process that will require vigilance and constant interaction."

HUNT: So what was the context of your letter to *American Theatre* magazine?

LEVITOW: When I got to the [Theater Communications Group] conference, everyone was so excited. Everybody I talked to said "This is the greatest conference we've had in years, there's so much collegial feeling, we're all united behind the NEA crisis." People were having meetings outside of meetings to talk about the NEA situation. It was great. There was so much enthusiasm, there was less hesitancy in talking to each other. . . . People were more friendly and gregarious. There was a strong presence of women.

HUNT: Was it intentional, do you think?

LEVITOW: Yeah, sure. There was a highly visible female presence at the conference. There was tremendous participation. Emily Mann had just taken over the McCarter, Joanne Akalaitis was at the Public. Lisa Peterson presented her performance piece of Virginia Woolf's work. Anne Bogart was very present.* But when I went to dinner with Darrah Cloud, Gordon Edelstein came to our table and asked if we knew that there had been a meeting of the black theater caucus, and they weren't having fun at all. They were feeling completely left out. They were feeling that no one was attending to their concerns and that racism, essentially in hiring, was still very present in American theater and that all this togetherness was actually exclusive, that their concerns weren't being addressed in this national congress. As he was saying that, I thought "white women, yes; black men, no." Interesting. There were women everywhere. There were white women everywhere. There weren't women of color, there were white women. Interesting to take note of that.

The next morning was Fugard's presentation. Lee Richardson stood up and said, "Mr. Fugard, I say this with all respect for your work because it's made a big impact on the way we understand the political situation in South Africa . . . but how do you feel, as a white man, writing the black man's voice?"† It was a direct question and Fugard answered it directly. "I am rigorous with myself," he said. "I ask myself: What am I doing? Do I have a right to be doing this? I'm just a person who happened to have been at a certain moment of history and had certain skills and certain opportunities, and something happened because of it. I feel honored to have been able to help give voice to people who had no voice." And Lee said, "How do you see the racial situation in the United States?" And Fugard said, "I'm glad you brought that up because in my opinion your racism is much more insidious than mine." He said, "Mine is easy, you know exactly who's on which side because it's all very overt. But in the United States, you have very subversive racism and it is much harder to understand it, to pinpoint it and then to defeat it." Lee said, "It's interesting that you would say that, because . . . ," and he started pointing out

*Anne Bogart is a director and the recently departed Artistic Director of the Trinity Repertory Company in Providence, Rhode Island.

†Lee Richardson is a free-lance director and the former Artistic Director of Crossroads Theatre Company in New Brunswick, New Jersey.

people in the auditorium who were black, saying, "See, this person is a set designer, this person is a costume designer, this person is a director, this person can't get work outside of work on material about African-Americans. And we feel that racism, we feel excluded. We feel the conference should be paying attention to that." Well, people were in the spirit for reconciliation, and suddenly the sixties were back, and everyone was saying, "Let's *do* something about that, let's *do* something about this." During the break, those black artists were accosted by artistic directors saying, "Get me your resume." Great, but kind of funny at the same time. Then later that day, Debbie Baley from the Perseverance Theatre proposed that TCG take national responsibility for a campaign to support the NEA, and everyone went "Unanimously! Yes!" It was like 1968. "Yes!" Every hand went up. A spokesperson for the black caucus said, "There's racism in the American theater—we need a task force on it and TCG should take charge." And the hands went up: "Yes! Absolutely, let's stop it, let's defeat it!" Then Jim Nicola from New York Theatre Workshop got up and said, "We need to take a stand about the homophobic elements in the campaign against the NEA. We want a resolution passed by the body that says 'we don't support homophobia' " and everybody went "Yes!" and the hands went up again.

HUNT: What happened to the women?

LEVITOW: The women didn't need to be passing resolutions. There wasn't a woman there who felt we were ripped off. I mean, I didn't feel that way. I'd just gotten $12,000. And a lot of attention.

I rode with Molly Smith and other friends back to New York City. Molly had gotten a grant from the Rockefeller Foundation to put together a truly multicultural theater company. Molly's people went around the state and auditioned every racial and cultural group that's in Alaska and brought the performers back to the Perseverance Theatre in Juneau. They'd just come out of the first year of this ambitious effort, and it was hard because the logistics of making something like that happen were awesome. This multicultural thing: Does it mean that we white people get to invite over the Chinese for the opera and the Japanese for the Noh and bring Chocolate Bayou up from the South? Is it like being an anthropologist, collecting all these wonderful artifacts from all these different cultures? It's nice to have that permission, that enthusiasm for the process of reeducation. So on this drive back into New York, we were aware that we *seek out* being influenced by other cultures. Most of us are making a conscious effort, certainly in artist/intellectual circles, to be liberal and careful. But one of the people in the car said, "You know, I saw a project at one of the Puerto Rican theater companies in New York and it was sexist. I don't want to support that. I don't need to see plays where guys are macho and they treat women like those women were treated in that play." And I said, "That doesn't make sense to me. No, we must go see those plays. And we can't go saying, 'Gosh, I wish you guys would catch up,' or 'I'm not interested in black theater, it's so loud and everybody's always emoting so much,' or 'I'm not interested in Hispanic theater because it's always macho.'"

We've become very selective about what we will let ourselves be told by the Other. We're willing to let the Other in, but only in ways that please us. We don't want the Other in if the Other is going to tell us things we don't want to hear and in ways we don't want to hear it. And I feel like there's a really big glitch there. There's a big problem. Because we have to hear what we don't want to hear. We have to hear what we don't know how to hear. The way multiculturalism has been constructed up to this point is "You can come to our house," not "We're going to your house."

HUNT: Can't that work, though? Wasn't it working for LATC to invite Latino artists to be in residence there, to create the Latino Theatre Lab within the confines of the white-run LATC?

LEVITOW: Well, it was working, for a time, probably because the Lab was relatively self-sufficient. Bush [Bill Bushnell] gave over so much independence to José Luis.* They pretty much did what they wanted to do, and Bush didn't define what kind of Hispanic theater could come in. Whereas at the Taper, Manuel Puig's *Mystery of the Rose Bouquet* was a piece that *happened* to be Latin, and it happened to be cast with white actresses, it happened to be directed by a white director, and it happened to be a story that was humane, funny, touching, and just a little bit mysterious. It was very comprehensible, it was completely accessible.

*José Luis Valenzuela was the Director of the Latino Theatre Lab at LATC.

HUNT: It was a good crossover piece.

LEVITOW: Yes, and it was selected out of the stuff that's hard to watch, and weird and disturbing, and brings up a lot of concerns you don't want to see, including anger and frustration and intercommunity bickering.

HUNT: Maybe this is a redefinition of what it is to be politically correct: to take hold of what's difficult to grasp, what's uncomfortable rattling around in your brain.

LEVITOW: I think we can have positions about how we'd like the world to be for ourselves, but if we want to have multiculturalism, we are going to have to live amongst the people the way they live, not the way we want them to live. I'm trying to talk about a way of assembling art and culture that is not assimilationist. I assimilated; I'm from an immigrant family. Many people will assimilate toward the dominant culture but that process of assimilation has aesthetic and cultural attributions. If you assimilate toward the dominant culture in the U.S., then your play is going to happen in a theater. George Wolfe's plays are historical now. They're about history, they happen in theaters. He's finding a positive way to cross over. Lee Richardson told me he asked Wolfe why he doesn't write plays about the present tense black experience, and George said because it's excruciating. *Spunk* is a collection of stories by Zora Neal Hurston. These stories were written between 1926 and 1942. *Spunk* is a great piece to watch, it's entertaining. It's an important contribution in the teaching of African-American history. However, it's not the same as that white middle-class audience going to spend even fifteen minutes in a contemporary African-American family context. We've given ourselves permission to . . .

HUNT: To taste.

LEVITOW: Yes, we've given ourselves permission to go out and have dinner at different international restaurants every night. Because we love it and now we talk about how much we love it. Ooooooh, I love soul food, I love Thai. And it's sincere, but it's an incomplete exchange. I started noticing that a lot of people were still pissed off. And I thought, "Why are you guys still so pissed off? Aren't things getting better?" "No, they're not getting better." Well, how come we don't know that? Because we're not going there. We're still not going there.

HUNT: And that comes out of fear, you think, fear of the strange, the Other?

LEVITOW: I think it is. I'm on the multicultural task force at UCLA. It's pretty interesting to watch a huge institution like UCLA deal with problems of cultural diversity. Pretty interesting to listen to the students themselves and try to hear what they're asking for and not just decide what they're asking for. I thought I had an idea what they're asking for. I thought they wanted a way in. But I don't think anymore that that's what they want. There *are* some ways in. They want to stop feeling like the *only* thing they can do is come in. They want us to come over.

HUNT: But why is this your crusade?

LEVITOW: Well, that's a really good question and I've been asking myself that a lot. I started to give myself some shit about it. I need to be rigorous, like Athol Fugard. I need to constantly ask myself what is important to me about it. Surely there's an identification with "outsider" status. I mean, I'm a female, and as a Jewish female who was raised by a paranoid Eastern European grandmother, I have an identification with outsider status that is pretty fundamental. I'm accustomed to thinking that I'm always going to have to knock at the door and hope that somebody will let me in, rather than thinking that I have a right or that I have a key. I don't have the key.

HUNT: But the intensity of your being part of this crusade has been growing over the last two years or so.

LEVITOW: Partly by circumstance. I mean, I didn't ask to be on the multicultural task force at UCLA: somebody called me up and said "would you please" and I said "well sure," not really knowing what it meant. In fact, they asked me before the Diaspora, the black theater students, did their demonstration. I hadn't known there was a problem; I just showed up in September and started teaching. I certainly noticed that there wasn't a lot of cultural diversity present in the department, both in terms of curriculum and in the profile of the faculty and students. It's something I care about a lot, and it's something that's very much of-the-time; there are eruptions everywhere, really. When I sat down in the advanced playwriting class at UCLA, I asked, "What are you guys concerned about in your writing?" These are six playwriting students in their first year of graduate work at UCLA and five of them are white; one is female and the rest are male. Of the males, one said he wanted to write for women, develop a woman's "voice" that is truthful. Another said he wants to break out of his own cultural bias and write people of other cultures and understand how to do that. And then two of them said, "I want to write about the disappearing life-style of my people." They meant white people. These kids are 20, 22. "I want to write what it's like to be a white male in America right now. I want to write what it's like to know that none of the perks that my dad had will be mine." I told this to Edit Villareal, who teaches Chicano Studies at UCLA and she's also head of the playwriting program. I said, "Edit, this is what the playwrights were saying this morning, isn't that interesting?" Some of them want more of this multicultural stuff and some were saying they want to talk about the fear . . .

HUNT: The backlash.

LEVITOW: These are decent people, but one of them is talking about the shadow and the fear, and the other is talking about the possibility and the hopefulness that this change is going to bring. It's happening, and these young artists want to talk about it. Edit said that white kids in her Chicano studies class come up to her and say, "I wish I had culture like this. I don't have anything or anybody." These kids don't believe they have a cultural heritage. They feel lost.

HUNT: How does all this affect your actual work?

LEVITOW: Well, when I wanted to make a movie, I asked Evelina Fernandez if we could adapt her play, which is set in East L.A., and so I spend a lot of time over in Montebello, on the East Side of L.A. I grew up in L.A., my father was born in Boyle Heights, but I've never spent more than drive-by time there.* Until now. Now I hang out there sometimes, partly to get the work done, partly just to hang out with the people I'm working with. In a way, I'm trying to test my theory. Maybe my contribution is to go there myself, not stay home and let people come to me. And part of that effort is to let Evelina's voice speak, to let that culture say what it wants to say rather than my defining what I want the culture to say. The story itself is about an

*Boyle Heights is a community in East Los Angeles that was originally populated by Jewish immigrants and is now populated by Latinos.

older woman having a baby, and whether or not she should have an abortion. It's not anything radical, aesthetically or politically. But it brings—and this is a significant fact—it reveals a couple of individuals who might be labeled and then misunderstood and then, perhaps, dismissed. This film gives these individuals an opportunity to speak and be human and funny.

HUNT: You're exerting a great deal of effort in being rigorous, as Fugard said, about your own motivations. Do you think that this is a one-way street? You did an interview when *Etta Jenks* opened in Los Angeles where you expressed some concern that you were being ghettoized, that you were too often asked to do plays about women in crisis.

LEVITOW: To tell you the truth, I find I'm inclined to continue doing women's plays. I would pick Evelina's play over somebody else's play. I would pick Darrah Cloud's next play or her adaptation of *O Pioneers!* over something else. When I make lists of who I'd like to work with again, the list reflects my personal desire to keep putting women's work forward. I invite Phyllis Nagy to the Taper, I try to get a commission for Marlane Meyer, I try to get Darrah's play on the boards.

HUNT: Is it as hard for women artists as it was when you did the *Etta* interview [in 1988]? Is progress being made?

LEVITOW: (pause) Yeah, I think there probably is. There's more of a track record than there was, say, ten years ago, so people are less frightened. They don't think, "Ooh, it's a play by a woman, it might just fall apart." They think, "Oh, it's a play by a woman and directed by a woman, that's OK." There are more women running theater companies now. But it's still possible that we're getting these jobs because we can't get film and television jobs. Men are leaving theater to go do film and television, which is where the money and the glamour is. A lot of the people who hire now are more familiar with the experience of having a woman work at their theater. Probably most people have had *a* woman work at that theater, so it's no longer the first time that someone has to do it. But it's not gotten to the point where it's gender-blind hiring. People still tend to hire people like them, people they're more comfortable with. The men are more comfortable with men. But the women are hiring women, or some of them are.

HUNT: Is it significant that many women directors are "putting forward" and directing plays by men?

LEVITOW: If one asks, "Is the writing of women coming forward?" I don't know, that's a different question. The directing opportunities for women are changing. I think the competency question has pretty much been addressed. I mean, there are enough women who've managed to get from the beginning of a production to the end of a production. The evidence would show that you can still get a hit, you can still get a rave review and be female. The answers to the big-budget questions, like Broadway, that probably still hasn't shifted very much. In regional theater, if the perspective is that hiring a woman director is risky, then that's followed by the perspective that says "you can afford a bad show, you can afford to hire two women out of six shows because you know you'll get by, there's a safety net." There's no safety net on Broadway, and there's no safety net in film, so that's still one of the reasons women are having a rough time getting into film directing. Women writers, though, I don't know.

HUNT: When the Taper asks you what you want to do, you say, "I want to work with Marlane, I want to work with Darrah, I want to work with Connie, I want to work with Phyllis." You're there as a personality force, as an energy force that they have invested in and you're telling them, "I want to take your investment and move it over to these people." But writers so seldom talk to the powers that be. Are artistic directors responding to you or to the writing?

LEVITOW: Well, that's a good point. It's possible that if I were bringing in projects by male writers I would be getting work up faster at the Taper than I'm able to do now. They're willing to let me do a project, but they haven't responded to any of the material I've submitted. It may be that the artistic director of this particular institution doesn't respond to women's writing. And neither do some members of his staff. So *Miriam's Flowers* isn't going into Taper Too, and *O Pioneers!* is not part of the subscription season on the main stage. The writers I'm interested in aren't writing so-called mainstream material. They don't want to; it's not the kind of writing they do. So when you ask if it's a one-way street for the female experience—that women can go to the man's house, but the men don't really want to come to the women's house—I think those writers might be evidence that that's true.

HUNT: The women's "house" is writing?

LEVITOW: Yes, and there are people who don't really want to hear the story the way those women are telling the story. But, just like the situation of the black theater artists at the TCG conference: that is the story that wants to be told but doesn't want to be listened to. It's a different kind of language and subject matter. More unpleasant, more unassimilated.

HUNT: The paradox is always that when plays by women that are about that feminine sensibility get produced, the audiences respond tremendously. The critics often don't.

LEVITOW: Yes, they really don't.

HUNT: And that's also true of multiculturalism. So what do you do? Do you just wait for all these old white guys to fade away?

LEVITOW: It's not just the old white guys who have this problem; it's the young white guys and the young white women, too. A lot of us are putting up a lot of obstacles to real interchange. If it were just gender and age, then why aren't our friends' plays getting done? We have young women running theater companies, and they're not picking that stuff either.

HUNT: But with women artists, there are no culture-specific theaters, other than the Women's Project in New York. There is no Inner City Cultural Center for women. You do have to wait to be invited up onto the Hill.

LEVITOW: Yes, you're right. Women's work gets done because someone gets tired of waiting to be invited.

HUNT: It seemed that when we were at LATC, there was a lot of writing by women getting done, there and elsewhere. That doesn't seem to be as true now. How come?

LEVITOW: This is how I taught my feminist theater class: I said if you can identify with a question about the distribution of power in relation to gender, then you can identify with a question about the distribution of power in relation to race, sexual preference, class, or anything else. Women know what it's like to have power withheld because of something that is involuntary, something that one didn't choose to be true. There are a lot of analogies about how things are or aren't happening for women in the same ways they are or aren't happening for other disenfranchised groups. Any black theater artist would identify those times when suddenly everybody wants to do black theater, and then, just as suddenly, nobody wants to do it anymore. There are times when everybody wants to do the next Latino play, and then nobody wants to do it anymore. Maybe that's what happened when we were at LATC. Feminism was hot for awhile, but feminism is far from hot now.

HUNT: Do you think these trends occur because there's money to back them up?

LEVITOW: Well, it was probably hot because there was some money available for it, but also it may have just been trendy. But feminism isn't trendy now, that's for sure.

HUNT: The immediacy of these issues, the changeableness of them— does that have a connection to the fact that you only direct new plays? Can the classics address the sociopolitical connections that you need to make as an artist?

LEVITOW: I'm sure they could, but not for me.

HUNT: You seem to learn a lot from the playwrights that you work with. You talk about getting inside Evelina's world, and I know that's also true with Mickie Cruz and Marlane and Darrah. Does it have to do with wanting to be around a living experience, an energy force?

LEVITOW: Yes, I'm sure it does. For example: I like Lorca very much, so I've read a lot about him, I directed *Yerma*. And I feel sympathy with something central to his work, but it's not an immediate experience. It's described. When I work with my "new play" students at UCLA, we talk about how much energy you put into knowing the universe of the person who's writing that play. Invariably the students say, "This would be great for us to use on our classical pieces." And I say yes, that's right, it would be good for you to do that. It would be great. So you go spend six months trying to get as intimate with Chekhov as you just got with your writing buddy. There are so many intangible things that are never described in books, and I guess some directors just make all sorts of intuitive leaps based on what they read. They read and read and read, and when they've immersed themselves in that person, they begin to explore their own response to the material. I think that's the right process, and I read a lot when I'm preparing my work, but I don't feel that I'm able to know that artist from description the way I'm able to pick up things from the artist in person. These are things that are unnamed but knowable. So

I much prefer the immediacy of working with a living author. Also, it broadens my world tremendously. I'm so private and solitary in so many ways that by having these unnamed but knowable experiences with other people, my living experience is bigger.

HUNT: And is that how it feels? That your life gets bigger?

LEVITOW: Yeah, sometimes. "Oh, we're going here now. Oh, great, let's go there." I probably wouldn't go by myself. The writer goes. The writer says I'm gonna go over there, there's a dark alley, I'm gonna go walk down there and open that door. Writers are terribly curious and they'll go. But I'm extremely fearful, so I like to go with somebody else.

HUNT: You're teaching new play development now. What is that like? What skills are necessary in new play work? Many artistic directors seem to choose to direct classics much much more than they choose to direct new work. I was talking to Heather McDonald about this, and she wanted to know why Garland Wright doesn't direct new plays. Why doesn't Bob Falls direct new plays?* These are people that I need to learn from, she said, and they don't do it. Part of it is, per-haps, a matter of ego. When you work with Mickie Cruz, you turn around to her and ask her, "Is this supposed to be funny?" When you do that, you're choosing to report back to this other fearless warrior. But Garland is not reporting back. He only has to be concerned with what Garland wants it to look like.

LEVITOW: That's right. He asks, do I think it's funny? And if he thinks it's funny, he makes it a joke and if he doesn't think it's funny he makes it not a joke. He might ask an actor.

HUNT: But in doing new plays, the director is answerable to one more person, and it's a big person, with some pretty scary stuff on the line. Doing world premieres is a very high-pressure business.

LEVITOW: I do listen to the playwright a lot and I probably should hold on to my own ideas a bit more. There've been times I knew something was wrong and I didn't say, "We're not doing this." As I

*Heather McDonald is the author of the plays *The Rivers and Ravines*, *Available Light*, and *Dream of a Common Language*. Garland Wright is the Artistic Director of the Guthrie Theatre; Robert Falls is the Artistic Director of the Goodman Theatre.

do it more and more, I'll become able to balance listening with telling. It is so interesting to me how one's personality so fundamentally informs what one does. I don't think it's programmatic for me that I like talking to Mickie, I just really like talking to Mickie. She's fun to know, and she takes me places I've never been, and I love that. So I don't mind asking, "Is that funny?" I don't mind saying that because that's how I learn about her and it's how I get to go take a trip someplace I've never been before.

HUNT: So you're not doing it just to make the play better, you're doing it to make your life bigger?

LEVITOW: Oh, I'm sure I'm doing it *mostly* because my life is bigger. Happily, though, finding the right answer makes the play better, because I'll have found out the perfect answer instead of a made-up answer. Most people do plays about what they know. I don't do very many plays about what I know.

HUNT: But isn't there a whole section of the audience that wants to see what they know?

LEVITOW: There was a guy that stood up in the Circle Rep audience of *Each Day Dies with Sleep* and said, "Well, this doesn't have anything to do with life as *we* know it!" And I thought "Of course it doesn't, that's why we're doing the play!"

HUNT: One of the things I'm curious about is this bicoastal career you've been having: *Etta Jenks, The Stick Wife, Each Day Dies with Sleep*—all done on both coasts. What's the difference?

LEVITOW: I was trying to explain to Kathleen Dimmick at the Taper why she could have fun out here in California because she wasn't sure she could, having just moved here from the East Coast. And I said, you can, because in the West we're still inventing and reinventing ourselves. Our theater work has that energy. We haven't seen everything that's gone before; we're not referring back to a recent production which refers back to another production, which refers back to another production. Each thing we do is new to us and we're making up the rules pretty much as we go along. And that's the fun part. It can be a collage of things that don't belong together, it can be whatever we say it is, because we're out here in the West and nobody can stop us! So oftentimes the work is a little wilder. It has a certain energy and vitality to it.

HUNT: Is it more innovative?

LEVITOW: Not necessarily. It's not necessarily more innovative because innovation is based on what came before. But we don't really pay much attention to what came before, because everything is constantly brand-new and we're only interested in what's new. That's very much the personality of the West Coast in general but certainly Los Angeles and California in particular, and it's reflected in the theater here. It feels like gold rush time, and we're building the town out of the prairie.

You go back to the East Coast and it's exactly the opposite. Everything is seen in relation to something else. Everything is compared to the work that came before. Not surprisingly, like other aspects of the East Coast, there are traditions and rules and hierarchies in East Coast theater. Who you aspire toward, what good aesthetics are. No one works out of context—you're always *in context*. Now, because it's in context, people have a very lively framework for discussion, so people can speak of the work in relation to this piece or the piece that they saw that this author did before. The audiences and the artistic community and the critics can articulate this generation of writers vs. the generation of writers that came before, how directing styles are changing, the history of the institution at which you're working. The eastern audience has probably seen more over the years, so they've watched the art form itself develop through different stages. And they see the work in context with their own experience. They compare Lois Smith's performance in one play with her performance in another and with Jessica Tandy's performances, with other great American stage actresses who they've seen.

HUNT: How does it affect your work?

LEVITOW: I think that the move from West to East is productive for me because the first productions here are new, new plays, and there's a lot of vitality about the fact that we're doing it at all. And then, when we go back East, we . . .

HUNT: We get nailed.

LEVITOW: We didn't always get nailed. We got nailed one out of three times. That's not horrible. It's just that that was the last time, so that's what's horrible about it. The most recent scars are the most painful. The first time we ever did *Stick Wife*, at LATC, we were amazed by it. By the time we did it at Hartford Stage, it became a production with certain aesthetic elements, and we had the opportunity to sand and polish. A lot of the spontaneous invention that birthed the first time was refined the second time.

HUNT: But with *Stick Wife* you had the advantage of stirring things up with a new cast and a full rehearsal period. With *Etta*, there were a few new cast members. With *Each Day*, it was the same cast, shorter restaging time . . .

LEVITOW: *Each Day* had its own problems because *Each Day* had its own problems. I can't really ascribe its problems to the fact that I didn't get to try it again. Although I think it would have been much better if I had gotten to try it again, but. . . . In *Etta*, Didi O'Connell, John Nesci, and Ebbe Roe Smith: all three of them had spent time in New York, doing a lot of productions in New York, and they weren't intimidated by it.* And, in fact, I remember talking to Didi before we went, and she said don't worry, we'll be fine, because I know what this feels like, and I think the audience will appreciate the writing and they'll like the way we're doing it. And Nesci said the same thing. He never doubted that it would go over, and he's spent time in both places. We didn't have that experience on *Each Day*. With *Each Day*, there was tremendous pressure, which we tried to evaporate, but it wouldn't seem to go anywhere. There was a lot of tension in the cast about performing in New York at that level of exposure, at Circle Rep. As to the play itself—we knew that our work was incomplete and that was a lot of pressure to put on the cast. They knew that something wasn't quite right, so they couldn't feel like they were coasting in, which had been the feeling with *Etta*. They felt like we were kind of limping in, and that's bad.

HUNT: Are you conscious of making different aesthetic choices when the production will be moving to New York?

LEVITOW: Yes, I am. I mean, it took me three times to get it. Of course, you know, failure is the best teacher. I didn't quite understand how it worked so well on *Stick Wife*. I wasn't even sure how it was working on *Etta*, but now, having added *Each Day*, I can see

---

*Deirdre O'Connell, John Nesci, and Ebbe Roe Smith played leading roles in the New York production of *Etta Jenks*.

something of what we were doing. I remember this from my work in Seattle. A lot of times in the provinces, which I think Los Angeles in some ways still is, the work is dominated by its energy and vitality, not by its subtlety and refinement. The fact that you do it at all, the energy with which you do it, is oftentimes convincing to us, because we've gotten it up out of nothing. But when you go back East, everybody sort of assumes "Well, we've been doing that for centuries here, so the fact that you *do* it is not that interesting. We want to see your skill level in relation to someone else's." Now, with *Each Day*, I was doing a show at Circle Rep; I was being reviewed by the same people who review Marshall Mason! It's scary. *I* never put myself in comparison with Marshall Mason. I don't do that, but I was at Circle Rep, and I was a director just like he's a director. And José's a writer just like Lanford Wilson is a writer. Nobody is giving us a break for being young and enthusiastic: people are expecting us to live up to certain expectations and those expectations are based on a comparison with the peer group. So while it was exciting to be compared with the peer group, it was also a lesson in, you know, well, what does that mean? Aesthetically, because New York theater is so poverty-stricken, most people have dismissed any emphasis on design. They don't seem to expect spectacle to the same degree that West Coast audiences do. We're still quite seduced by spectacle. We have the space. We have the budgets. And the audiences are charmed by it. I think of a piece like Schweizer's production of *Kingfish* at LATC, which was such a smash. There were many things about the production that were very ingratiating to the audience, but certainly the sound, light, and picture show were a good portion of what was endearing about it. It was beautiful. But because theater is so poverty-stricken in New York, people are used to walking into places like Playwrights' Horizons or Circle Rep, which are no bigger than this living room, and the walls are falling down, the seats are incredibly uncomfortable, the bathroom looks like something you should be scared of and get out of as fast as you can. The sets: you can see the tape lines; it's just hard to disguise the mechanics of the visuals in such a small space. The budgets are limited, it's impossible to get a prop, the work it takes to get the right prop in New York is unbelievable. So people don't really expect the spectacle to be that fabulous and they don't care if it isn't as long as the acting and the writing is *exceptional*. That's what they want to see. Certainly *Each Day Dies with Sleep* was heavy on spectacle, and it made a lot of people very . . . I mean, some people loved it, and they thought the spectacle was great, but other people certainly felt that it was completely overwhelming. And I thought, well, certainly it was never meant to be overwhelming, but in our large space at Berkeley, it wasn't so overwhelming. . . . New Yorkers would've been fine if I'd just cut the slides, cut the sound cues, just gotten those actors talking with those words. Their interest is more on performance and text. It's definitely on understated vs. overstated performance.

HUNT: We're trained on it. We all did Shakespeare outside in the summer.

LEVITOW: Right. We're used to more "performance," and the taste in New York is much more understated. I've watched actors very carefully, and it's remarkable how much the New York actor undercuts the overtly theatrical choice. In L.A., the actors don't give you the theatrical choice at all; they opt for believability. L.A. actors acquire a different set of skills in doing film and television, and one of those skills is to go with the first choice. In theater, their job is to reveal the unexpected. But in film and TV, their job is to fulfill the expected. New York actors are self-revelatory, whereas L.A. actors *look* like they're self-revelatory. Also—and I actually came to appreciate this—in L.A., I don't think we consider authenticity a vital quality that we desire in our lives. The authentic, the unpretentious—

HUNT: The authentic what?

LEVITOW: We'd rather buy a new chair than strip an old chair, and it is so much the opposite back East. Lack of pretension and authenticity is all-important. And there's a high degree of sensitivity to what might seem pretentious. The coasts are quite opposite in that regard.

HUNT: It's a complicated dichotomy. Maybe the East Coast is pretentious about their authenticity?

LEVITOW: Maybe. The eastern critics congratulate you for what you've got, but you get criticized for what you're faking. Here, we *accept* some kind of hype. Here, everything is conjured. We live in a desert and we've conjured a garden. You get admiration and respect for that within the community of artists. Back there, everybody's got a Geiger counter about conjuring, so the theater tends to be re-markably honest. Good New York actors are very honest, and the good New York directors keep them honest. It's to the bone; it's the straight goods. Out here we can bullshit a little bit, we make fan-tasy. We let our imaginations go—we encourage our imaginations to go, and sometimes we're a bit dishonest. We'll be dishonest for the effect. And that doesn't go over too good back there.

HUNT: Heather McDonald was telling me about what provoked her to write *Dream of a Common Language*, and she said she was curious about the number of women artists who, when they reach a certain age, i.e., ours, they stop. They just stop.

LEVITOW: I tell you, sometimes I feel like that. I just feel like turning the power off. Stop now. And it's really not frustration or burnout. When you're climbing to the top of the mountain, you can only imag-ine what's at the top, and so it's exciting because your imagination is filled with all the potential of what could be there. And I'm at a position now where at least I can see it. I think I can see where I'm going. I can see what a life in the theater is.

HUNT: What is it?

LEVITOW: Well, for a director, it's running a company in a relatively large American city, if you're lucky, with a reasonable budget and reasonable visibility. If you're not lucky, then it's running a com-pany in a smaller town, less visibility. It's teaching, if you're lucky in a large university, if not, at a smaller school. The visibility of your work, and your ability to interact with colleagues would depend on where you end up. Or it's free-lancing and bopping around like a crazy person, 130 days a year being somewhere else. Living in a hotel room for six weeks, no family with you, your friends are on the tele-phone. Meeting a production team for the first time, hoping that they like you well enough to bring you back the next time. Then the six weeks are up and all those friendships: poof!

HUNT: You don't sound like you're much in favor of the free-lance option.

LEVITOW: I'm definitely not in favor of the free-lance option. I'm not sure I'm in favor of any of the three of those options, quite frankly. I don't think those are very promising options.

HUNT: Gordon Davidson's not teaching, Bob Falls isn't teaching.

Robert Woodruff is still free-lancing, but for most of our leading directors, teaching and/or free-lancing don't seem to be the top of the mountain.

LEVITOW: Gordon's experience is totally different. Gordon was a founding director, Donovan Marley was a founding director, Bill Bushnell was a founding director. I mean, those guys . . . it must be very different for them. They started a business, they invented it from scratch and it began to thrive. You can tell I'm a westerner, because it's much more appealing to me to have entrepreneurial adventures where you start from nothing and something happens than to just fit into the existing system.

HUNT: You're not considering starting a theater.

LEVITOW: I'm not considering starting a theater. But I am considering running one. I got headhunted the other day, my first time. I'm so excited! So I'm trying to think about that. What would that really be like? Five years of my life, going to donor brunches and trustee meetings. And there's teaching, which is exciting, but it's hard to find an environment where professionals really mesh in an academic setting. And I am not a trained academic. I am from the professional world and I had a very good experience at UCLA, but I'm watching myself and other fellow professionals as we try to interact in an academic setting, and I don't think full-time teaching would be a very good choice for me.

HUNT: So what's left is the combo plate approach. That's what you've done this year—you've got free-lancing gigs, you're attached to the Taper, you're teaching a little bit.

LEVITOW: This year is the combo plate year, that's right. That's what this is.

HUNT: And has it been more satisfying than spending 130 days out of town? Your phone bill's down.

LEVITOW: Yes, my phone bill's remarkably down, as a matter of fact. I don't have to get on airplanes as often, and I was getting so sick of that. So the combo plate is good right now, but it's not financially better. For me, though, it's more stimulating because there's change and variety in what I'm doing.

HUNT: When you first started having associate artist meetings at the Taper, you talked about Woodruff's being one of the foremost directors in the country and not being able to get his teeth fixed, the irony of being affiliated with this very successful institution and not being able to get a decent health plan.

LEVITOW: Yeah, the Taper isn't helping me to get a health plan. But UCLA did, so I now know that if a horrible thing happened to me I'd be OK. It's the first time I've felt that way in years, and it's not thanks to any theater institution I've worked for, and it's not thanks to the directors' union. It's thanks to a brief but very rewarding full-time affiliation with a university.

HUNT: What ends up happening, then, is that when artists get old enough to comprehend they're not going to live forever, they have to get at least halfway out, begin teaching, looking for other sources of support.

LEVITOW: Every director I know is trying to get a television job. Robert Woodruff did a *Wise Guy* episode. The list of theater directors who are now making efforts to direct film and television: it's everybody. Literally everybody. Not even *most* people. I'm so late, and I live in Los Angeles, what have I been doing for five years? I've been living here, but I wasn't ready.

HUNT: What makes you ready?

LEVITOW: Good question.

HUNT: Why now, why not before?

LEVITOW: I didn't know how to compare the skills. I'm not sure I had the confidence. I grew up here, and I have a lot of personal demons about film and television.

HUNT: Because of growing up here or because your dad was in it?

LEVITOW: Both. Because I met a lot of strange characters, young actresses trying to get work. I found out how murky the world can be here. I met a lot of people who were hustlers and they didn't in any way feel like artists. And then my dad. Some demons about entering my father's world and what was the priority of the people who were in it. But I have to honestly say that of the people I've met so far, being in this AFI Directing Workshop for Women project, they are quite exceptional. They're smart, they're educated, they love art of all kinds, they often come from backgrounds in the theater, they're energetic. They're very disciplined about doing their work, because they've got to do the same things as one does to get a play together in half the time and with four times as many details. So whatever pre-conceptions I've had about John Steppling movie sleazebos, they're actually kind of impressive people. Fortunately, I don't seem to be hanging out with the people in John Steppling plays.*

HUNT: Thank God.

LEVITOW: Thank God. But here's an interesting thing: UCLA is a school of film, television, and theater and they're not going to separate them. They're going to start telling students they can study all three, which will be pretty much the UCLA gimmick, claim to fame, because there won't be another school in America that does that.

HUNT: We were talking awhile ago about what's wrong with the regional theater, the death of theater in America.

LEVITOW: Oh, were we talking about that again?

HUNT: And you were saying that theater is an art form that is based in literature, and that the reason, perhaps, that theater is decaying, or whatever's happening to it, is because the school systems are not turning people out who are literate and who are acquisitional about getting literary experiences and verbal experiences. If you combine film, TV, and theater, what happens to theater?

LEVITOW: Beats me. I tell you, I can only imagine it dies a painful, horrible death. We had a meeting yesterday at UCLA about new play development, where it should fit in the curriculum. Do you have to know theater before you can learn screenwriting, do you have to know how to write a play before you can write a screenplay? And where should we put the screenwriting component, should it be in the middle, should it be at the end, where?

HUNT: What did they decide?

LEVITOW: Well, they stuck it in the middle. And I raised my hand and I said, "Excuse me but it seems like a big philosophical choice we're making here. Shouldn't we decide whether the students need to accomplish theater before they try screenwriting? It is a different way of doing things, a different way of looking at things. Seems to me, if you can write a play, you can write a screenplay, but if you can write a screenplay you certainly cannot necessarily write a play."

*John Steppling is a Los Angeles playwright whose work often examines the darker, or darkest, side of Hollywood.

They listened. And then we took screenwriting out of the middle and put it at the end. It was so odd, because it was such a small moment, and yet of great import.

HUNT: Why is it, then, that playwrights, when they start writing for television and film, don't come back to theater? Do you think it's purely economics?

LEVITOW: No, I don't. Because as I begin to work on this movie, I find myself losing a kind of belief in theater. I feel that whatever has disappointed me about making theater—the disrespect that the artists get, the lack of audience enthusiasm in many ways, the difficulty of putting together the projects, the number of times that it fails for unbelievable reasons that you can never quite figure out, the few times that it really succeeds, the energy that it takes, the eternal optimism and faith you have to have to make a play—I find those concerns coming to the foreground instead of being in the background. It's so easy to be defeated by the difficulties of doing it. Film is not like that. Film is seductive. It *does happen*. It gets done. The locomotive starts going and it keeps going. They give you food, they feed you well, there's coffee, there's always a little table with little refreshments, the chairs are comfortable, the buildings are clean. And people get their work done. They're not jerks. They're smart, they're lively, they're funny, and it gets done.

HUNT: And why? Because the payoff is so great? Why can't that happen in the theater?

LEVITOW: Because it's business. It's big business. Film is a successful business and theater is not a successful business. Part of me knows that this is a Pollyanna point of view, because this is my first film adventure. But what's seductive as much as anything is you get your work done. You come in with an idea and, OK, it gets pushed around here and there, but it's more or less creative. It's not like everybody's a demon, they just compromise here and there, they're willing to take the nips and tucks. In nonprofit theater, we take nips and tucks by virtue of our own limitations. The nips and tucks in television happen from the outside. Someone says "You better nip and tuck here." There's more freedom in the theater, you can do whatever you can accomplish. Physically. With your own energy. Whatever you can muster together, you can say in the theater, and someone might come in to watch it. You can't say whatever you want to say in film and television, but it will get done. You'll have a product, you'll have fulfilled something. And they'll pay you. You can live in a house and buy some groceries, you know?

HUNT: Did you think you'd do this? When you first started in theater, did you think you'd eventually make this transition into film?

LEVITOW: No, I didn't.

HUNT: When you first started directing, what did you think would happen?

LEVITOW: I thought I was going to be a great theater director. I thought there was something called greatness in the American theater. First, I wanted to be a great actress, and then I wanted to be a great director. I thought you could be great. Who are the great ones of our generation?

HUNT: Who do you think are the great directors?

LEVITOW: I admire Garland Wright tremendously. I admire Mark Lamos, Dan Sullivan. I very much admire Robert Woodruff's work. I've only seen a couple of things of Emily Mann's and I liked *Annulla* very much. I admire Joanne Akalaitis. There are people I admire, but I don't think they have the kind of stature that I once imagined one could have in the theater. These artists aren't being treated like national treasures, like in Japan. It may be that the society, the culture, isn't giving these artists the permission or the recognition, somehow, to be treasured.

HUNT: But that was the idea.

LEVITOW: To me, sure. Yes. I wanted to be a great artist. I wanted to be like Rembrandt. I wanted my art form to have greatness.

HUNT: What were the things that made you start thinking that wasn't possible?

LEVITOW: I don't know. It might be my own limitations, Mame. It might just be me going, well, I'll never be a great artist. Maybe it's been seeing myself in context with other people and realizing that the things I like, some people love and some people hate. I would always prefer to work on The Gang's plays than anything else, but that's not going to get grocery money. Maybe I've done the best I can do and that's what it is. Or maybe if I do have it, whatever "it" is, it's going to be expressed in very idiosyncratic ways.

HUNT: Would you have done your career differently, made different choices along the way?

LEVITOW: Oh, no. I don't think so. I feel extremely fortunate, actually. The ultimate pretension to me has often been to describe myself as an artist at all. My father was a painter, so I used to go to the art museums all day long. When I think of great artists, I think of that. My standard is very, very high. And I think very few people measure up. Maybe it's the striving toward, not the sense of having accomplished it, that's supposed to be the deal. I would like to strive for great art, I would, and I do, but the context in which we work is . . . it's not prohibitive, but it's not terribly conducive. You sort of feel a little foolish sometimes, you feel a little pretentious. You strive to be a great artist. And nobody quite knows how to help you do that.

HUNT: What kind of impact do you think you've had on your art form?

LEVITOW: I think it's having been present at the debuts of some of these writers. That's what it's been.

HUNT: On the drive up here, I was thinking of the last day of the New Works Project in '88, when *Etta* had opened and *Kingfish* had a reading and we were sitting in that office, not able to move, but knowing that this was a magical moment, that life was not going to be the same, really, for any of us. Because it wasn't a fluke any more: Marlane was the genuine article. And it became clear that weekend.

LEVITOW: Yeah, well, you know, she's freaky. Her talent is freaky. Her whole life is of another . . . she's got something. I think you and I were very fortunate to be part of the birthing of a little school.

HUNT: How did it happen?

LEVITOW: I didn't find those plays, you found those plays. You cared deeply about it. You were interested in new writing and when the play hit your desk, you responded to it.

HUNT: But there were a lot of circumstances that contributed to that two-and-a-half-year period of time at LATC. The longer I'm away from it, the more it perplexes me. When I moved to Berkeley Rep, I remember glibly telling people that I was going to see if I could do it again. And the interesting thing is that I have not done it again.

LEVITOW: Yes, there were specific conditions that made it possible. One was, once again, Bill Bushnell's really valuable ability to let his staff do what they wanted to do within certain limitations. He let José

Luis and the Latino Lab do whatever they wanted to do, and they created a phenomenon. Bush and Diane White gave them the freedom to be creative.* They put lots of limitations on things, because they were the managers of a large institution. But they also gave us that freedom. We had *very* few limitations to what we wanted to do, Mame. There were almost no rules at all, it just had to be cheap. So if you and I wanted to sit around and come up with this weirdo idea and try it, Bush would say, OK, go ahead, see what you can do with it. That was incredible. Other artistic directors just don't give complete freedom to their employees like that.

HUNT: The critic Charles Marowitz said in an *L.A. Times* article that Bush was the white patriarch inviting all these minority cultures in, when he should let the artists themselves run things. Do you think that's an accurate statement?

LEVITOW: Well, no, it's not a very accurate statement, because in many cases he did let the artists run things. It is true, though, that he wanted to be the papa, the patron. I'd have to disagree with Charles's criticism of that. Very few other people perform the balancing act as successfully as Bush did. He didn't ask very much of the artists in terms of obeisance. He liked to show up in the lobby after a show and hang out with the gang. That's what made him feel paid back.

HUNT: Why is it, then, that a theater that was inviting in people like José Luis Valenzuela and Milcha Sanchez-Scott and Darrah Cloud . . .

LEVITOW: And us . . .

HUNT: And us, and Marlane Meyer and David Schweizer and Reza Abdoh. LATC has been the most threatened theater in the state of California almost from the moment it opened its doors.

LEVITOW: But who was threatening it? Not the audience. Institutionally they had their own personality problems, which is a fact of life. And they were also being threatened by external politics. When Bush conceived the Theatre Center, he was never concerned, really, about whether it was fair to other arts institutions in Los Angeles or in the state of California. That didn't concern him. He was just out to get as much as he could get, and he would say it that way.

HUNT: He's very much a part of that West Coast entrepreneurship.

*Diane White was the Producing Director at LATC.

LEVITOW: Yes. He's not going to feel guilty about whether or not the $21 million that goes to the Theatre Center is $21 million that didn't go to a hundred other theater companies. I remember him saying at one point that he was astounded that more theater managers of his time didn't choose to go with more entrepreneurial energy. He couldn't believe that Ron Sossi, for example, was willing to work at an Equity-waiver level. Bush was going to just keep pushing until he had a big Equity house. Ron is still running the Odyssey Theater as a very successful nonunion house, twenty years after he started it. Now that's not about Bill Bushnell getting a grant from the Community Redevelopment Agency; that is truly about Ron's decision not to turn it into a larger, profit-making venture.

HUNT: There are a lot of different leadership models now. There's the laid-back style of the guys at South Coast Rep, there are the people at the Globe and Seattle Rep, who are moving things to Broadway. There are people like Bush and Mr. Papp, who are entrepreneurs, and as long as you can hold on to the corners of your magic carpet, you can ride it with them. There are people like Ron who say, OK, we're a certain size, let's hold on to this. What kind do you think you'd be?

LEVITOW: That's tough, because I haven't thought that hard about it. The one time I spent time thinking about it was for the Eureka. The reason I considered it was because I want to do my friends' plays. That's what I would do.

HUNT: That's sort of the Greg Mosher model.*

LEVITOW: Yeah, I'd do my friends' plays. Marlane Meyer, Mickie Cruz, Darrah Cloud, Phyllis Nagy, Connie Congdon, José Rivera, Gary Leon Hill, Donald Margulies. But an artistic director needs to ask certain questions: Who are you having a conversation with? Who wants to have a conversation with you? And what do you want to talk about? Plays are the means of having that conversation. And I'm not sure a lot of people want to talk about the work that I like. Maybe my disenchantment has to do with the kind of material I'm interested in. Seattle's Empty Space repertoire—*Kaspar* and *Tooth of Crime* and Heiner Müller plays and Kroetz plays—those were the plays I fell in

*At the time this interview was conducted, Gregory Mosher was the Artistic Director of Lincoln Center. He is now the theater's Resident Director.

love with, and I still prefer writers who are writing at the edge of society with the same edginess in style and subject matter. It's that midlevel theater that doesn't seem to be there for us.

HUNT: What happened to it?

LEVITOW: I don't know. I think sometimes it's economic, that it fell away. I wonder what happened to the Empty Space audience. Did they stop going to theater altogether? Did they move on to Seattle Rep? Do they just go to movies now? Have they all had children so they're home with their babies? Do they watch performance art instead because it's more interesting than half-baked experimental theater? Maybe our generation just dropped out of seeing plays. What are they doing? Why don't they want to go see an interesting, intellectually stimulating piece of theater?

HUNT: My brother says he'd rather go to dinner than subscribe to a theater, because he can be spontaneous about when he goes. At dinner, one can have a conversation and it's like having a family. I think most of our generation is so far apart from our families now that what we're looking to do is re-create a family experience, not an artistic or spiritual experience.

LEVITOW: But the artistic experience used to be a family experience. When I was in Seattle, you could go to the Empty Space and feel like you were with your people. You could go to the Empty Space and recognize the background and the interests and the enthusiasms of the people in the theater with you. You could look across the house and think: "I bet that would be a great person to have dinner with. I bet we like the same things and enjoy the same movies." There was a feeling of family in that theater, or certainly neighborhood.

HUNT: A sense of the tribe.

LEVITOW: Yes, tribe. So what is our tribe doing?

HUNT: I felt like the people who came to see things at LATC were my tribe, for the most part. They were curious. You talk about taking journeys to places you've never been: LATC audiences wanted to go places they hadn't been before, and that's why they came there. They wanted to see this crazy Norwegian do *Three Sisters*. Could it be some bizarre geographical phenomenon, that when I go to northern California, I lose my tribe?

LEVITOW: I don't know where they are either. When I go to South

Coast Rep or the Taper, I wonder how I can have a conversation with these people. That's my job as an artist; aren't we supposed to be talking about something? Isn't live theater a dialogue? I need to have a dialogue with peers, with colleagues, with people who are of my tribe. But I don't know where our theaters are any more, so I don't know where we can have that dialogue. When I go to George Coates Performance Group or Robert Longo, I can see people in the audience who have that look of curiosity. Performance art or dance. But they're not at the theater. That's very discouraging to me as an artist.

"I keep things away from absolute clarity," Roberta said a few days after the initial interview, "because to me, the act of making theater comes from a kernel of curiosity that is *almost* undefined. I hope to recognize a moment of truth, but I prefer to seek that moment from the exception rather than the rule."

Postscript: The Los Angeles Theatre Center gave its last performances on October 13, 1991. At the time of this writing, the Latino Theatre Lab was sleeping in the lobby of the theater, hoping to gain enough of a foothold that the City of Los Angeles would let them continue to produce their work.

Cinema and Theology

André Bazin

he cinema has always been interested in God. The Gospel and the Acts of the Apostles were the first best-sellers on the screen, and the Passions of Christ were hits in France as well as in America.[1] At the same time in Italy, the Rome of the first Christians provided filmmakers with subjects that required gigantic crowd scenes, which were later seized upon by Hollywood and are still present today in films like *Fabiola* [1948] and *Quo Vadis?* [1951].[2] This immense catechism-in-pictures was concerned above all with the most spectacular aspects of the history of Christianity. These films were simply amplified variations on the Stations of the Cross or on the Musée Grévin.[3]

The hagiographies appeared a little later. As the cinema is in itself already a kind of miracle, it was absolutely appropriate to show a rain of roses pouring down or springs gushing out of arid sands. Several films were made about Saint Thérèse of Lisieux and Bernadette Soubirous; the latest of these films, an American one [*The Song*

of *Bernadette*], is only a few years old.[4] Here the cinema exploited above all the popular belief in miracles. This vein is not exhausted, and our children will probably one day see a *Golgotha* in 3-D after a color *Quo Vadis?* We must note, however, that the hagiography has evolved considerably. *Monsieur Vincent* [1947] is a saint's picture without miracles, and Rossellini seems not to have emphasized too much the stigmata and the enchantment of the birds in his *Flowers of St. Francis* [1950].[5] Also made last year in Italy, *Heaven Over the Marshes* [1949] tells the story of little Maria Goretti, who was canonized soon after the completion of this film (Figure 1). *Heaven Over the Marshes*, which still has not been released in France despite its director's being awarded first prize at the Venice Film Festival, is the prototype of the accursed film that is likely to upset both Christians and nonbelievers alike. In it, sainthood isn't signified by anything extraordinary, either on the physical or the psychological level. Divine grace doesn't manifest itself in nature as the product of a tangible causality; at most, it reveals itself through some ambiguous signs that can all be explained in quite natural terms. Psychoanalysis or even her simple decency, heightened by a naive piety, could very well account for Maria Goretti's martyrdom, which, all things considered, is little more than a common news item: "Murdered by a Farmhand Whose Advances She Had Rejected!" From this point of view, I would consider *Heaven Over the Marshes* the first theological film to assert, through the very nature of its characters, story, and events, the total transcendence of grace, which occurs at the expense of apologetics, of Christian propaganda that likes to suppose that sainthood is conferred a priori on saintly lives. Hence the embarrassed reaction of Catholic circles to this film.

There is also a third category of religious movie, built upon a principle that perhaps represents an advance on Stations-of-the-Cross films and hagiographies. I'm talking here about the priest's or nun's story. I have to check this point, but I think we owe the international vulgarization of this type of film to America. The Catholic minority in Hollywood, whose influence is great, found in the cinema a remarkable tool of propaganda. The myth of the "cool" priest who loves sports and jazz easily overshadows the austere reality of the Protestant pastor with a large family. Bing Crosby in a cassock turned

Figure 1. *Heaven Over the Marshes*, 1949, directed by Augusto Genina. Courtesy of the Museum of Modern Art (New York), Film Stills Archive.

out to be irresistible.[6] I myself preferred Spencer Tracy in *Boys' Town* [1938] and the ex-gangster priest [Pat O'Brien in *Angels with Dirty Faces* (1938)]. Hollywood decadence! The same trend has not taken hold in France, where in fact we have had to suppress the typically Gallic tradition of the ribald monk and the red-nosed priest. Thank God, our cinema has remained relatively free of this new trend, and even if we have had to put up with *My Priest Among the Rich* [1952] and *Clochemerle* [1947], at least we have done so with an embarrassed smile. For its part, Tino Rossi's Sunday calling in *Fevers* [1941] must be considered a mere episode.[7] But let's get back to serious films.

The first one is relatively recent: *Angels of the Streets* [1943], written by Robert Bresson, Jean Giraudoux, and Father Brückberger (Figure 2). In it, for the first time in the cinema, the problems of the spiritual life are described, if not in indisputable terms, then in any case in their intellectual, moral, and social ramifications. We are entitled to think that Robert Bresson's art in the forthcoming *Diary*

Figure 2. *Angels of the Streets*, 1943, directed by Robert Bresson. Courtesy of the Museum of Modern Art (New York), Film Stills Archive.

of a Country Priest [1951] will be no less rigorous.[8] Here again, as in *Heaven Over the Marshes*, there can be no question that what we are witnessing is greater sophistication in the treatment of religious themes. But in the three varieties of films that we have just examined, these themes are explicit and visible, since their protagonists are obviously martyrs, saints, priests, or monks. Although the artistic conscience of the filmmaker may have managed to interiorize the drama or lift it to an authentic religious level, it still rested on a glamorous myth, which is to say an extrinsic one for the most part: the wonder of sainthood or the mystery of priesthood. It's almost a filmmaker's trick: to give human dimensions—moral and psychological ones—to protagonists whose glamour in the eyes of the public derives precisely from their *difference* from common mortals.

Almost none of this holds for a film like *La Symphonie Pastorale* [1946], in which the conflict is primarily moral and owes its intensity solely to the will of the protagonists (Figure 3). This is not to say

Figure 3. *La Symphonie Pastorale*, 1946, directed by Jean Delannoy. Courtesy of the Museum of Modern Art (New York), Film Stills Archive.

that the movie has no religious significance, but only that this significance does not imply any a priori ideas, not even the idea of God; the only thing implied is *faith* in God. The protagonists are answerable to nobody but themselves; their damnation, like their salvation, is internal. Faith is the operative mechanism in the trap that the pastor sets for himself; it is the moral alibi for his sin. One may say that this complete interiorization of the religious problem was dictated by the Protestant nature of the subject, whose adaptors [Jean Aurenche and Pierre Bost, from the novella by André Gide] and director, incidentally, had the same [Catholic] education as André Gide. And one can talk at length about a "Protestant cinema" in connection with Roger Leenhardt's *The Last Vacation* [1948]. The term is appropriate, but it could very well be that the filmic Protestantism of Aurenche, Bost, and Delannoy was the best vehicle for a Catholic novelist in the cinema.

The history of religious themes on the screen sufficiently reveals the temptations one must resist in order to meet simultaneously the requirements of cinematic art and of truly religious experience. Everything that is exterior, ornamental, liturgical, sacramental, hagiographic, and miraculous in the everyday observance, doctrine, and practice of Catholicism does indeed show specific affinities with the cinema considered as a formidable iconography, but these affinities, which have made for the success of countless films, are also the source of the religious insignificance of most of them. Almost everything that is good in this domain was created not by the exploitation of these patent affinities, but rather by working against them: by the psychological and moral deepening of the religious factor as well as by the renunciation of the physical representation of the supernatural and of grace.[9] As for "mysteries," the cinema has been able to evoke only those of Paris and New York. We're still waiting for it to deal with those of the Middle Ages. To make a long story short, it seems that, although the Protestant sensibility is not indispensable to the making of a good Catholic film, it can nevertheless be a real advantage. And I see the evidence for this in the [1950] film based on Henri Queffélec's novel: *God Needs Men* [a.k.a. *Isle of Sinners, Island Priest*] (Figure 4).

What was already present in Queffélec's novel, and was fully retained by the filmmakers, is first and foremost the absolutely *natural* character of events. This story is thus no less interesting to a nonbeliever than to a believer. It takes place a century ago on the island of Sein, a rugged and barren tract off the Brittany coast upon which lives a small community of fishermen and pillagers of shipwrecks. Their way of life and their mentality are so primitive that they have caused the parish priest, a native of the mainland, to flee. But now that the priest is gone, this community, which the diocese considers a parish of savages and heathens, feels a strange emptiness; it can't go on without a priest, with an empty church. In the absence of a real priest, the former sacristan takes care of the candles, cleans the church, and makes the people say their prayers on Sunday morning. One day he even speaks to them, and to everybody's surprise, including his own, what he says is precisely what the parish priest had never been able to say. His moral authority begins to increase. Of course, he doesn't lose his head: he knows full well that he is not a priest, that he does not have the rights of a priest, except perhaps those that a layman may assume in order to save what he can of the souls in

Figure 4. *God Needs Men*, 1950, directed by Jean Delannoy. Courtesy of the Museum of Modern Art (New York), Film Stills Archive.

this parish. But little by little, the community pressures him to such an extent that he must identify with his function. He is not allowed to pardon sins, but should he refuse to hear the confession of a dying woman or of a murderer? He will hear their confessions, if only to alleviate the suffering of such people or to save them from despair. And since he has heard them, since he is capable of keeping a secret that nobody will understand better than he, why should he refuse to give them absolution? The penitent would feel himself cleansed of his sin more by him than by the Pope in person. The false priest struggles with his scrupulous conscience; he does not disregard what ordination means, the powers it confers and without which he remains a poor devil. But he also feels that the confidence placed in him is like an almost irresistible calling, and that, wretched creature though he may be, he is nonetheless not unworthy. To live up to this confidence, he is forced to conform his life more and more to the model of the priesthood: he gives up his job, calls off his marriage, and moves into the rectory. This asceticism makes him resemble even more what the community wants him to be; it seems that nothing distinguishes him from a priest anymore, from a *good priest*, from the parish priest that the diocese is incapable of sending to the island. After numerous crises of conscience, he gives in and agrees to say mass.

Meanwhile, the diocese becomes concerned over the strange things happening on the island and finally sends a new priest. He's an old man who comes accompanied by his prejudices and the state police; he is at once frightened and frightening. What he sees scandalizes him, and the islanders for their part reject him; they prefer their false priest to this stranger in a cassock. Only one man could save the situation. But that man, who has relentlessly fought against the temptation of equating himself with a priest and who has given in only reluctantly—at least that's how he defends his actions—that man is overcome by dizziness at the sacrifice that the new priest is demanding of him. Was everything he did completely meaningless, was it all a sham? It isn't pride that is growing in him, just common sense, the sense of his usefulness, of the work he has accomplished. Does the real priest, who has the power of turning bread into the Body of Christ, also have the power of making men better than they are, as he has? Here the film cuts itself a bit short and definitely betrays the book in the process. After a spectacular manifestation of the false priest's independence (a "burial" at sea), the schism is avoided and all the islanders go to the real mass said by the real priest.

One can see in this theological happy ending a craftiness whose intent is not particularly pure. I fear that our Protestant filmmakers have let their own apologetics show through here: *in cauda venenum*, or the sting is in the tail. In the novel, the bishop gives in—twice: first, by allowing the sacristan to enter the seminary. But the stubbornness of the islander and his age prevent him from absorbing this delayed education, and he cannot be ordained. He goes back to the island, wishing only for peace and to be able to return to his normal occupation as a fisherman. Then, for the second time, the community pressures him to such a degree that he is forced to commit the same sacrileges. The schism would no doubt have manifested itself this time had not the bishop resigned himself at long last to consecrating this strange vocation and ordaining the priest of the Island of Sein. This final reconciliation of the Catholic hierarchy and the priestly sacrament with the Christian community may very well be a historical accident, like the regularization of a free state, but it is nevertheless far more meaningful than the capitulation imagined by the filmmakers, a capitulation that guarantees the rebelling island- ers the best role and the audience's sympathy. The spectacle-of-an- ending substituted by the filmmakers, and made possible by the addi- tion of the new, legitimate priest, guarantees the audience's laughter; it superficially resolves the crisis, but it doesn't solve anything.

Although this ending is likely to reassure the Catholic viewer, it leaves the Protestant one feeling secretly victorious, even exalted, over its evasion of the real issue. Of course, I don't reproach Aurenche and Bost for their veiled Protestantism here, but I do reproach them for no longer playing fairly, for cheating on both the dramatic and the religious levels. However, I will grant them extenuating circum- stances. Film being what it is, I'm not certain that the ending of the novel would have been possible on-screen. First, because of the simple necessity of dramatic concentration, a concentration that the novel does not require. Second, and above all, because the structure of the film narrative is completely different from what it was in the book, in that it is a *tragic* structure. According to the logic of the action (which is not the same thing as the psychology of the characters or the religious tendencies of the filmmakers), I would say that this conflict is irresolvable; the irreducible nature of the contradiction is evaded by the happy ending, which has about as much meaning as the classical Hollywood "they got married and lived happily ever after." The novel can escape this happy ending and satisfy us through a de- nouement that is at the same time credible and orthodox, because it can tolerate protractedness, which tragedy refuses to do. Just when the spectator is counting on the healing effects of time and patience, or on the good offices of the king, the curtain falls.

The truly religious meaning of the book isn't affected as much as one might fear by this tendentious denouement. The story, as we see it unfold on the screen, doesn't aim for a moment at resolving the question, but rather at posing it in terms of a tragic dialectic, and Delannoy couldn't have given it a more pressing form. The religious meaning achieves a maximum rigor and efficiency here because it simultaneously respects the sociopsychological reality and the transcendence of the sacred. It is, let us say, an apologetics set in relief. Although the sacerdotal reality transcends the natural order, it nonetheless springs from a social and historical milieu. As long as the priest remains part of the community, we are more aware of his shortcomings than of the community's need for him. Thus only after the islanders have chased away their parish priest does their need for a priest become obvious. These primitive beings, pillagers of shipwrecks as others are smugglers, discover that they can't live without a priest. The sacrament is part of their social economy; it is necessary for the elimination of sin. Deprived of its religious organ, society poisons itself, its blood becomes tainted. In front of the empty tabernacle, this community of murderers and thieves discovers that it is irremediably Christian. Since no priest is given to them, they decide to create one, and the one they create obviously deserves the office: out of his mouth come the words of Truth and Life that the parish priest hadn't been able to utter. However, as not only the calling but also a kind of grace gradually asserts itself in him, the absence of the priestly sacrament makes itself felt. All his sacrifices, all the good that he does for his brothers, can't change anything. What he incurably lacks is made even more poignant by the fact that we can't see what ordination would add to his natural capacities; it seems that it would not even add grace, which appears to inhabit him already as a result of the function he fulfills.

Two scenes are particularly significant in this regard. The first is the one in which the roof of the church is damaged by the storm, and the rain drips drop after drop into the holy-water basin. How could we not see in this a sign of the Lord's distinct approval? The other concerns the hosts, which are made with a flatiron by the women of the village so that the false priest can say mass, and which the new priest throws onto the ground. They are indeed only small pieces of bread. But even the most irreligious viewer will gasp at the horror of this gesture and will understand the grievous fear of the sacristan, who attempts to tiptoe softly on his clogs so as not to dirty what *could be* the Body of Christ. The sacramental reality is made palpable here by its absence, as in the geometric theorems that one can prove only *ab absurdo*.[10]

Although the film has modified the book somewhat, it has by no means done so in order to reduce its religious significance. On the contrary, since he was less subject to dramatic requirements, and since he was able to count on the reader more than the filmmaker could count on the viewer, the novelist seems to have insisted less on the clash of religious forces, on the forging of religious significance: his book was above all a sociopsychological novel in which a casual reader could have interested himself for its human and historical picturesqueness. This is not for a moment to suggest that the film is better than the novel; on the contrary, I think that the book had a discreetly accomplished style that the film betrays in the process of moving the center of gravity of the subject from open-ended religious narrative to closed-off *theological tragedy*. Without turning away from the natural, historical, social, and psychological data provided by the book, the screenwriter has altered their dialectics. For once, the change of titles in fact conforms to the spirit of the adaptation: from *The Parish Priest of the Island of Sein* to *God Needs Men*, one goes from the particular to the general, from the moral to the theological.

Are you aware that *La Symphonie Pastorale* is the biggest box-office success since the Liberation? Although predictions in these matters are unwise and uncertain, if one could place bets on movie hits, I would wager a lot on *God Needs Men*. At first glance, one might have thought that, in order for the adaptors to bring a unique and relatively austere book to the public, they would have had to "humanize" the subject.[11] They could, for example, have made a love story out of it: the elements were there, since the false priest renounces marriage. It is to their credit that they managed to avoid doing this—but we expected no less from Aurenche and Bost. What is more astonishing is that they were allowed to make *this* film. For it means that a truly religious problem interests the general audience more than a sentimental drama. Thus the adaptors demonstrated that, in dealing with a religious subject, it is possible to renounce not only the facile and traditional conflict between love and duty, between eros and agape, not only the pomp and splendor of history and liturgy, but also the moral wonders of hagiography.

Given the exceptional value of this film and its wide success, the reservations one might have about it could only be concerned with details. These details are significant enough, however, to leave us with a certain dissatisfaction. The adaptation has at least one regrettable weakness: the character of the actual priest. Here again, Aurenche and Bost have not played fairly. The revolt of the islanders, and even more so of the false priest, is too easily explained by the stupidity of the new priest. Moreover, the casting of Jean Brochard, which was more appropriate in the comic *Clochemerle*, was itself an act of heavy-handed anticlericalism. The scandal thus loses its theological rigor and becomes almost accidental. The real choice is not between a false but appealing priest and a real but repugnant and stupid one. It is between the two halves of the priesthood, between consecration by the community and consecration by the sacrament. For, although it is true that the sacristan is worthy of being a priest in the eyes of his brothers, he can't give them what even the most unworthy of defrocked priests could. But the best of priests wouldn't do for these people, who wouldn't recognize themselves in him. The highest religious achievement of this work is in fact its reminding us of an eminent Christian truth that the last few centuries of Catholic history have dangerously shunted aside, but that the experience of the missionaries is bringing back to the forefront: namely, the communal origin of the priesthood. This "heathen" island, by defending its false priest, is perhaps not making any less Christian a statement than the Catholic hierarchy that becomes indignant at their sacrilege. The truth that the islanders are unconsciously promoting is, as it were, the complementary opposite of the truth to which the miserable priest of *The Power and the Glory* bears subjugated witness. Thus it is absurd that the viewer should be made to side with the sympathetic sacristan against the foolish priest: the tragedy lies precisely in the impossibility of choosing, in the inevitability of the scandal, which would be the same if the diocese had sent a "good" priest.

Moreover, the quality of the mise-en-scène is not quite sufficient to meet its objective. Material circumstances beyond Delannoy's control probably forced him to shoot most of the film in a studio; few scenes were shot in Brittany, and the physical landscape therefore plays only a secondary role. It would indeed be rather easy to adapt the film as it exists to the stage. This lack of a natural setting for the action could have been a major weakness, but Aurenche and Bost's adaptation makes us almost forget the artificiality of Delannoy's means. This moral and metaphysical drama barely needs the excuse of human geography to justify its existence. This is a bit of cleverness on the part of the screenwriters, but it is not a cinematic virtue, for, from a strictly cinematic point of view, it is better to make fatality tangible through things than through actors, and Delannoy succeeded remarkably in doing this with the snow in *La Symphonie Pastorale*. The sea does not play nearly the same role here.

The acting—except for Brochard, who, as I have noted, is miscast—is astonishing in every respect. Pierre Fresnay, whom we admired so much in *Monsieur Vincent*, seems to me to be far superior here. The character of Vincent de Paul was relatively easy to play for such a skillful character actor. By contrast, the elemental protagonist of *God Needs Men*, who struggles against events that go beyond him but who nevertheless manages to cope, required a flawless mastery of simplicity. Almost by a miracle, Fresnay's aristocratic and slightly southern accent becomes here a rugged tongue, a kind of barking of the soul.

Appendix: List of Directors

Henri Diamant-Berger, *My Priest Among the Rich*, 1952

J. Stuart Blackton, *The Life of Moses*, 1909

Alessandro Blasetti, *Fabiola*, 1948

Robert Bresson, *Angels of the Streets*, 1943

————, *Diary of a Country Priest*, 1951

Alain Cavalier, *Thérèse*, 1986

Pierre Chenal, *The Scandals of Clochemerle*, 1947

Maurice Cloche, *Monsieur Vincent*, 1947

Michael Curtiz, *Angels with Dirty Faces*, 1938

Robert Darène, *Bernadette of Lourdes (Il suffit d'aimer)*, 1960

Maurice de Canonge, *Thérèse Martin*, 1938

Jean Delannoy, *Fevers*, 1941

————, *La Symphonie Pastorale*, 1946

————, *God Needs Men*, 1950

————, *Bernadette*, 1988

Cecil B. De Mille, *The Ten Command-
ments*, 1923
———, *King of Kings*, 1927
———, *The Sign of the Cross*, 1932
Julien Duvivier, *Golgotha*, 1935
Edison Studios, *The Passion Play*, 1898
Louis Feuillade, *Mater Dolorosa*, 1910
John Ford, *The Fugitive*, 1947
Augusto Genina, *Heaven Over the
Marshes*, 1949
Enrico Guazzoni, *Quo Vadis?* 1913
———, *Fabiola*, 1917
Alice Guy-Blaché, *La Vie du Christ*, 1906
William Keighley and Marc Connelly,
The Green Pastures, 1936
Henry King, *The Song of Bernadette*, 1943
Roger Leenhardt, *The Last Vacation*, 1948
Mervyn LeRoy, *Quo Vadis?* 1951
Leo McCarey, *Going My Way*, 1944

———, *The Bells of St. Mary's*, 1945
Fred Niblo, *Ben Hur*, 1926
Sidney Olcott, *Ben Hur*, 1907
———, *From the Manger to the Cross*,
1912
Nicholas Ray, *King of Kings*, 1961
Roberto Rossellini, *The Flowers of St.
Francis*, 1950
Martin Scorsese, *The Last Temptation of
Christ*, 1988
Alf Sjöberg, *The Road to Heaven*, 1942
Victor Sjöström, *Therese*, 1916
George Stevens, *The Greatest Story Ever
Told*, 1965
Norman Taurog, *Boys' Town*, 1938
William Wyler, *Ben Hur*, 1959
Ferdinand Zecca, *Quo Vadis?* 1901
Ferdinand Zecca and Lucien Nouguet, *La
Passion*, 1903

Notes

André Bazin's "Cinema and Theology" was translated by Alain Piette and Bert Cardullo and edited by Bert Cardullo. It was first published in French in *Esprit* 19 (February
1951): 237–45. It is translated into English here for the first time with the permission of
Madame Janine Bazin. It will be included in *Bazin at Work: Major Essays and Reviews
From the Forties and Fifties*, trans. Alain Piette and Bert Cardullo (forthcoming, Rout-
ledge, 1992). Unless otherwise indicated, all notes have been supplied by the editor,
Bert Cardullo.

1 For example, in America: *The Passion Play* (1898); *Ben Hur* (1907); *The Life of
   Moses* (1909); and *From the Manger to the Cross* (1912). In France: *Quo Vadis?*
   (1901); *La Passion* (1903); *La Vie du Christ* (1906); and *Mater Dolorosa* (1910).

2 In Italy: *Quo Vadis?* (1913) and *Fabiola* (1917). In America: *The Ten Command-
   ments* (1923); *Ben Hur* (1926); *King of Kings* (1927); and *The Sign of the Cross*
   (1932). In America subsequent to the publication of Bazin's essay: *Ben Hur* (1959);
   King of Kings (1961); *The Greatest Story Ever Told* (1965); and *The Last Temptation
   of Christ* (1988).

3 The Musée Grévin is a famous museum of wax figures in Paris—the Parisian
   equivalent of the waxworks exhibitions of Madame Tussaud (1760–1850) in London.

4 Saint Thérèse of Lisieux (also known as Saint Thérèse of the Child of Jesus) was a
   French Carmelite nun, born as Thérèse Martin, whose saint's day is 3 October; she

lived from 1873 to 1897 and was canonized in 1925. Films: *Therese* (1916); *Thérèse Martin* (1938); and *Thérèse* (1986).

Saint Bernadette Soubirous (1844–1879) was a peasant girl who had a vision of the Virgin Mary at what has become the shrine of Lourdes. Films: *The Song of Bernadette* (1943); more recently, *Bernadette of Lourdes* (*Il suffit d'aimer*) (1960) and *Bernadette* (1988).

5   The script of *Monsieur Vincent* was co-written by Jean Anouilh. Saint Vincent de Paul was a French priest (1580?–1660) who founded charitable orders; his saint's day is 19 July.

6   In *Going My Way* (1944) and *The Bells of St. Mary's* (1945).

7   *Clochemerle* is also known as *The Scandals of Clochemerle*. Tino Rossi (1907–1983) was a popular (Corsican) tenor of French radio, operettas, music halls, and films.

8   See André Bazin, "*Le journal d'un curé de campagne* and the Stylistics of Robert Bresson," in *What Is Cinema?* trans. Hugh Gray (Berkeley, 1967), 1: 125–43.

9   Bazin's note: Except, of course, for films whose supernatural quality is both pervasive and authentically religious, like *The Green Pastures* [1936] and *The Road to Heaven* [1942].

10 Bazin's note: It is perhaps worthwhile to recall here that the same Aurenche, in a script of *Diary of a Country Priest* that its author, Georges Bernanos, vehemently rejected [in the end, Bresson directed the film from his own screenplay], had introduced precisely this theme of the desecrated host, which was not present in the novel. One would be tempted to see in this an obsession on the part of the screenwriter.

11 Bazin's note: We must, of course, take into account what part publicity plays in the choice of a title. John Ford's *The Fugitive* [1947], based on Graham Greene's *The Power and the Glory* [1940], was released in France under the title *God Is Dead*. The change of titles had absolutely no intrinsic justification here, as it did in the case of *God Needs Men*, but at any rate it demonstrated that, in France, God is commercial. An interesting comparison could be made between Greene's *book* and Delannoy's film [*God Needs Men*, directed by Delannoy in 1950], which is, as it were, its negative instance.

The Passion of St. Charles:

Martin Scorsese's *Mean Streets*

Jim Hosney, Jacquelyn Wollman,
and Jesse Ward Engdahl

Note. The reason Milton wrote in fetters when he wrote of Angels &
God, and at liberty when of Devils & Hell, is because he was a true
Poet and of the Devil's party without knowing it.—William Blake

oice-over on a blackened screen: "You don't make
up for sin in Church. You do it in the streets
or at home. And the rest is all bullshit." Full
shot of Charlie (Harvey Keitel) awakening from a
bad dream. He gets up, walks over to the dresser,
and looks at himself in the mirror. A siren's wail
rises above the sound of the traffic outside. Cut to
Charlie going back to sleep. The opening bars of the Ronettes's "Be My
Baby" blare from the soundtrack, continuing throughout the following sequence. Side view of an 8-mm projector that turns toward the
audience. Charlie's home movie begins, with the projector creating
an 8-mm frame within the 35-mm frame. The title *Mean Streets* cuts

across both frames. The remaining credits appear over Charlie's home movie, which opens with a full shot of Charlie and Michael (Richard Romanus). What follow are shots of a birthday cake, Teresa (Amy Robinson) holding a baby, Uncle Giovanni (Cesare Danova), Charlie shaking hands with a priest and then putting on his dark glasses, balloons rising in the air, the lights of the San Gennaro festival.

In this opening sequence, Martin Scorsese establishes the major concerns of *Mean Streets*. Charlie's opening words immediately make the viewer aware of religion as a central element of the film. Because he was raised in an Italian-Catholic environment, Catholic conceptions of women and sexuality, sin and penance, martyrdom and sainthood obsess Charlie and motivate his actions. Charlie's desire to achieve martyrdom and secular sainthood stems from his self-preoccupation, which Scorsese establishes in this opening sequence when Charlie looks at himself in the mirror. The first sound from the outside world is the wail of a siren, prefiguring the world of violence in which a modern saint must seek his martyrdom.

Scorsese moves from the universal concerns of religion to the specific concerns of Charlie's contemporary world with his use of the Ronettes's "Be My Baby." The song posits an uncomplicated view of male/female relationships, antithetical to Charlie's own experiences. The female singer could almost be Teresa, who is always asking for Charlie's love, yet the words "I love you" are impossible for him to say. His sexual problems stem from his inability to see women outside the Catholic stereotypes of mother and whore; the repeated lyric "Be my little baby" takes on an ironic dimension.

Although Charlie's conflicts with religion and sex seem resolved in his home movie, this comfortable, middle-class resolution is achieved only at the expense of a vital element within Charlie, the anarchic energy represented by Johnny Boy (Robert De Niro), who is conspicuously absent from the home movie. Furthermore, an indication comes within the home movie that Charlie's conflicts are indeed unresolved; he puts on dark glasses after shaking hands with the priest, signifying a barrier between himself and the Church.

The road of excess leads to the palace of wisdom.
He who desires but acts not, breeds pestilence.
—William Blake

Formally introducing Charlie in a church, Scorsese opens the sequence with Charlie at the altar proclaiming his unworthiness: "Lord I know I'm not worthy . . . to eat your flesh . . . not worthy to drink your blood." But he expresses dissatisfaction with conventional forms of penance; he wants to create his own penance, because "it's all bullshit except the pain of hell." For Charlie, the pain of hell is twofold—physical and spiritual—with the spiritual the greater of the two. This speech on the pain of hell becomes a voiceover when Scorsese cuts to Charlie in Tony's bar, which is bathed in a hellish red light. The lighting and editing indicate Tony's bar as the arena in which Charlie must seek his penance. The camera follows behind Charlie as he dances through the bar, acknowledging friends and making his way to Diane (Jeannie Bell), the black topless dancer onstage; the ease of his performance renders this a familiar ritual. When a fight breaks out at a table behind Charlie, the sudden eruption of violence leaves Charlie undisturbed because this, too, is a familiar ritual. These rituals are as familiar to Charlie as those of the Church.

Johnny Boy's entrance into the bar contrasts his personal anarchy with the patterns of behavior prevalent in the bar; he checks in his pants with the hatcheck girl. But the audience is hardly shocked by this performance, because they have already been exposed to Johnny's anarchic energy in his introduction, in which he blows up a mailbox for no apparent reason. Only Charlie is disturbed, for he realizes that Johnny Boy is his penance: "All right. Thanks Lord. . . . Talk about penance." We are reminded of Charlie's first words in the film, which stress this preoccupation. The soundtrack challenges Charlie's religious concerns with the Rolling Stones's "Jumpin' Jack Flash," an assertion of anarchic energy. The visuals, however, echo the imagery of the church, as a stained-glass window behind the bar now becomes visible and the lights in the bar replace the candles in the church.

Charlie's desire for martyrdom becomes explicit in a discussion with Teresa at the beach. Although he expresses his admiration for the nature-loving St. Francis of Assisi, Charlie hates the ocean, sun, grass, trees, and heat; he loves mountains, but skyscrapers are his mountains. Because Charlie clings to Italian ideas of the importance of family ties, he is shocked by Teresa's disavowal of her cousin Johnny Boy: "He's like an insane person." He tries to use the example of St. Francis to defend his support of Johnny Boy, but Teresa deflates Charlie's conscious identification with St. Francis by reminding him that "St. Francis didn't run numbers."

Scorsese underlines Charlie's confusion about sainthood through the character of Teresa. Her namesake, Theresa of Avila, one of the great saints of the Counter-Reformation, was the subject of Bernini's sculpture *The Ecstasy of St. Theresa*, a piece that confuses sexual and religious ecstasy, although it occupies a prominent place in the church of Sta. Maria della Vittoria. But Theresa of Avila's description of her religious experience when an angel pierced her heart with a golden arrow also confuses sexual and religious ecstasy: "The pain was so great that I screamed aloud; but at the same time I felt such infinite sweetness that I wished the pain to last forever." Scorsese's Teresa has epilepsy, a disease associated with deity and religious experience. Charlie is unable to reconcile Teresa the saint with the Teresa he calls "a cunt."

Charlie associates sex with death and, hence, his own martyrdom. In the hotel sequence in which Charlie and Teresa are in bed together, he describes a dream in which he has sex with Teresa but prematurely ejaculates blood. After pretending to shoot her with his finger, he tells her "you're killing me" as they playfully wrestle on the bed. Charlie's inability to reconcile sex with his religious attitudes is visually reinforced by the bar imagery that often blocks Charlie's view of Teresa: he looks through the bars of his window to see her undressing; later he watches her dress in the hotel room through the bars of his fingers as the venetian blinds cast horizontal shadows across her body.

In the next sequence, Scorsese both underscores and mocks Charlie's sense of martyrdom with a shot in which Charlie's head is aligned with tapestry pictures of John F. Kennedy and Robert F. Kennedy, two contemporary Catholic martyrs. Charlie then seeks purification from the sex of the previous sequence by washing his hands in the men's room of a restaurant. This act of cleansing himself is accompanied by an act of self-reflection, looking at himself in the bathroom mirror, which reminds us of the precredit sequence and reinforces his self-preoccupation. The Italian music on the soundtrack signifies his Italian-Catholic background that stresses the division of woman into mother and whore.

Charlie self-consciously identifies himself with Christ at a private party in Tony's bar for a returning Vietnam veteran. "I have come to create order," he proclaims, as water is poured into his drink over his fingers in imitation of the priest during the communion ritual. Tony (David Proval) and Charlie proceed to parody Pilate's interrogation of Christ before the Crucifixion:

TONY: Art thou the King of the Jews?
CHARLIE: Dost thou say this of thyself or have others told thee this of me?
TONY: Am I a Jew?
CHARLIE: My kingdom is not of this world.

In Scorsese's original screenplay, the party is a costume party to which Charlie comes dressed as the crucified Christ, complete with stigmata. Scorsese views Christ's violent crucifixion as a human sacrifice, a level of martyrdom to which Charlie aspires.

But the martyrdom at the film's conclusion, in which violence and blood become elements in a religious experience of purification, is Johnny Boy's martyrdom, not Charlie's. After Johnny mocks Michael by pulling a gun and refusing to pay him the money he owes him, Charlie and Teresa attempt to drive Johnny Boy to a hiding place. But Michael and his hit man (Martin Scorsese) overtake them. Johnny is shot in the neck and Charlie is shot in the hand; the car goes out of control and crashes into a fire hydrant; Teresa's hand goes through the windshield. Blood literally spurts from Johnny Boy's neck, an image which has religious significance for Scorsese: "To me, I like the idea of spurting blood, it reminds . . . it's like a . . . God, it's . . . it's really like a purification, you know, the fountains of blood." Johnny Boy becomes the unwilling martyr for Charlie's sins. A close-up of Charlie's bloodied hand on the steering wheel reminds the viewer of Christ's stigmata. Charlie and Teresa survive to become the happy parents in the home movie.

This ending makes the beginning of *Mean Streets* possible. In order to become the middle-class father in the home movie, Charlie must suppress the Johnny Boy aspect of his personality. Hence, his victory is pyrrhic because Johnny Boy is a potential source of vital energy. Throughout the film, Charlie is concerned with maintaining the status quo; anything that disturbs this equilibrium poses a threat to him: Johnny Boy's anarchic energy; Teresa's sexuality; Diane's blackness. (He arranges to meet the topless dancer in the Village, but drives by her in a taxi instead because he is afraid of being seen in the Village with a black woman.) Johnny Boy understands this concern and mocks it when he calls Charlie a politician during their confrontation in Charlie's parents' apartment. As politician, Charlie is unable to synthesize the divergent elements of his life. Johnny Boy cannot be a player in Charlie's movie. But Scorsese never shows Johnny Boy's actual death because, unlike Charlie, he does not want or need to rid himself of this vital life force. Thus *Mean Streets* becomes Scorsese's home movie, representing an alternative view, one that celebrates a marriage of heaven and hell.

> The tygers of wrath are wiser than the horses of
> instruction.
> Exuberance is Beauty.
> Improvement makes strait roads, but the crooked
> roads without Improvement are roads of Genius.
> —William Blake

Anticipating the Romantic movement in England, William Blake exalts energy ("Eternal Delight"), emotions, impulses, and sensuous life in *The Marriage of Heaven and Hell*, and he attacks the fetters that reason and conventional morality place on one's life. Within this work, Blake creates a dialectical tension that is one source of the work's vitality: "Without Contraries there is no progression. Attraction and Repulsion, Reason and Energy, Love and Hate, are necessary to Human existance." He synthesizes religious and aesthetic passion, but he rejects conventional religious systems. Another source of the work's vitality is Blake's self-reflexivity, evident through his Romantic redefinition of Milton in "The voice of the Devil." By calling attention to another poet, he is also calling attention to himself as a poet—he is Milton's successor.

Martin Scorsese creates similar tensions and syntheses within *Mean Streets*. Although Scorsese does not completely reject Catholicism in his synthesis, he values the sensuous, aesthetic qualities of the Church's rituals rather than its conventional moral strictures, which makes his Catholicism as passionate and vital as his film. He announces his own self-reflexive intentions with the deliberately self-conscious shot in the opening sequence in which the 8-mm projector is turned on the audience. Later in the film, Scorsese will indicate his heritage as a filmmaker through direct quotations from other films, John Ford's *The Searchers* (1956) and Roger Corman's *The Tomb of Ligea* (1965).

Scorsese acknowledges the importance of energy through a direct reference to Blake's "The Tyger," a major poem in his *Songs of Experience* (1794). After the fight in Joey's pool hall (the "Mook" sequence), Tony takes Charlie, Johnny Boy, and Jimmy "the Mook" (Lenny Scaletta) into the back room of his bar and unveils two cages, each containing a lion cub. He confides to Charlie: "Really wanted to get a tiger, Charlie, y'know . . . like in William Blake and all that." The tiger is Blake's symbol of fierce strength, which is terrifying in its possibilities of destructiveness; but, at the same time, it is impressive and admirable, a challenge to the idea of a benign creator. Inhabiting the forests of the night, the tiger represents a burning quality combining wrath, passion, and ardor ("Tyger! Tyger! burning bright"). The rhythms of the poem stress the tiger's energy, vitality, and power. Scorsese's allusion to "The Tyger" in this sequence has a twofold effect. First, the audience is surprised by Tony's literary reference because it seems out of character. Second, the viewer realizes that Johnny Boy is Scorsese's symbol of fierce strength, both terrifying in his possibilities, yet impressive and admirable.

In the following sequence, the reference to Blake is both amplified and qualified. Charlie comments on the depressing atmosphere of Tony's place and talks about the kind of place he would like to own: "I'd call it something like 'Season of the Witch' " (Scorsese's original title for *Mean Streets*). This reference to Donovan's song "Season of the Witch" evokes the flower child mysticism of the mid-1960s. However, this world of free sexual expression and glorification of nature is totally alien to Charlie's worldview. But when Tony mocks Charlie's allusion, Charlie retorts: "Who's the guy with William Blake and the tigers?" Charlie realizes that Tony's tigers are, in fact, tame lion cubs, not the free, fierce spirits of Blake's poem. They are kept hidden in a back room, locked in cages, because Blake's ideas are not a viable part of Tony's existence. Johnny Boy rejects both these worlds when he mocks witches and tigers: "Will you guys shut up with the witches and tigers!" He has no need for these symbols because he personifies the force and mystery of Blake's tiger.

Like the unanswered questions of Blake's "The Tyger" ("What the hammer? What the chain? / In what furnace was thy brain?"), Johnny Boy's behavior remains unexplained. Why does he blow up a mailbox in his introductory sequence? Why does he borrow money from everyone? Why does he fire a gun from the rooftop? Why does he beat up a young passerby? Why does he purposely spend the money Charlie has given him for Michael's payment? These unanswered questions yield an explosive enigma—Johnny Boy. Tossing a firecracker, which resembles a stick of dynamite, off a rooftop, Johnny Boy yells "It's back to Bataan!" This cry evokes Edward Dmytryk's film *Back to Bataan* (1948) in which John Wayne leads American soldiers into victorious battle in the Philippines. But Johnny Boy is not attempting to identify with John Wayne and American heroism; his action is an expression of his nihilistic energy. This same energy is evident when he sets fire to the ten dollar bill rejected by Michael. Johnny Boy delights in mocking Michael, even though he knows that this action will force Michael to seek revenge. Fire remains merely a tool for Johnny Boy— it has no symbolic connotations.

But for Charlie fire has a more traditional meaning, the fire of hell. He is fascinated by it, yet, at the same time, fearful of it, because fire represents an important part of his martyrdom—pain. In his introductory sequence in church, he holds his finger over a holy candle, the first indication of his fascination with fire. Later, he will hold a match to his finger and will place his finger over the flames of a grill in a restaurant kitchen. However, he always withdraws his finger before he gets burned, just as he will never complete his martyrdom. Charlie's relationship to fire is similar to his relationship with Johnny Boy. He will always withdraw before he gets burned, although he remains fascinated. Obviously, Charlie never comprehends the Blakean proverb: "The tygers of wrath are wiser than the horses of instruction."

Scorsese's use of Blake in *Mean Streets* is both self-conscious and self-reflexive. When Tony alludes to Blake's "The Tyger," he sounds like a character in a film by Jean-Luc Godard, a filmmaker whose characters are constantly stepping out of their roles in order to quote from diverse literary, artistic, and philosophical sources. This self-conscious narrative device becomes visually self-reflexive when the fires of Blake's tiger become the fires in the sequence from Roger Corman's *The Tomb of Ligea*. Johnny Boy and Charlie watch a movie that mirrors Johnny Boy's fascination with fire and destruction as well as Charlie's association of fire with hell; on a subconscious level, this sequence could mirror Charlie's fear of female sexuality dragging him into the fires of hell. The audience watching Johnny Boy and Charlie watching a film are being reminded that they, too, are seeing a film, a form of fiction. In an earlier sequence this stylistic device is used when Charlie, Tony, and Michael go to the movies and Scorsese visually quotes from John Ford's *The Searchers*, the fight between Martin Pawley (Jeffrey Hunter) and Charlie McCorry (Ken Curtis). This sequence becomes even more self-reflexive through Charlie McCorry's cry "Fight fair, Marty!"

Perhaps most self-reflexive of all is Scorsese's role in *Mean Streets* as Michael's hit man. At the end of the film, it is Scorsese who kisses his gun before shooting his own characters. In fact, Michael's directive to him, "Now's the time," takes on added meaning because now is the time to end the film. The first time we become aware of Scorsese, he is arguing with Charlie in a comic scene outside the restaurant in Little Italy:

CHARLIE: Hi, Shorty.
MARTY: Fuck you, Charlie!
CHARLIE: Shorts, you must be having illusions of grandeur.

Most of the humor in this sequence comes from the fact that it is the director playing opposite the star of his film. Scorsese's sense of humor keeps the self-reflexive quality in this film from ever becoming pretentious.

Although some may view these self-reflexive sequences as stylistically disruptive, we see them as manifestations of the filmmaker's exuberance. Like Blake, Scorsese rejects "strait roads," conventional narrative form. Instead, he enjoys disrupting his narrative through the use of self-conscious devices which, conversely, lend added power to the narrative. Martin Scorsese's *Mean Streets* is one of the most cinematically and intellectually exciting American films of the 1970s because Scorsese follows "the crooked roads without Improvement," Blake's "roads of Genius."

The Church of the Desert: Reflections on *The Sheltering Sky*

Jody McAuliffe

ut now he was awake . . . In the next room he could hear his wife stepping about in her mules on the smooth tile floor, and this sound now comforted him, since he had reached another level of consciousness where the mere certitude of being alive was not sufficient . . . Later he would climb down from the high bed and fling the window open and at that moment he would remember his dream. For although he could not recall a detail of it, he knew he had dreamed. On the other side of the window there would be air, the roofs, the town, the sea. The evening wind would cool his face as he stood looking, and at that moment the dream would be there. Now he only could lie as he was, breathing slowly, almost ready to fall asleep again, paralyzed in the airless room, not waiting for twilight but staying as he was until it should come.
—Paul Bowles, *The Sheltering Sky*

The dreamer wakes. The rowboat approaches the shore of French North Africa. In Bernardo Bertolucci's film version, Ryuichi Sakamoto's mournful theme introduces the menage: Kit, Tunner, and Port, the first tourist/travelers to this place since World War II. Tunner is a tourist, Port a traveler, and Kit half and half. A tourist thinks about going home as soon as he arrives. A traveler might never go back at all. Port and Kit: two professionless artiste intellectuals. Tunner: a rich man whose only work is giving dinner parties on Long Island. Who else would have the desire or means to journey in hope of meeting his own little prince in the desert, maybe even eat some sand? Americans about to be reinvented, seeking to escape the war, lift back the curtain.

"What makes the desert beautiful," said the little prince, "is that somewhere it hides a well."
—Antoine de Saint-Exupéry, *The Little Prince*

The film begins with its central image: the face of Port upside down. And John Malkovich conveys all the pale, baked, existential dread you could ask for. Though the implication is that we will see this world from his point of view, Bertolucci embraces Kit's psyche as he constructs their journey: every image is an omen.

ESTRAGON: (restored to the horror of his situation). I was asleep! (Despairingly.) Why will you never let me sleep?
VLADIMIR: I felt lonely.
ESTRAGON: I had a dream.
VLADIMIR: Don't tell me!
ESTRAGON: I dreamt that—
VLADIMIR: DON'T TELL ME!
ESTRAGON: (gesture towards the universe). This one is enough for you? (Silence.) It's not nice of you, Didi. Who am I to tell my private nightmares to if I can't tell them to you?
VLADIMIR: Let them remain private. You know I can't bear that.
ESTRAGON: (coldly) There are times when I wonder if it wouldn't be better for us to part.
VLADIMIR: You wouldn't go far.
ESTRAGON: That would be too bad, really too bad. (Pause.) Wouldn't it, Didi, be really too bad? (Pause.) When you think of the beauty of the way. (Pause.) And the goodness of the wayfarers. (Pause. Wheedling.) Wouldn't it, Didi?

VLADIMIR: Calm yourself.
ESTRAGON: (voluptuously). Calm . . . calm . . . The English say
           cawm. (Pause.)
—*Waiting For Godot*

In the French colonial café Port insists on telling his dream to Kit
and Tunner. This is the dream from which he awoke in that opening image:

PORT: I had the strangest dream yesterday . . . I just remem-
       bered it.

An old streetcar RATTLES into view and stops outside in the sun,
crowded with haggard PEOPLE in tattered clothes.

KIT: Oh, Port! Please! Other people's dreams are so dull!
PORT: I know it's boring, but I won't remember it if I don't tell
       it. (he looks back at the streetcar) I was on this train . . .
       and I thought "We're going to crash into a big bed with the
       sheets all in mountains." . . . I was thinking that if I wanted
       to I could start at the beginning—and live my whole life
       all over again. So first I thought "No, I can't go through all
       that God-awful stuff all over again" . . . And then I saw the
       trees out of the window and I thought "Yes! I'd go through
       anything just to smell the countryside the way it smelled
       when I was a child . . ." But then I realised it was too late.
       Because just while I was thinking "No", I'd reached up to
       my mouth and broken off my teeth—as if they were made
       of plaster . . . The train had stopped and I was holding my
       teeth in my hand and I wanted to cry—but I couldn't. Then
       I woke up.

At this moment the Pozzo and Lucky of Bertolucci's *Sheltering Sky*
enter the picture to complete it: Eric and Mrs. Lyle—the grotesque
fading aristocracy, lumbering through Africa in a white Mercedes,
denigrating the Arabs all the while. Mrs. Lyle is a writer of travel
guides who browbeats her son; her face is straight out of a painting
by Ensor. Eric, falling apart with the pox, tiptoes about, embodying
his mother's description of Arab behavior.

The omnipresent image of the red desert butted against a blue sky
translates quite directly into the relationship between Kit and Port.

Her color is blue: icy, cool, and unapproachable. He is bathed in a red of overheated eroticism, whether through the glass of the Grand Hotel or in the late afternoon sun.

Witness his dream: Port is the proverbial accident looking for a place to happen. He scrapes with death on his first night. When Kit won't tell him why she doesn't "trust" Tunner, he storms out into the street. He meets an Arab who asks him what he is looking for. Nothing. Urging him that life is short, the Arab leads him to a whore. The path is a descent into hell, down a ladder into darkness toward a small camp glowing like hot red coals in the distance, the burning core of existence. Malkovich reveals Port as a smug American who thinks he can take what he pays for without losing anything, an overly smart, arrogant, charming sensualist. He peppers his performance with well-chosen, barked shouts and explosions that surprise, but are absolutely necessary. He escapes the whore's tent with his wallet intact, but her male companions nip at his heels like dogs trying to drag him down. It is only a matter of time. He has betrayed Kit and she will betray him with Tunner.

When he arrives back at the hotel, Tunner urges him to look at himself in the mirror: "Have you seen yourself?" The first part of this movie is crowded with mirrors. Some of the shots are set up through as many as two. The café has a wall of mirrors. Their presence depicts the swollen self-consciousness of these characters. As they travel deeper and deeper into the Sahara, Kit remarks that there are no mirrors. Mirrors and the consequent ability to see oneself emerge as last vestiges of civilization, as significant as running water.

In the central scene of this film Port takes Kit to a place he misses more than anything in this world. His love for the desert terrifies his wife. This landscape, moonscape of empty desert met at the horizon by a block of blue sky, is like the empty scape where Gogo and Didi wait interminably for Godot. A patch of sunlight isolates Kit and Port on a bank overlooking an abyss in the long shadows of late afternoon. Wearing sunglasses, they look like a 1950s couple about to watch a bomb blast in Nevada. As they make aborted love on this shoal, the long-awaited reconciliation in this church of the desert, Port sees the sky as "so strange, almost solid, as if it were protecting us from what's behind." But there is nothing behind, only absolute night. Kit thinks

Port can live alone, without her. She wishes she could be like him, but she can't. Debra Winger reveals Kit's lack of self in her slightly stilted, affected delivery. Her words seem not to be her own. Port thinks they fear the same thing: loving too much. Here, too, they echo Gogo and Didi. "Let's leave here." "Okay. Okay." The same questions nag both these couples: "Can you be happy here?" "Happy? Happy, how do you mean?" "I mean could you like it here?" "How do I know? God, I wish you wouldn't ask me questions like that." All four are preoccupied with meaning, and beset by the difficulties of embracing one another.

"Where are the men?" the little prince at last took up the conversation again. "It is a little lonely in the desert . . ."

"It is also lonely among men," the snake said.

The little prince gazed at him for a long time.

"You are a funny animal," he said at last. "You are no thicker than a finger . . ."

"But I am more powerful than the finger of a king," said the snake.

The little prince smiled.

"You are not very powerful. You haven't even any feet. You cannot even travel . . ."

"I can carry you farther than any ship could take you," said the snake.

He twined himself around the little prince's ankle, like a golden bracelet.

"Whomever I touch, I send back to the earth from whence he came," the snake spoke again . . .

"I can help you, some day, if you grow too homesick for your own planet. I can—"

"Oh! I understand you very well," said the little prince. "But why do you always speak in riddles?"

"I solve them all," said the snake.

And they were both silent.

—*The Little Prince*

In Ain Krorfa a funeral crosses their path. Over a supper of bug-ridden soup, Kit remarks that Port thinks you get used to everything and she wonders out loud if that's good or bad. Tunner calls this getting used to everything "the end of progress." Port's descent, fired by his jealousy of and annoyance with Tunner, escalates. After Eric Lyle steals his passport, Port has to run faster to escape Tunner's effort to return it to him. Port is turning cold. He and Kit see a troop of native cavalry training on their perfect white horses, their capes flying in the wind. Bertolucci frames Kit's face in a close-up, registering her premonition of the Arab merchant caravan that will carry her away after Port's death. Husband and wife discover they are standing in a graveyard whose markers bear no names, no dates. Kit lies down. Port performs a brief mock ceremony over her body, takes his hat off to honor her grave. She asks: "Don't you think we should stop?" And the camera sweeps back to the horses in the distance, a throwback to another era altogether.

The second use of the shot of Port's head upside down occurs during his fevered delirium. In a masterful stroke of adaptation, Bertolucci and collaborator Mark Peploe collapse Port's trip to a whorehouse and his obsession with a blind girl into yet another dream, a function of his disease. His entire journey is a kind of dream fulfillment of his first nightmare—of the train crashing into the mountain of white sheets and his not being able to open his mouth and scream because he's cracked his teeth. The blind girl gives him the pattern of his death throes in a dance that culminates in seizure. After arriving in El Gaa and joking about the accommodations, Port falls and bites his tongue. He says that he always wondered what it would be like to do that. This remark epitomizes his dilettante's desire to taste life in all its dimensions of pain and pleasure. He resembles the protagonist of Bowles's "A Distant Episode," a linguist in search of a little box made from camel udders. The Reguiba, a shady element, cut out his tongue, dress him in tin cans, and he willingly dances for the caravan. Eventually, the sound of classical Arabic restores him to consciousness— pain—and he runs like "a holy maniac" straight into the setting sun.

"You understand . . . It is too far. I cannot carry this body with me. It is too heavy."
—*The Little Prince*

Port's snake is typhus. In his last moments of lucidity bathed in red light, he says that he has always lived for Kit without knowing it, and now she's going away. She protests that she isn't going anywhere, not realizing that in a sense it is she who is dying, because now she will have to live for him. The night comes closer and closer until his light dies. The red gets smaller and smaller until it disappears, leaving them in the gray of the Foreign Legion barracks. Her grief for the loss of him, someone to talk to, is heartrending. The desert is silence.

In the third and final use of the image of Port's face upside down, his eyes are wide open, dead. The camera pans right to reveal Kit's face upside down, with her eyes closed. Then her eyes open. As the result of a kind of horrifying experiment, his point of view has been successfully transfused into her. And the gesture has cost him his life, though his death throes are still to come. She is a peculiar kind of Frankensteinian creature who steps out into the icy blue moonlight. Like the hero of Antonioni's *The Passenger*, she reinvents herself— she really gets lost.

The opposition of these forces of fire and ice, red and blue, desert and sky are purified and distilled in the last movement of the picture. There is very little dialogue. Kit hitches up with a merchant caravan, and one of the owners becomes her lover. Bertolucci opted to cut the rape of Kit by the other owner; he is interested in a different kind of journey, a less violent, more internalized and mature experience of this profound landscape. The desert has always held a special lure; it is the closest place to hell on earth. In Christian tradition, privation in the desert yields enlightenment, a sense of true vocation. (One of the most shockingly powerful and deeply romantic cinematic images is Marlene Dietrich walking into the desert to follow Gary Cooper at the end of *Morocco*.) Kit slowly becomes a part of this landscape. She gives away her explorer's hat. Her lover buries her western clothes and disguises her as a boy to keep her secret from his wives. But when he leaves home on his next trip, she reveals herself as a woman to his wives, abandons her role in this household, and is suffocated by the crowd in the marketplace. This scene is a late nod to an earlier scene in the novel when Kit is trapped in a railcar and forced to stare into the face of death in the person of one horribly disfigured Arab.

She drifts from reunion with Tunner back at the Grand Hotel, and instead of losing herself on a streetcar only to end up at the end of the line, as in the novel, or disappearing in a crowd as in the screenplay, she runs into the author of her story, Paul Bowles, in the café.

To his question, "Are you lost," she replies, "Yes," and smiles as if she's finally found her reflection. I can see why Bertolucci wanted to put Bowles in the film. His face is like the desert itself. And here's somebody who lived to tell about it. But his presence diminishes the weight of the lives of these characters, these postwar searchers not so different from ourselves. Their story does not profit by being delimited as metafiction. Better she should disappear into an eternal crowd, more powerful an image than the streetcar of 1949, than into the character of Paul Bowles. Port and Kit's story wants to be an ultimate refutation of American individualism, to herald the end of progress.

The future belongs to crowds.
—Don DeLillo, *Mao II*

What the Streets Mean:

An Interview with Martin Scorsese

Anthony DeCurtis

hen I grew up in Greenwich Village in the fifties and early sixties, the neighborhood was not the bohemian theme park that it is today. Of course, there was a strong, long-standing and genuine bohemian presence—the writers, painters, poets, beats, and political progressives who constituted the reverse image of the mainstream fifties of conformity and McCarthyism. There was also a significant, though subterranean, gay presence, one that would explode onto the surface in the late sixties after a riot at a bar on Christopher Street called the Stonewall.

But the Village that I grew up in was an Italian neighborhood, a place where you were defined by what parish you lived in, where everybody went to church on Sundays and the kids went to Catholic schools, where the streets were lined with fruit and vegetable stands and everybody knew that if your apartment was robbed, if your purse was stolen, if anything went wrong, you didn't call the police, you went to the mob. The mob guys hung out in bakeries, in barber-shops, in the storefronts with blackened windows they called social clubs. These guys hated problems in the neighborhood that were not specifically connected to their own activities—such problems only served to confuse things, to antagonize the bought police, to create more problems. They would listen to you and, in order to enforce the notion that only certain types of crimes were permitted in this neighborhood, they often would help you.

The instinctive clannishness of the immigrant community, the code of silence that ruled all mob-related activities, and the simple fact that in this country, then or now, the lives and needs of working-class, ethnic people—too isolated, untrusting, and proud to make demands of the government, too unpolished and prole for the right wing, too independent and unfashionable for the left—don't matter much, created the sense that, in terms of the larger world around us, we didn't exist. In the eyes of others, we were invisible.

This was especially true for the children and grandchildren of the Italians who came here from the old country. The old-timers, the "greaseballs," the ones who, as we used to say, still seemed as if they "just got off the boat," simply recreated, to as great a degree as possible, the lives they had lived in Italy. But we, their offspring, grew up with television and the New World imperative to invent a "better" life. We were taught not to speak Italian, to obey the authorities, to do well in school. We were the hyphenates: Italian-Americans. My father, not a man especially known for his restraint, would stop a roomful of conversation dead if he happened to overhear someone call me Tony. "His name is Anthony," he would announce absolutely. "Tony is a hoodlum's name."

But in our rage we became hoodlums anyway. No one—at least no one we knew, least of all our parents and grandparents—had the slightest idea how anything really worked, how we were really supposed to create our New World lives. The old country receded, but America—the land where Americans lived—seemed no less foreign than it ever had. Our grade schools—Our Lady of Pompeii, in my case—were jails of discipline, repression, and superstition. We lived nowhere but the streets, but we owned the streets. We'd get high, occasionally steal, indulge in exultant vandalism, but our primary rush was violence.

Essentially, the subjects of our violence were people who lived in the American culture from which we felt excluded. Of course, given where we lived, we engaged in some perfunctory gay-bashing, though the gay men fought back—the spark that would eventually kindle the Stonewall?—which greatly discouraged and frightened us. The main problem with gay-bashing, however, was that, despite how it shored up our sexual identities, it didn't provide much of a kick. In some deep way we understood that the gays, after all, were ultimately as excluded as we were. What could it mean, therefore, to victimize them?

Our enemies, then, in this class war became people whom we called "tourists," a category that applied to anyone who walked the streets of our neighborhood and who was white, middle- or upper-class, and seemed to have more options than we did. They were people we envied and, while we affected a streetwise condescension toward them, we in fact hated them. While it often seemed emotionally useful to have women watch us intimidate and assault their escorts, we never attacked women—too easy, and sex wasn't the point. Nor did we rob anyone. That seemed petty, beneath us. It wasn't about money.

It was about exerting control over our streets, and violence for the sheer, ecstatic fun of it, for the explosion of release. It was wilding. If we were aimless, if we had no idea where we were going, we would make it dangerous to go where we were. If we were invisible, we would enforce our presence, make ourselves matter.

Long after I had left that world behind—the police were becoming too intolerant of our mayhem; I had too many troubling memories of people we'd hurt—and consciously determined, as a friend put it, "that it was upward-mobility time," I saw *Mean Streets* by Martin Scorsese. Scorsese had grown up nearby, in Little Italy, the neighborhood next door. The kids from that neighborhood were at least as bad as we were, but we regarded them as hicks, sort of the way northern Italians to this day regard Sicilians, or urban Italians regard their rural compatriots. Even so, *Mean Streets* was the first time I had seen the world I had known growing up represented in a work of art. I was so astounded that virtually every other aspect of the movie was lost on me. Here was someone who clearly shared all the contradictory feelings of coming from a place that continued to mean so much, even while, for hundreds of reasons, it had to be judged and rejected. Rejected, but acknowledged. Acknowledged, and perhaps even honored.

From that point on, the films of Martin Scorsese haunted me. For me, watching *Mean Streets*, *Raging Bull*, or *GoodFellas* is like looking through an album of photographs from my youth, like disappearing into a world of my past, a world that still, in many ways, for better or worse, often seems more substantial than the worlds I move in now. I was thinking about all this when I went to interview Martin Scorsese in the fall of 1990, shortly before *GoodFellas* opened.

Martin Scorsese's apartment sits seventy-five floors above midtown Manhattan and offers an imperial view that encompasses Central Park and the Upper East Side, extending out toward the borough of Queens, where Scorsese was born in 1942. The calming grays and blacks and whites of the living room's decor combine with the apartment's Olympian height—so high as to eliminate almost all street noise—to make New York City seem a distant abstraction, a silent movie playing in Martin Scorsese's picture window. *Mean Streets* it's not.

For *Mean Streets*, you would have to go to the roof and look the other way, behind you, down toward Little Italy, the Italian ghetto on the Lower East Side where Scorsese came of age in the fifties and sixties. Scorsese returned to that neighborhood—or at least to a virtually identical neighborhood in the East New York section of Brooklyn—with *GoodFellas*, which is based on Nicholas Pileggi's book *Wiseguy*, the story of the middle-level Irish-Sicilian mobster Henry Hill and his twenty-five-year career in the criminal underworld.

The movie reunited Scorsese with his homeboy, Robert De Niro, for the first time since *The King of Comedy*, in 1982, and assembles a veritable who's who of superb Italian-American film stars, including Ray Liotta, Joe Pesci, Lorraine Bracco, and Paul Sorvino. Scorsese himself wrote the screenplay with Pileggi. Grisly, funny, violent, and riddled with moral questions posed by matters of loyalty, betrayal, and personal honor, *GoodFellas* also returned Scorsese to the themes that pump at the heart of some of his most urgent films, most notably *Mean Streets* (1973), *Taxi Driver* (1975), and *Raging Bull* (1980).

Though the usually dapper Scorsese is casually dressed in jeans and a faded blue shirt, he is anything but relaxed for the interview. He didn't realize the interview would involve so much time—at least two hours. What about the other things he'd arranged to do? His two daughters, Catherine and Domenica, would soon be coming by the apartment (he had recently separated from his fourth wife, Barbara De Fina). He needs to make some phone calls, change some things around, work some things out. After we start to talk, he moves back and forth between a chair that serves as something of a command center—located, as it is, next to a phone and a movie projector and opposite a wall with a pull-down screen on it—and a place closer to me on the white couch.

Scorsese speaks in the style of a born-and-bred New Yorker. He formulates his thoughts out loud, as if they were terrifically important but continually in flux, in need of constant refinement. Asked a question, he starts talking immediately, stops abruptly, starts and stops again and again until he finds his groove. He gestures for punctuation and emphasis, fires off staccato bursts of insight when he's on a roll, laughs wildly at his own improbable characterizations and verbal excesses. At times, the sheer nervous energy of his intellect propels him out of his seat, and he speaks while standing at his full height—he's quite short—for a minute or two. He walks over to a cabinet several times for nasal and throat sprays to ease the effects of the asthma that has afflicted him since childhood. He alternately concentrates on me with a ferocious intensity and seems to forget I'm there at all.

A filmmaker in a kind of tumultuous internal exile, Scorsese sits edgily poised in splendid isolation over the city that remains one of his most fertile obsessions—and looks to the future with hope and apprehension.

DeCURTIS: I want to start with *GoodFellas*. Obviously you have returned to some familiar terrain. What brought you to that specific project?

SCORSESE: I read a review of *Wiseguy* back when I was directing *The Color of Money* in Chicago, and it said something about this character, Henry Hill, having access to many different levels of organized crime because he was somewhat of an outsider. He looked a little nicer. He was able to be a better front man and speak a little better. I thought that was interesting. You could move in and get a cross section of the layers of organized crime—from his point of view of course. Which could be true—maybe, who knows? It's what he says. You get into two different areas there. What he says the truth is— you have to take his word for it, which is . . . I don't say it's doubtful, but it's like . . .

DeCURTIS: It's a version.

SCORSESE: The second element is really the most important one: his perception of the truth. Where, you know, if somebody gets shot in a room and there's five people who witnessed it, you'll probably have five different stories as to how it happened. You know what I'm say- ing? So you have to take that all into consideration. But that's what fascinated me about the book. So I got the book and I started read- ing it and I was fascinated by the narrative ability of it, the narrative approach.

DeCURTIS: Henry has a real voice.

SCORSESE: He's got a wonderful voice and he has a wonderful way of expressing the life-style. He reminds me of a lot of the people that I grew up around. It had a great sense of humor, too. So I said, "This will make a wonderful film." I figured to do it as if it was one long trailer, where you just propel the action and you get an exhilaration, a rush of the life-style.

DeCURTIS: That acceleration at the end of the film is amazing, when Henry is driving around like a madman, blasted on cocaine, trying to deal for guns and drugs while the police helicopter is following him, and, through it all, he keeps calling home to make sure his brother is stirring the sauce properly for dinner that night.

SCORSESE: Yeah. The sauce is as important as the helicopter. That's a whole comment about drugs, too. When I read about that last day in the book, I said I'd like to just take that and make it the climax of the film. Actually, the real climax is him and Jimmy in the diner. A very quiet moment.

DeCURTIS: When you talk about the world you grew up in, as it happens, it is virtually the same world I grew up in. I went to Our Lady of Pompeii in Greenwich Village.

SCORSESE: Great!

DeCURTIS: On Bleecker Street.

SCORSESE: It was the West Side, though. You were on the West Side. That's a funny thing, on the East Side, we didn't have the influx of other cultures, that very important bohemian culture.

DeCURTIS: My family was Italian and working-class—I wasn't part of that. I grew up in a world as enclosed as the one that you describe. But there was always this sense that there was something else. I mean, when I was a kid, the *Village Voice* office was around the corner. So when it got to the point where like, as kids, everybody was getting in trouble with the police, I had a very clear vision that there was some way out.

SCORSESE: That there was another world. We didn't know that.

DeCURTIS: It's a very clear distinction. The bohemian world of the Village was like another world, even though you only lived a few blocks from the Village.

SCORSESE: I never went to the Village until I enrolled at NYU in 1960. I grew up on the East Side. From 1950 to 1960, for ten years, I never ventured past Houston Street, past Broadway and Houston. I think my father took me on a bus when I was five years old or something. I remember Washington Square. I was on a double-decker bus. And I remember a friend of mine, I was about nine years old, his mother took us to the Village on a little tour to see the little houses and flowers. It was like a wonderland, because they had flowers. It was a very different culture.

I was used to, you know, wonderful stuff, too, on Elizabeth Street, which was five grocery stores, three butcher shops all on one block. Two barbershops. And it was barrels of olives—which was great. Growing up down there was like being in a Sicilian village culture. It was great. But you come from there so you know. It's complicated to explain to people who didn't grow up in it.

DeCURTIS: It is. When I'm trying to tell people about it, I refer to your movies. I don't know any other representations of it.

SCORSESE: A good friend of mine I grew up with just sent me a letter.

He just saw *GoodFellas* and he said he had just spent a sleepless night remembering what a great and incredible escape we both made from that area, from that whole life-style.

DeCURTIS: I first saw *Mean Streets* after I had left New York to go to graduate school in Indiana. I had never been west of New Jersey, and I saw *Mean Streets* . . .

SCORSESE: In Indiana!

DeCURTIS: And it was like, "Wow, somebody got it. There it is."

SCORSESE: That's the whole story of *Mean Streets*. I mean, I put it on the screen. It took me years to get it going—I never thought the film would be released. I just wanted to make, like, an anthropological study; it was about myself and my friends. And I figured even if it was on a shelf, some years later people would take it and say that's what Italian-Americans on the everyday scale—not the Godfather, not big bosses, but the everyday scale, the everyday level—this is what they really talked like and looked like and what they did in the early seventies and late sixties. Early sixties even. This was the life-style.

DeCURTIS: Why was it important to do that? To document that?

SCORSESE: Oh, you know—myself. I mean why does anybody do anything? You know, you think you're important so you do a film about yourself. Or if you're a writer you write a novel about yourself or about your own experiences. I guess it's the old coming-of-age story.

Actually there were two of them for me. *Who's That Knocking on My Door?* and *Mean Streets*. *Who's That Knocking* I never got right, except for the emotional aspects of it—I got that.

DeCURTIS: I watched it recently and was struck by how strong it was. How do you feel about it at this point?

SCORSESE: I dislike it. Only because it took me three years to make. And, you know, we'd make the film and we'd work on a weekend and then for three weeks we wouldn't shoot and then we'd work another weekend. So it wasn't really a professional film to make. It took three years to make. The first year, '65, I cast it. We did all the scenes with the young boys and we had a young lady playing the part of the girl. But later on we came up to about an hour and ten minutes and there was no confrontation. The young girl was always seen in flashbacks and asides. It was all between the boys. So you never understood what was happening between the Harvey Keitel character and the girl. The conflict was, of course, being in love with a girl who is an outsider, loving her so much that you respect her and you won't make love to her. Then he finds out she's not a virgin and he can't accept that. It's that whole Italian-American way of thinking, of feeling.

Finally we got it released. We got it released by '69, when we were able to put a nude scene in it. In 1968, we shot a nude scene. In '68 there was a new tolerance about nude scenes. Very old, wonderful actors and actresses were playing scenes in the nude—it was very embarrassing. We had to get a nude scene. We shot it in Holland, because I was up in Amsterdam doing some commercials for a friend of mine. We flew Harvey over and we got the young ladies there and we did this nude scene. I came back, kind of smuggled it back into the country in my raincoat, put it in the middle of the film and then the film was released. But it was still a rough sketch to me. I wish . . . ah, it's the old story: if I knew then what I know now it would be different.

DeCURTIS: One of the most interesting parts of the movie is the sexual fantasy sequence while the Doors's "The End" is playing.

SCORSESE: Well, that was the scene done in Amsterdam. That was fun.

DeCURTIS: The Oedipal drama in the song underscores the Oedipal struggle of the Keitel character. Using that song also captures the way that you were profoundly affected by what was going on culturally in the sixties. But for the characters in your movies, the sixties don't seem to exist. Their world is . . .

SCORSESE: Medieval! Medieval. Well, that's the thing. When I was about to release the film, we were having a problem getting a distributor and my agents at William Morris said to me, "Marty, what do you expect? You have a film here in which the guy loves a young woman so much that he respects her and he won't make love to her. Here we are in the age of the sexual revolution, and you're making a movie about repression! Total sexual repression. Who's going to see it? Nobody."

Yeah, I mean, that was my life. When I went to Woodstock in '69, I mean, it was the first time I started wearing jeans—afterwards. I took cufflinks; I lost one of the cufflinks. Certainly it was having come from that neighborhood and living there completely closed in, like in a ghetto area, not really leaving till the early sixties to go to the West Side. So I had one foot in the university and the other foot in *Mean Streets*, you know, that world, that life-style. I became aware of other people in the world and other life-styles, other views, political and otherwise, much later. But I was quite closed off. It was like somebody coming out of the Middle Ages going to a university.

DeCURTIS: In a documentary that was done about you, you said that you would see certain things when you were young and you would say, "Why don't you ever see this in a movie?" I was wondering about what it was you were seeing, or what you felt was missing then in the movies?

SCORSESE: I think it is the way people behaved. I'd be sitting and watching something on television. My uncles would be in the room. My mother would be there. One of my uncles would say, "That wouldn't happen that way. It's a good picture and everything else, I really enjoyed it, but, you know, what would really happen is such and such. He would do this and she would leave him and the guy would kill the other guy." They would work up their own versions of the film noir that we were watching, and they were actually much better. My uncles' and my mother's and father's ideas were much better than what we were watching on TV. And it had to do with what was based in reality. What would really happen.

DeCURTIS: That's an interesting aspect about your movies. Obviously you're completely soaked in film history and you've seen a million movies. But your movies never become just movies about movies. There's never anything cute or clever about them. Even when Henry in *GoodFellas* says, when the police are coming for him, that things don't happen the way they do "in the movies," it doesn't seem contrived. Of course, you got that from the book.

SCORSESE: I was going to take that out, but I left it in because I felt it had more of an honesty to it. I hoped it had an honesty to it, if you understand. I always find that sort of thing too cute or too self-conscious or something—though I don't mind being self-conscious at all. I like Joseph Losey's films. You see the camera moving, it's very self-conscious. But it took me years to get to understand the precision of it and the beauty of that, you know? And I don't mind the self-conscious aspect. What I do mind is pretending that you're not watching a movie. That's absurd. You are watching a movie and it is a movie.

But Henry did say, "They don't come to you like you usually see in movies." So he's not talking about this movie. He's talking about other movies that you see. And I was even thinking of saying, "I know you're watching this as a movie now." I was even thinking of putting that in. Then I said, no, it gets too—what's the word for that?—maybe academic to get into that. There's a falseness about that that I wanted to avoid here.

DeCURTIS: It seems exactly like what he would say.

SCORSESE: It just sounded right to me, you know what I'm saying? It sounded right in the context of the way he was speaking and all, so I just let it go.

DeCURTIS: That approach to things relates well to the subterranean world you deal with in *GoodFellas* and some of your other movies. You depict a real world of consequences, in which people don't get a lot of chances to make mistakes. There is a clear sense that if you step out of line, if you do the wrong thing, you're going to pay for it.

SCORSESE: That's very important. These guys are in business to make money, not to kill people, not to create mayhem. They really want to make money. And if you make a big mistake, you bring down heat on them, you bring attention to them, you cause strife between two crime families, somebody has to be eliminated. It's very simple. Those are the rules. Very, very simple. I mean, you can't make that many big mistakes. You don't rise in the hierarchy if you do. It's very much like a Hollywood situation where, you know, how many pictures could you make that cost $40 million that lose every dime? You can't. It's purely common sense. And so they work out their own little elaborate set of rules and codes.

DeCURTIS: It's also a means of working out a certain version of the American dream. In *GoodFellas* Henry says he'd rather be a wise guy than be the president of the United States.

SCORSESE: It's better, because you can do anything you want. And you can take anything you want, because, like Henry says, if they complain, you hit them. It's very simple. It's more exciting, and the opportunity is endless. And this is the great country for it to happen to, because the opportunity here is endless, usually.

However, I always quote Joe Pesci, who pointed out that wise guys have a life cycle—or an enjoyment cycle—of maybe eight or nine years, ten years the most, before they either get killed or go to jail and start that long process of going in and out like a revolving door. I try to give an impression of that in the film when Henry gets to jail and says, "Paulie was there because he was serving time for contempt. Jimmy was in another place. Johnny Dio was there." I mean, this is like home for them. Then the life begins to wear you down. The first few years are the exuberance of youth. They have a great time— until they start to pay for it. Tommy [DeVito, played by Pesci] starts doing things, just unnecessary outbursts. Look why Jimmy [Conway, played by De Niro] goes to jail—because he beats up some guy down in Florida. It's a long story in the book; in the film, it's totally un-important as to why they're even there. We did it so quickly to show you how, just as fast as it happened, that's as fast as he could go to jail for something he forgot he did.

DeCURTIS: Tommy and Jimmy in *GoodFellas* are, like Travis Bickle in *Taxi Driver* and Jake La Motta in *Raging Bull*, walking powder kegs. What interests you about characters like that?

SCORSESE: There are a thousand answers to that. It's interesting. It's good drama. I'm attracted to those kind of characters. And you see part of yourself in that. I like to chart a character like that, see how far they go before they self-destruct. How it starts to turn against them after awhile—whether it's shooting people in the street or arguing in the home, in the kitchen and the bedroom. How soon the breaking point comes when everything just explodes and they're left alone.

DeCURTIS: You once said that the La Motta character in *Raging Bull* never really has to face himself until he's alone in his prison cell, hitting his head against the wall.

SCORSESE: Totally. That's the one he's been paranoid about all along. I mean, it gets to be so crazy. If his brother, and if Tommy Como, and if Salvie and if Vicky did everything he thought they did—he can do one of two things: kill them all or let it go. If you let it go, I mean, it's not the end of the world. But, no, no, he's got to battle it out in the ring. He's got to battle it out at home. He's got to battle it everywhere until finally he's got to deal with that point where everybody else has disappeared from him and he's dealing with himself. He didn't let it go. And ultimately, ultimately it's *you*.

DeCURTIS: Is that the source of all that violence, of all that paranoia and anger?

SCORSESE: Oh, I think it comes from yourself. I mean, obviously it comes from Jake. It comes from your feelings about yourself. And it comes from what you do for a living. In his case, he goes out in the morning and he beats up people. And then they beat him up and then he comes home. It's horrible. It's life on its most primitive level.

DeCURTIS: But that doesn't account for the sexual paranoia.

SCORSESE: Well, yeah. I don't know if it does. But I really am not a psychiatrist. It just comes from the fact that the guy is in the ring and you feel a certain way about yourself. When you're punching it out you feel a certain way about yourself. You could take anyone, you see; the ring becomes an allegory of whatever you do in life. You make movies, you're in the ring each time. Writing music—if you perform it, you're in the ring. Or people just living daily life, when they go to their work—they're in the ring. And, I think, it's how you feel about yourself that colors your feelings about everything else around you. If you don't feel good about yourself, it takes in everything that you're doing—the way your work is, the people who supposedly love you, your performance with them, your performance in loving, your performance of lovemaking—everything. You begin to chip away at yourself and you become like a raw wound. And if a man spits across the street, you say he spit at you. And then you're finished. Because then nobody can make a move. You'll think, "Why did you look at me that way?" Who's going to be with you? Who can stay with you?

DeCURTIS: At the end of *GoodFellas*, you leave Henry in a more problematic spot than the book itself does. Is there any reason for that?

SCORSESE: It's not about Henry, really; it's about the life-style. It's about all of them together. Henry's the one who gives us the in; he opens the door for us, but basically, it's about all these people. So it's more a comment on the life-style than it is on Henry. I mean, he's just left out in God knows where, annoyed because he's not a wise guy anymore. I was more interested in the irony of that. There wasn't a last paragraph in the book saying, "Now I know what I did. I was a bad guy, and I'm really sorry for it"—none of that. Just, "Gee, I can't get the right food here." It's right in line with when he says as a kid, "I didn't have to wait in line for bread at the bakery." I mean, it's the American way—getting treated special. It's really a film about that. It's a film about getting to a position where you don't have to wait in line to get served in a store.

DeCURTIS: A significant issue in the arts in recent years, and particularly, in your case, with *The Last Temptation of Christ* and *Taxi Driver*, has been various attempts at censorship. What are your feelings about that?

SCORSESE: Obviously, I'm for freedom of expression. I was very glad that *The Last Temptation of Christ* was able to be made by an American company, that I didn't have to go to Europe or to some other country to get the money for it. That's what this country is about, to be able to do something you believe in. I'm for freedom of expression, but in each generation there are threats to it, and you have to keep battling and fighting. I'm concerned about the educational system because it seems to be at a low level at this point in our history and that means that a lot of kids are not learning about this, are not learning that they have to fight for this freedom in this country. I don't necessarily mean going to the Mideast. I'm talking about fighting for it at home, fighting for it in your school, fighting for it in your church. Because they have a low level of education, many people are not going to know that. They're going to take it for granted and it's going to become worse and worse of a problem and there's going to be fewer people to make sure that we secure these rights, to take the right stand.

That's all I'm concerned about. I personally don't like a lot of the stuff I see—it's offensive to me. But that's what it's about. You have to let it go. As far as my personal way of dealing with subject matter, I can't let anybody tell me, "Don't do that, it will offend people." I can't do that.

On one level, when I'm dealing with a Hollywood film, that means I have to do a certain kind of subject matter that will make a certain amount of money. If I decide to make less money, that means I can take a risk on subject matter. So the only criterion on the films I'm willing to take risks on is that it be truthful, that it be honest about your own feelings and truthful to what you know to be the reality around you or the reality of the human condition of the characters. If it's something that's not honest, not truthful, then it's a problem. If you don't believe in it, why are you making it? You're going to offend people to make some money? What for? It doesn't mean anything. The money doesn't mean anything. All that matters is the work, just what's up on the screen. So that's it. I'm not like some great person who's out there undaunted, fighting off all these people. I didn't think any of this stuff would really cause trouble—let alone *Taxi Driver*. *The Last Temptation*, I knew there would be some problems, but that's a special area for me. I really demand that I get to speak out the way I feel about it, even within the Church, the Catholic Church. Some of my close friends are still priests and we talk about it. I just heard from one today, and they support me.

DeCURTIS: But you must think about the potential impact of your movies. I remember your saying that you were shocked when audiences responded in an almost vigilante fashion to the end of *Taxi Driver*.

SCORSESE: To *The Wild Bunch*, too, they reacted that way. I was kind of shocked.

DeCURTIS: It would suggest there's some kind of fissure between your moral and spiritual concerns and how the films are perceived.

SCORSESE: No, I went to see the film that night and they were reacting very strongly to the shoot-out sequence in *Taxi Driver*. And I was disturbed by that. It wasn't done with that intent. You can't stop people from taking it that way. What can you do? And you can't stop people from getting an exhilaration from violence, because that's human, very much the same way as you get an exhilaration from the violence in *The Wild Bunch*. But the exhilaration of the violence at the end of *The Wild Bunch* and the violence that's in *Taxi Driver*—because it's shot a certain way, and I know how it's shot, because I shot it and I designed it—is also in the creation of that scene in the editing, in the camera moves, in the use of music and the use of sound effects, and in the movement within the frame of the characters. So it's like . . . *art*—good art, bad art, or indifferent, whatever the hell you want to say it is, it's still art. And that's where the exhilaration comes in. The shoot-out at the end of *The Wild Bunch* is still one of the great exhilarating sequences in all movies, and it's also one of the great dance sequences in the movies. It's ballet.

Now *Taxi Driver* may be something else, I don't know. It may be something else entirely. The intent was not necessarily the reception I saw. I know it can't be the reaction of most of the people who have seen the picture. I was in China in '84 and a young man from Mongolia talked to me at length about *Taxi Driver*, about the loneliness. That's why the film seems to be something that people keep watching over and over. It's not the shoot-'em-out at the end. As much as I love the shoot-'em-out at the end of *The Wild Bunch*, I wouldn't put it on for fun. If you put it on for fun, that's something else. That's a whole other morbid area.

There's an interesting situation going on. There's lots of movies that have been cut and movies that appear on video with scenes put back in and you begin to get these esoteric groups in the country, people who become obsessed with getting the complete film. The films can range anywhere from *Lawrence of Arabia* to some very, very shlocky horror film that shows dismembering of bodies and disemboweling of people, so that you can see every frame of disemboweling. That's something else. I can't think about that. I don't know what that is.

DeCURTIS: Living in New York, obviously violence is around you all the time.

SCORSESE: Oh come on. I just took a cab on 57th Street, we're about to make a turn on Eighth Avenue, and three Puerto Rican guys are beating each other up over the cab. *Over* it—from my side, onto the hood, onto the other side. Now, this is just normal—to the point where the cabbie and myself, not a word. We don't say anything. He just makes his right turn and we move on. It's at least two, three, four times a year that happens. I'm not in the street that much, but it would happen much more if I were.

DeCURTIS: But complaints about violence in your films don't bother you?

SCORSESE: It's never stopped me. You do the subject matter because you think it's going to make a lot of money—I don't do it. I just don't do it, you know? If I'm making a more commercial venture—I mean a more commercial venture like *The Color of Money*—it's something else. It becomes a different kind of movie and I think you can see the difference. My new film will be something else. It's a more mainstream commercial film for Universal Pictures.

DeCURTIS: What are you doing?

SCORSESE: It's a remake of *Cape Fear*, the 1962 film directed by J. Lee

Thompson, with Robert Mitchum and Gregory Peck. Bob De Niro wants to do it. It's more of a commercial venture. You do have a certain kind of responsibility to the audience on a picture like that because, number one, you have certain expectations from the genre, the thriller genre. You work within that framework and it's like a chess game. You see if you can really be expressive within it. I don't know if you can, because I always have that problem: loving the old films, I don't know if I can make them. You become more revisionist. I mean *New York, New York* was obviously revisionist. But *The Color of Money* I went half and half, and it should have been one way, I think.

DeCURTIS: *New York, New York* pitted its period style against completely unnerving contemporary emotions in the plot.

SCORSESE: The reality of the story. That was conscious. That was a love of the old stylization, you know, a love of those films, but then showing what it really is like as close as possible in the foreground. That's, I guess, what they call revisionism and that's why the picture—besides being too damn long, it's sprawling—didn't catch on.

DeCURTIS: Are there any new directions in which you'd like to move your work?

SCORSESE: I find I have a lot of things in mind and I want to be able to branch out and go into other areas, different types of films, maybe some genre films. But there's no doubt, even if I find something that's dealing with New York society in the eighteenth century, I usually am attracted to characters that have similar attributes to characters in my other films. So I guess I keep going in the same direction. I'm fascinated by history and by anthropology. I'm fascinated by the idea of people in history, and history having been shown to us in such a way that people always come off as fake—not fake but one-dimensional. And I'm interested in exploring what they felt and making them three-dimensional. To show that they're very similar to us. I mean, they're human beings. So just because the society around them and the world around them is very different, it doesn't mean that they didn't have the same feelings and the same desires, the same goals and the same things that haunt us in modern society. And in going into the past, maybe we can feel something about ourselves in the process.

DeCURTIS: It seems like that was a lot of the impetus behind *The Last*

Temptation of Christ, too, a desire to portray Christ in more three-dimensional terms.

SCORSESE: No doubt. To make him more like a person who would be in this room, who you could talk to.

DeCURTIS: There's a genuine concern with spiritual issues in your movies, at the same time that there is also a brutal physicality. How do you square that?

SCORSESE: It's just the struggle, that's all. The struggle to stay alive and to even want to stay alive. Just this corporal thing we're encased in and the limitations of it and how your spirit tries to spring out of it, fly away from it. And you can't. You can try. People say you can do it through poetry, you can do it through the work you do, and things like that. Thought. But you still feel imprisoned. So the body is what you deal with, and it's a struggle to keep that body alive.

DeCURTIS: You spend a great deal of time thinking about the world that you grew up in. But you are no longer part of that world. Does that create any complexities for you?

SCORSESE: Oh, because you left it behind doesn't mean that you don't have it. It's what you come from. You have an affinity to it and very often you have a love of it too. I can't exist there now. I don't belong there anymore. But I can damn well try to make sure that when I use it in a film like *GoodFellas*, I make it as truthfully as possible. What's wrong with that? It's part of your life, and if you try to deny that, what good is it? A lot of what I learned about life came from there. So you go back and you keep unraveling it. For some people it was the family, for other people it's the state. I don't know. Me, it was the subculture.

DeCURTIS: What things do you learn there?

SCORSESE: People are usually the product of where they come from, whether you come from a small farm in Iowa and you had your best friend next door and you went swimming in the old swimming hole—in other words, whether you had an idyllic American childhood—or you were a child in Russia or you were a child on the Lower East Side. The bonds you made, the codes that were there, all have a certain influence on you later on in your life. You can reject them. You can say, "Okay, those codes don't exist for me anymore because I'm not of that world anymore," but the reasons for those codes are very strong. The most important reason is survival. True survival. It's very simple. Food, safety, survival. It comes down to that. That struggle of the human form, the corporal, the flesh, to survive—anything to survive. And you learn in each society it's done a different way. In each subculture another way. And all these rules are set up and you learn them and they never really leave you. It's what everybody learns when you're all kids in the street or in the park. I think those things you carry with you the rest of your life.

And then, of course, it causes problems in that your response to certain stimuli at that time was one way, and when you get the same sort of stimuli now, you've got to be very careful you don't respond in the street fashion. Because they're different people. They don't really mean it. It's something else entirely. It's very funny because, you know, it's like I've seen people do things to other people that I said, "My God, if a guy did that, if that woman did that to me or a friend of mine back in 1960 or in that neighborhood, they wouldn't be *alive*." And you have to realize it's a different world. You just learn your way in and out of it, how to get in and out of the moral inlets of this new world, whatever the hell it is. I don't know what it is. Basically I'm here, in this building. I stay here. Here in this chair. That's it. I answer the phone. They let me out to make a movie. People come over to eat. That's it. I mean, I just do my work and see some very close friends. That's all. So that's what it comes down to. So in a funny way all the trauma of trying to find the new ways to react to the same stimuli in these new societies, it's kind of past me, I guess. I'm past that, which is good.

If you go to a cocktail party, someone comes over to you . . . like, I don't know, some strange *insult* occurs. You know, "How *dare* you!" You know, in the old days, in those neighborhoods, certain people, if you stepped on the guy's *shoe*, you could die, let alone come over and *insult* him. He'd kill you. It's so funny. Oh you'd be surprised how the insults come—it's just wonderful what they do. And people wonder why you don't want to talk to anybody. But it's fascinating. One person in a university, in the academic world, was introduced to me. We were having a few drinks after the David Lean American Film Institute dinner, and the woman said, "I must say I'm an admirer of *some* of your films, because, after all, I am a woman." Who needs it?

Who needs it? Who needs it? I mean, look, I make a certain type of film and that does bring out certain things in certain people. What can I say? So you try to avoid it.

DeCURTIS: Don't you have a sense of losing touch with things?

SCORSESE: No. I mean, you come from a certain time and place. I can't turn and say, "Well, gee, I'll only listen to rap music now." I can't. I mean, I still listen to older rock & roll; I listen to the music that I like. You come from a certain time and place and you can't . . . I mean, maybe there are some people who can, some artists, let's say, a painter or a novelist or some filmmakers who can keep up with the times and move along with what audiences expect today. I just think we are of a time, and the generations that come after us, we'll either still speak to them or we won't. We'll maybe miss two or three generations, and then a third or fourth generation will pick up what we did and it will mean something to them. But, I mean, you take a look at, in the early sixties, when you had the French New Wave and the Italian New Wave, with the jump cuts and the freeze frames, the destruction of the narrative form. You had a lot of Hollywood directors trying similar things, and it didn't work. And the guys who remained, the guys whose work stayed strong, are the ones who were not swayed by what was fashionable, who stayed true to themselves. And it's hard because they got rejected. Billy Wilder—everything from the mid-sixties on was rejected. Especially, I think, one of his greatest pictures: *The Private Life of Sherlock Holmes*. There were a lot of others who tried these flashy techniques and now you look at their films and they don't come out of an honesty, they don't come out of a truthfulness. And I don't say they were phonies. But they were saying, "Hey, that's a new way of doing it, let's try that." But if you can't tell the story that way, tell it the way you know how to.

DeCURTIS: What do you think is the flash stuff now?

SCORSESE: I think the formula—what do they call them?—high-concept pictures, probably. A high-concept picture has a basic theme. You can say it in one sentence: "A fish out of water." But you know, high-concept pictures have been around for a long time under different guises. In some cases they were very beautifully made vehicle films for certain kinds of stars. Bette Davis. Clint Eastwood. If you went to see a person, you knew what kind of film you were going to see. Okay, there were a lot of films that were like that, but they had a little more style to them, they had better actors in them, they were better written. But now the more money that's spent on a film, the bigger the audience has to be. Which means it's got to make more money. So you've got to cut it down to the best common denominator that you can get—and probably the lowest—so that it reaches more people.

A lot of it is, I think, the flash kind of cutting that goes on. The man who broke that into films originally was Richard Lester with *A Hard Day's Night*. You really saw the influence of television commercials on the film, and it worked. And now—this is old hat what I'm saying, really, it's really not even very good—the influence of MTV, let's say, over the past eight years on movies, maybe the audience attention span is a bit of a problem now. Things have to move faster. And you feel that. But, I mean, you can be true to yourself. You can really do it in this business, but it has to be for a price. Everything's for a price.

DeCURTIS: Your movies have been pioneering in their use of music, but now with MTV, everybody's using music.

SCORSESE: Well, I think they're using it cheaply. I think they're using it unimaginatively. I think they're using it basically to say, "Okay, it's 1956." They're using it to tell you which period you're in.

DeCURTIS: In your movies, the relation between the song and the scene takes on so many aspects. I was thinking about the scene in *GoodFellas* where that corpse is rolling around in the garbage and the coda from "Layla" is playing.

SCORSESE: That was shot to "Layla," you know. We played a playback on the set. All the murders were played back on the set to "Layla," to that piece, because it's a tragedy. A lot of those people, they didn't really deserve to die. It's like the unveiling, it's like a parade, it's like a revue, in a way, of the tragedy, the unfolding tragedy. It has a majesty to it, even though they're common people. You may say "common crooks," I still find that they're people. And the tragedy is in the music. The music made me feel a certain way and gave a certain sadness to it, a certain sadness and a certain sympathy.

DeCURTIS: One term you've used to describe the making of *Raging Bull* is "kamikaze filmmaking." What did you mean by that?

SCORSESE: What I meant was that I threw everything I knew into it, and if it meant the end of my career, then it would have to be the end of my career.

DECURTIS: Did you honestly feel that?

SCORSESE: Absolutely, yeah. I don't know exactly why, but I did. I just felt it would probably be the end of it, but I might as well throw it all in and see what happened.

DECURTIS: But why, because it might prove too much for people to take?

SCORSESE: Well, I was making a certain kind of film. Films at that time . . . don't forget, it was the beginning of the Reagan era. Sylvester Stallone had created his own new mythology and people were more into that. I mean, after the experience of New York, New York, I realized the kind of pictures I was going to make, even if I was dealing with genre . . . this is why I was telling you about the new thriller, Cape Fear. It's a very interesting situation, because I don't want it to be necessarily revisionist the way New York, New York was. But on the other hand, I want to find my own way in it. Now, does my own way mean, automatically, the undermining of a genre picture in traditional terms, which means that it will not be satisfying to an audience the way the traditional hero films, like all the Rocky movies, are?

Anyway, that was the mood of the country. And Raging Bull comes out. Who's going to see it? Who cares about this guy? Nobody— that's what I thought. And maybe some people would say, "Well, you were right, because nobody saw it." The film came out a week before Heaven's Gate and the whole studio went under. It only made a certain amount of money. The whole mood of the country was different. Big money was being made with pictures like Rocky and eventually the Spielberg-Lucas films. I mean, New York, New York was a total flop, and it opened the same week as Star Wars. We're all close friends, George and Spielberg and myself. But at that time they were the mythmakers, and to a certain extent still continue to be. So at that time I knew which way the wind was blowing and I knew it certainly wasn't in my direction. Therefore I just did the best I could with Raging Bull, because I had nothing and everything to lose. I knew that I'd probably get movies to make in Europe or something. But I'm an American. I have to make movies about this country. So what do you do? You just say it's the end of your career, but you don't know any other way to do it, and you do it that way. That's what I meant by kamikaze. You just put everything you know into it. It takes a certain kind of passion to do that. *Taxi Driver* had a kind of kamikaze effect too. Passionate. That's another movie I didn't expect anybody to see. It was done out of real love for the subject matter and for the characters. Or, I should say, out of empathy with the characters in it.

DeCURTIS: When you talk about *Cape Fear*, it seems that you want to make a genre film on your own terms without subverting the genre.

SCORSESE: *Subverting* the genre, I think, would be a problem. What I hopefully will do will be to try to blend the genre with me, in a sense, with my expression of it, with the elements that I'm interested in and see if it doesn't derail it too much. If it enhances it, and I get the best of both, that would be great. I don't know if I can. I mean, I still wouldn't be interested in doing—as much as I adore them—the old musicals. As much as I *adore* them. I have no words for them, some of them are so beautiful. I still wouldn't be able to do that. I wouldn't be interested in doing that. I still want to do something with a musical where it's got an edge to it. But I think I would be able to, this time, get a clearer idea of how to approach it.

DeCURTIS: What's the difference now?

SCORSESE: *New York, New York*, we made it up as we went along. We had a pretty good script by Earl Mac Rausch and we didn't pay any attention to it. The two methods of filmmaking—the improvisatory style and the old studio style, where you have to build sets—didn't blend. You're wasting money that way, because the set was built and you would improvise yourself into another scene. And then you'd have to *reimprovise* yourself *back* into that set. It was crazy. I think we got some real good stuff out of it—and some real truth about that world and relationships between creative people. But I think it could have been more concise, maybe shorter. Maybe there was too much music. The repetition of scenes between the couple was really more like *life*, where a scene repeats itself and repeats itself and repeats itself until finally . . .

DeCURTIS: It becomes tension-producing watching it; it's very unsettling.

SCORSESE: And that's the idea. The way, if you're in a relationship with someone and you've talked it out and talked it out and talked it out and you can't sit, you can't go in the same room! That was the idea. Maybe in that case, it's successful—but I don't know if it's entertainment. I can guarantee you, you're not going to have the head of a studio say, "Marty, let's make a picture where the people get so tense—and it's a musical, okay? And people come out thinking about their own lives, oh my God, and their four marriages, and they get upset—and we'll give you fifty million dollars to make it!" No! They're not going to do it.

DeCURTIS: That's like when you told a studio head who asked you why you wanted to make *The Last Temptation of Christ* that you wanted to understand Jesus better.

SCORSESE: I said that to Barry Diller, and he didn't expect that, Barry. It was very funny. He kind of smiled. He didn't really expect that. It was really funny. It's true, though. And I had to learn that that picture had to be made for much less money. You're that interested in something personal—"We'd like to see what happens with it, but here's only seven million. You can do it at seven, not at twenty-four."

DeCURTIS: You've said over and over that you don't see yourself as especially literary. But on the other hand you'll talk about *The Gambler* as a model for *Life Lessons*, your contribution to *New York Stories*, and, of course, *The Last Temptation of Christ* was based on the Kazantzakis book. Why do you downplay that aspect of your work and your thinking?

SCORSESE: I guess I'm still cowed a little by the tyranny of art with a capital A. And there has always been the tyranny of the word over the image: anything that's written has got to be better. Most people feel it's more genuine if you express yourself in words than in pictures. And I think that's a problem in our society. And, I've said it many times in interviews, I come from a home where the only things that were read were the *Daily News* and the *Daily Mirror*. Those were the two newspapers, and I brought the first book in. And there were discussions about whether or not I should bring the book in the house, too.

DeCURTIS: What do you mean?

SCORSESE: They were worried.

DeCURTIS: That you would become . . .

SCORSESE: God knows.

DeCURTIS: I mean my parents didn't graduate from high school either, but . . .

SCORSESE: They didn't graduate from grammar school, my parents.

DeCURTIS: My parents were obsessed with education and with my going to school.

SCORSESE: Oh, no. Mine, no. Mine wanted me to continue because they understood one thing: you go to school, you make a little more money. It's as simple as that. But what I was doing then was out of the question. First I was going to be a priest and that was one thing. They could take that. To a certain *extent* they could take that. But when I started to have books come in the house and go to New York University, which was a secular situation, not a parochial, not a church-oriented place, obviously . . . it was in the sixties, you know? They're not educated people. They said the college is too liberal. It's communist. That sort of thing.

DeCURTIS: Were they paying for you to go there?

SCORSESE: My father paid, yeah. They both worked in the garment district. They paid. So having difficulty reading . . . I mean, I'm not a fast reader, although I'm forcing myself to read as much as possible now. I'm sort of catching up on books that I should have read twenty years ago, forcing myself to read a lot. And usually in certain areas, like ancient history or historical novels, good ones, strong ones. And trying to get to read faster that way.

There are certain kinds of films that are more literary-based. Joseph Mankiewicz's pictures are on a more verbal level—and I love them. *All About Eve, Letter to Three Wives, Barefoot Contessa*. I like those pictures. They had a sense of dignity because of their literary background.

But then what do I make of my attraction to Sam Fuller? People say about Fuller, "Well listen to his dialogue. It's terrible." "Well, yeah, but the visuals and the way he's expressing himself with that move." You don't sit there and say, "Gee, look at that camera move." You get an emotional reaction. And then if it affects you enough and you're interested enough, you go back and you start playing around with it. You see why. "Why was that effective? Oh, gee, that's what he did. He moved that way. And that actor goes flying out of the frame here and the energy of that actor is still felt and you're flying into the wall."

I mean the same kind of visual intelligence you find in Douglas

Sirk, and yet I'm not able to enjoy the Douglas Sirk films, maybe because of the genre. At least now in the past ten years I've been able
to appreciate them in terms of visuals, in terms of the camera, the
lighting, the compositions. The genre just never attracted me when I
was young. It was over my head. I didn't know. And I sort of got past
the trash level, the lurid quality of *Written on the Wind*. But certainly
I didn't miss it in *Duel in the Sun*. I caught it there, and I enjoyed
it better in *Duel in the Sun*. The visuals were much stronger for me
in *Duel in the Sun*. King Vidor. I thought that was just phenomenal.
Granted, it's trash down to the very bone, the very core, the very
marrow, but wonderful, just wonderful. I prefer the excess and the
hysteria there.

I could talk about this for ages. The literary will always have the
upper hand here. It always will.

DeCURTIS: Even though it's become such a visual culture?

SCORSESE: Oh God yes. I mean look at the things taken seriously.
I was just going to point out in 1941—*Citizen Kane* came out that
year—if I'm not mistaken the best picture of the year, I think it was
Watch on the Rhine. [In fact, it was *How Green Was My Valley*.] Now,
come on, is that a movie? Is that a movie? A *movie* movie where
images were used in a certain way? It did have a certain emotional
impact. Look, the war was on, and we were about to be drawn into
it. It was very important that that film won at that time. And *Mrs.
Miniver* the next year. Very important, you know. But they're not . . .
I mean, I like Wyler too but *Mrs. Miniver* is not one of my favorites.

I mean the greatest casualty in terms of being honored is Alfred
Hitchcock. And his movies are purely visual. He was never given an
academy award. He got the life achievement award but was never
singled out for best director. *Rebecca*, I think, won the best picture of
the year, but I don't think he won director. Because, again, they said,
"Well, he's got clever scriptwriters and he does clever things with the
camera."

DeCURTIS: Was there a specific point at which you felt that in terms
of your own skill you could say exactly what you wanted to say
with film?

SCORSESE: Oh no. One of the great breakthroughs is to know that you
really don't know that much. That gives you a little more to learn. It

gives you hope that you always can learn more. And it makes you not arrogant. It makes you get on the set and it makes you realize, "All right, what am I going to do?" Not on the set—that is, in the mind. When I make a picture, in my mind I'm always on the set. I'm on the set right now for my next picture, picking up images. I put myself into a certain mode. I see fewer people and I just try to stay alone. It's a freeing thing to know that you really don't know that much. The best part is the hope to learn. And it keeps you in line with your material. Then there are bursts of inspiration. You do some things and *bang*. You say, "Okay, I'm going to approach that scene." You work it out on the page. You say, "Ah, that happens this way." Bang, you go this way. "And then we're going to move the camera here, and then we are going to shoot this way." And then you wonder how you thought it up, and you have no idea. You could also devise intellectual approaches, where a character is photographed with certain-size lenses up to a certain point in the film, then the lenses change as the story progresses. That's okay. That will work. I prefer the stuff that just comes out of nowhere. But, you know, you've got to *get* them from out of nowhere. I don't know where that comes from.

DeCURTIS: Well, how do you do it?

SCORSESE: I lock myself away, usually for about four or five or six days. In the case of *New York Stories* it was two days; I worked on shots. I try to lock myself away and just go to a hotel or stay home and play some music, walk around. Sometimes you do nothing for hours and then suddenly it all comes in a half hour. Sometimes it doesn't come. In some cases you find that for certain scenes you've got to find the location before you can even begin to estimate how you are going to do it. In most of the cases you can say, "No matter what the location is, I know that the camera is going to track, and I know it's going to track from left to right. I know it's going to go from this character to that character and I'm going to go with him." You make certain choices. You either pan them out or you track them out. They are different emotional statements that the audience feels. I can talk about rationalizing it and intellectualizing it for hours, but it is just a process where you have a clear mind and you try to let the story seep in on you and you're taken by it. You really fantasize the movie—practically frame by frame.

DeCURTIS: Which of your movies means the most to you?

SCORSESE: Well, *Mean Streets* is always a favorite of mine because of the music and because it was the story of myself and my friends. It was the movie that I made that people originally took notice of. But I certainly couldn't watch it. I've watched scenes of it. I could never watch the whole thing. It's too personal. I like certain elements of *Raging Bull*. I like the starkness of it. And the wild fight scenes. The subjective fight scenes, as if you were in the ring yourself, being hit in the ear. Frank Warner's sound effects are just so wonderful. I like the look of a lot of it. And I love Bob and Joe Pesci and Cathy Moriarty. And Frank Vincent. I love the performances. Nick Colasanto. It was just wonderful.

DeCURTIS: *Taxi Driver?*

SCORSESE: No.

DeCURTIS: No?

SCORSESE: I like Bob in it. Oh, I like everybody in it. Cybill Shepherd was wonderful there. Jodie Foster. But *Taxi Driver* is really Paul Schrader's. We interpreted it. Paul Schrader gave the script to me because he saw *Mean Streets* and liked Bob in it and liked me as a director. And we had the same kinds of feelings about Travis, the way he was written, the way Paul had it. It was as if we all felt the same thing. It was like a little club between the three of us. Paul Schrader and myself had a certain affinity, and we still do, about religion and life, death and guilt and sex. Paul and I are very close on that sort of thing. But I must say we merely interpreted it, and the original concept is all his. Now you know another guy can come along and say he merely interpreted it—and *ruin* it. I'm not being falsely modest. But you've got to understand that the original idea came from him. And that's something that I think over the years, when they say, "Martin Scorsese's *Taxi Driver*," that's something that can be very painful to Paul. It's really his.

Raging Bull is something else altogether. It came from Bob, and Paul helped us with it and then we worked it out again. We rewrote it, Bob and I, and the same thing with *The Last Temptation of Christ*. Paul worked on it and then I rewrote it myself with Jay Cocks. But the two that I feel most nostalgic for are *Mean Streets* and *Raging Bull*.

DeCURTIS: What about some of the other movies that people don't necessarily put in the first rank of your films?

SCORSESE: Well, on one level they were all hard work, learning experiences. In conjunction with, let's say, Ellen Burstyn in *Alice Doesn't Live Here Any More*, I needed to do something that was a major studio film that was for a certain amount of money and to prove that I can direct women. It was as simple as that. *After Hours* was trying to learn, after *The Last Temptation of Christ* was pulled away, how to make a film quicker. And *The Color of Money* was trying to do a real Hollywood picture, with movie stars like Paul Newman and Tom Cruise. But, you know, each one was a lesson, like going to school. And *Cape Fear* to a certain extent will be that way too. Although in *Cape Fear*—the key there is I got Bob De Niro. And that's like . . . it's fun. It becomes something else.

DeCURTIS: How would you describe your working relationship with De Niro?

SCORSESE: We're interested in similar traits of people. Like I said, we felt that we understood certain things about Travis. And it's very rare when three people, the actor, the director, and the writer all feel the same way about it.

DeCURTIS: What did you understand?

SCORSESE: You feel you understand the rage; you understand that you have certain feelings yourself. You're not afraid to say to each other, to the people who are seeing the movie, that those are aspects of ourselves. Many people have it under control. This character doesn't. He starts to act out his fantasies. You know, living in this city, at a certain point you may want to kill somebody. You don't do it. This guy does it. It's simple. He crosses over. But we understand those implications. Okay, we're talking violence there. But also the pain of romantic rejection. It doesn't mean that you're always rejected. It means that a couple of times when it happens you feel a certain way and you carry that with you for the rest of your life. And you can pull from it, you know?

Bob is not a guy who knows movies the way I know movies. He can't sit with me and Schrader and talk about *Out of the Past*, Jacques Tourneur's film noir. He doesn't know it. And yet that makes it purer because he's just relating to what's there. It's better. He doesn't have to bring anything to it. He's not taking any baggage with him.

King of Comedy and *Raging Bull* really stem from Bob. *Last Temptation* from me. *Taxi Driver* from Paul. *Mean Streets* came from me. It all kind of shifts and slips and slides around and we always find ourselves coming around. The roulette wheel keeps moving and we stop and we look at each other, and we're all in the same place: "Oh, it's *you* again." It's that kind of thing, where you seem to grow together rather than apart. It's good because there's a trust. And it isn't true where you say, "Oh, it's telepathy." Yes, to a certain extent there is telepathy involved, but not entirely. Once we're in the groove we very rarely have disparate points of view.

DeCURTIS: Well, so much experience has gone into making that telepathy real. It's not just something that happened out of thin air.

SCORSESE: No, no. And it doesn't mean it's easier. When there's a collaboration on that level, you expect the best from each other and you won't settle.

DeCURTIS: The two of you have created characters that have really entered the culture. How many times have you seen somebody imitate De Niro's scenes from *Raging Bull* or the mirror scene in *Taxi Driver?*

SCORSESE: We improvised the mirror scene. That's true. I did improvise him talking in the mirror: "Are you talking to me?" It was in the script that he was looking at himself in the mirror, doing this thing with the guns, and I told Bob, "He's got to say something. He's got to talk to himself." We didn't know what. We just started playing with it, and that's what came out.

DeCURTIS: You've become synonymous with the notion of a director with integrity. It seems, on the one hand, it must be tremendously gratifying. On the other hand, it seems like maybe it can potentially be paralyzing.

SCORSESE: No, I feel really good about it. I do feel gratified that people feel that the work is—I don't know what words you want to use—personal or uncompromising. No matter what happens, though, there are compromises. You can say, "Yes, I'm going to make *The Last Temptation of Christ* and give me $7 million and I can do it." But it's compromised at seven million. I would have liked certain angles.

I would have liked extra days for shooting. But, okay, that's artistic compromise, and what the film has to say is not compromised. But one has to realize it's scary, because you have to keep a balance. You want to get films made that express what you have to say. You try to do that, but it's a very delicate balance.

I'd also like the chance to do exactly what I'm doing now with *Cape Fear*, for example: try to do a great thriller and to give the audience what they expect from a thriller, but also to have those elements which make my pictures somewhat different. I will try. I tried in *The Color of Money*. I don't know if it was totally successful there. Sometimes it's a trade-off. You have to do a certain kind of film in order to get maybe two others of your own that you want. I'm in this period now where I want to start exploring different areas, and you've got to make use of each film you make. You've got to learn from it and you have to utilize it to get your own pictures made—the difficult ones, I should say, because they're all, in a way, your own pictures. And no matter *what* happens, the really hard ones, you're only going to get a certain amount of money for them anyway. So you've also got to think of making money for yourself for the lean years, when you have pictures you're only getting paid a certain amount to make. There are so many different variations. It's playing a game, a line that you're walking, taking everybody very seriously—the studios and what they need, what you need. And, see, every now and then you can come together. Like in *GoodFellas* we all came together. So that was the best of both worlds: $26 million to make a personal movie. That's very interesting. The rest, no, there's no guarantee of anything. Each picture you make you try to learn from, and you try to cover your tracks. I mean, every movie wastes money to a certain extent, but you don't do it to the point where . . .

DECURTIS: You create problems for yourself.

SCORSESE: Where you create real problems. But it's not that rational. It's not "My God how rational he sounds"—God forbid if I do—it's really a matter of being careful and smart. I mean, the artists coming out of America in film come from Hollywood. The Hollywood film. And I'm proud to be associated with Hollywood because of that. I mean, I lived in Hollywood over ten years. Even *then* they thought I was still living in New York. I live in New York. My parents are here, my kids are here. But I'm still a Hollywood director, and I'm always proud to be considered that by the rest of the world. To show that America, every now and then, will give me something to do, or give something to other guys—Stanley Kubrick, David Lynch—who do very specific, very personal pictures. There's so much fun involved sometimes that it's enjoyable. But it's dangerous.

An Interview with Stanley Kauffmann

Bert Cardullo

tanley Kauffmann was born in New York City in 1916 and was graduated from the College of Fine Arts of New York University in 1935. He spent ten years as an actor and stage manager with the Washington Square Players and has published a large number of short and long plays. He is the author of seven novels, published here and abroad, and worked for ten years as a book publisher's editor.

Since 1958 he has been active in criticism. At that time he became the film critic of *The New Republic*, with which journal he has been associated ever since, except for an eight-month period in 1966 when he was the theater critic of the *New York Times*. In addition to his film reviews, he has written a large number of book reviews for *The New Republic*; from 1969 to 1979 he served as both film and theater critic. He continues as film critic but wrote theater criticism for the

Saturday Review for five years, from 1979 to 1985. He has contributed reviews and articles to many other journals.

Mr. Kauffmann has received many prestigious awards and fellowships. In 1974 he was given the annual George Jean Nathan Award for Dramatic Criticism. He has received two Ford Foundation fellowships for travel/study and an Emmy Award for a television series about film that he conducted for five years on the PBS station in New York. In 1964 he was elected an Associate Fellow of Morse College of Yale University. Twice he has served as a juror for the National Book Awards. From 1972 to 1976 he was a member of the Theater Advisory Panel of the National Endowment for the Arts, and in 1977, of the Theater Advisory Panel of the New York State Council on the Arts. In the summer of 1978 he was a Rockefeller fellow at the Villa Serbelloni, Bellagio, Italy, and in 1979 he was given a Guggenheim Fellowship for the writing of his memoirs. Mr. Kauffmann received the George Polk Award for Criticism in 1982, the Edwin Booth Award from the City University of New York Graduate School in 1986, and the Birmingham Film Festival Award for Criticism, also in 1986.

He spent a total of five years until June 1973 as Visiting Professor in the Yale School of Drama and returned to that post from 1977 to 1986. From 1973 to 1976 he was Distinguished Professor of English, teaching drama, film, and literature, at York College of the City University of New York. Since 1976 he has been Visiting Professor in the Theater Program of the Graduate Center of the City University of New York.

Mr. Kauffmann has published five collections of film criticism: *A World on Film* (1966), *Figures of Light* (1971), *Living Images* (1975), *Before My Eyes* (1980), and *Field of View* (1986). He is editor (with Bruce Henstell) of the anthology *American Film Criticism: From the Beginnings to "Citizen Kane"* (1972). And he has published two collections of theater criticism, *Persons of the Drama* (1976) and *Theater Criticisms* (1983). A collection of his memoir pieces has been published under the title *Albums of Early Life* (1980). Further *Albums* have appeared in various journals.

CARDULLO: How has the academicization of film—in film courses, film departments, and film criticism—helped to shrink the audience for serious film? You brought that up in your "After the Film Generation" article, it fascinates me, and I tend to agree with you: the compartmentalization of film has done something to hurt students' interest in film. I'd like you to comment on that if you will.

KAUFFMANN: It's a paradox—the educational activities in film, the positing of film in college curricula that went on furiously from about 1960 on. At first, the effect was to make film more important, more necessary, more feverishly acquirable for students. I suppose that's still true of people who are film specialists, but I think the situation has changed for those who are just generalists about film, who are interested in film only as one of the increments of their cultural life. And this has a certain parallel, I think, with what happened long ago in literature. Let's assume that there were once people who read, read with pleasure and freely; then literature became for them a straitened, compartmentalized, curricular activity. At the beginning, I think the teaching of literature in colleges and universities helped people—I'm speaking always about the general person, not the specialist. But later, I think, it became for them a means of, in their minds, finishing with literature: "I've read my great books, now I'm free."

CARDULLO: Let me just add, to back you up, that I know I felt this way after I graduated from college, and I've talked to friends who have said, "After I left college, I didn't read a book for a year."

KAUFFMANN: That's conservative, a year. "I've read my books," a lot of them feel. I think that happened with film. I don't mean that people stopped going to films after they finished their film courses, which they took on their way to becoming doctors, lawyers, or just general good citizens. But that their interest in any kind of expansion or extension of themselves as the result of film experience, in taking any kind of trouble to see films, was something they associated with the moribund past, with note taking, exams, and papers.

CARDULLO: Well, as a college student in the early 1970s, I never took a film course, and I like that. What we felt then, I and my friends, was that we were discovering film along with frontline critics like you, and once film became part of the academy, it was as if that process of discovery had disappeared. It had been taken over by establishment academics.

KAUFFMANN: And in a certain sense, mummified. Going to a film was no longer a question of experience, but of visiting a tomb. That's of course regrettable for literature, for art history, for any art that gets studied systematically in the university.

CARDULLO: I think that for a while, this academicization of film hurt my interest in it—to see film being written about in third- and fourth-class journals, to see certain canons being established that had no business being established, was dispiriting.

KAUFFMANN: Once film got established as part of the curriculum, that meant people were teaching it, then *that* meant they had academic careers. They had to work for promotion in their departments, they had to please their deans, etc. I don't mean to disparage en bloc, with a grand gesture, all the people who are teaching film and writing about it in this country; we're speaking in the most broad, general terms here. You and I both know people whom we admire very much as individuals who are teaching film and writing about it from academic positions, but, in general, the most of anything is humdrum, and the most of film teaching and writing is humdrum. What does the humdrum person do when he is teaching film and needs to gain a certain stature for himself? He resorts to vogue, to critical vogue. It's easier to subscribe to a critical theory than to operate independently as a critical mind and talent. Again, it would be somewhat presumptuous of me to dismiss the great minds of critical theory who've been operating in our time: I'm not talking about them.

CARDULLO: I know what you mean, you mean the epigones.

KAUFFMANN: Yes, there are plenty of little epigones, less than epigones —mobsters, let's call them. Faculty mobs need to come under the shelter of some giant critical or theoretical wing because they can't fly on their own.

CARDULLO: This leads into a subject that I've thought about a lot lately, and that I'd like to bring up because you've been a part of it: the controversy over film as popular art versus film as high art. Often if you're an academic in a university looking to make your name, you attempt to "discover" certain directors, to induct them into the pantheon, and, in my view, and I think in yours, certain directors have been elevated in status, directors whom one would normally consider "popular," such as Frank Capra. You've been criticized in your career as being a literary or "highbrow" film critic, and in a recent letter to you at *The New Republic*, the writer brought up the fact that you have always stood strongly for the distinction between popular and high art in film. I'd like you to comment on that, because I think it is related to this whole issue of the academicization of film.

KAUFFMANN: Well, it's amusing because, depending on the day of the week, I get a letter berating me for this schism in my thinking, telling me that I'm snobbish toward pop film, or I get a letter applauding me for this schism but at the same time berating me because I seem to have become *less* snobbish of late toward pop film. I'm told, in the latter case, that I'm trying to please the yuppies who would rather rent *Ghostbusters* instead of any Bresson film. Of course, this is always strange to me—finding out how people read, what they find in you that you have no intent of putting there. I have never, in any way, taken a stance about film in terms of pop or high art. The distinction used to be posed in terms of American versus foreign films. I was told that I was prejudiced in favor of foreign films. It *never* was that way for me arbitrarily, categorically. What happened was that, if, in the course of a year, I reviewed fifty films, I discovered when I went over the list at the end of the year that forty of the ones I'd liked were foreign films. It's retrospective rather than prospective for me. The foreign versus American distinction got translated into the distinction between high art and pop art. I don't know how far we want to explore that now; it's been much belabored in the last thirty years. I certainly believe that there's a difference between the two. I'm not in favor of eradicating the difference, as some rather highly placed thinkers are; I certainly am not. I think that the differences are discernible and that those differences ought to be in the mind of the critic, ought to be in the mind of the intelligent viewer, without being prescriptive. And the matter is further complicated because—and this is where it becomes really muzzy because I seem to be coming to agree with the pop elevators—there *are* some pop films that are more than good entertainment, that become fine works of art. The first example that always comes to mind is *Some Like It Hot* (Figure 1). I think that *Some Like It Hot* is a great film, by any standards.

CARDULLO: Well, the elevation of *Some Like It Hot* comes in tandem

Figure 1. *Some Like It Hot*, 1959, directed by Billy Wilder. Courtesy of the Museum of Modern Art (New York), Film Stills Archive.

with the elevation of farce in dramatic literature to higher status than it has heretofore had.

KAUFFMANN: Yes, it's true that there has been a terrible, snooty prejudice against comedy as being lesser. There is a very fine book on Beethoven by J. W. N. Sullivan that I read when I was a college student, and he prefers the first, third, fifth, seventh, and ninth symphonies of Beethoven because the second, fourth, sixth, and eighth tend to be jolly. Well, you just extend that principle arbitrarily and you end up in a cement bag with the cement hardening. It's fundamentally in the brightest people that you see this attitude—and it's a stupid attitude, to be prejudiced thus against comedy. What you've raised is pertinent, but the final distinction between the comic and the serious is not between the low and the high, because there are people on both sides of this pop-art, high-art schism who take comedy very seriously. And what we come down to, finally, is what we want a film to be and to do, without derogating the film that pleases us but that doesn't do those things.

CARDULLO: Let's clarify our terms briefly. When students ask me what the difference between popular art and high art is, I say, "Popular art more or less *reflects* what's going on in society at a particular time, whereas high art *examines* and sometimes criticizes what's going on."

KAUFFMANN: That's a perfectly tenable and useful distinction. Another distinction, connected with what you've just said, is that popular art is made to make money.

CARDULLO: Right.

KAUFFMANN: *All* films are made to make money, but pop art is made *primarily* to make money. And serious films *hope* to make money but are made primarily because they say something for the people making them. Yet another distinction is between the impersonal, committee film that's cooked up by—

CARDULLO: By the Hollywood studios.

KAUFFMANN: By a *lot* of people around filmmaking, sometimes quite cleverly, and the film that is the project of one or two people who must make it, who want to make it, and who will do anything to make it.

CARDULLO: Say, a team like Zavattini and De Sica.

KAUFFMANN: Yes, there are many such examples, as you know, and there are lots of Americans who are trying to do that kind of thing.

CARDULLO: I'd like to address the corollary of what we've been talking about, and that is the insistent criticism over the years that your film reviews have a literary bent. I understand why people make this criticism of you, but I don't agree with it; I think it has to do with this distinction, again, between high art and popular art. And I'd like you to address this subject, if you would.

KAUFFMANN: Well, I've always been amused, because my critics don't know what my chief defect is. It's a defect I hope I've amended in the course of time—it was certainly there when I began. My defect wasn't that I had been writing novels; I think I published seven before I ever wrote film criticism—six, and the seventh came out later. It was that I approached films from the *theatrical* point of view, not from the literary one. I was educated for the theater, I worked for ten years in a repertory company, I'd written plays, I'd done some other work around the theater. Through these years I had always been going to films and loving them, but I always thought of them as secondary.

CARDULLO: As something a stage actor did when he couldn't get a New York theater job.

KAUFFMANN: Yes, when he, or a director or a writer, couldn't get work in the theater. I thought that it was wonderful to have films around, but they were like the vegetables around the roast: the roast was what mattered. And through a series of accidents, I became a film critic. And when I look back at some of those early reviews of mine, what I see is a theater person going to films.

CARDULLO: Your theater background is certainly clear in your analysis and criticism of acting.

KAUFFMANN: I hope that's true, I've wanted it to be, and I hope that it hasn't diminished. But I hope also that, through the years, I've learned more about film and about film values as such. I'm very anti the auteur theory, but I owe the auteur theory a debt. It made me look at films as films. And the auteur critics made me make the examination of purely filmic values part—not by any means the primary part, as it is with them, but certainly *a* part—of my criticism.

CARDULLO: It's interesting that you say you're against the auteur theory. I'm against it *and* for it because, on the one hand, as you suggest, it is good to look at film as an autonomous, unique art form. Please explicate the other side.

KAUFFMANN: The other side is summed up in one word: priorities. I can't be expected, I as an individual, can't be expected to leave at the door of the film theater all my experience of life and art, and concentrate only on what the film has to offer me. I can't be expected to leave at the door my knowledge, insofar as I have it, of psychology, of acting, of structure, of stories, of depth of theme, of political relevance, of social weight, etc., and say, "But ah, look at the way he panned across that room and then segued into that beautiful long shot."

CARDULLO: Max Ophuls is the prime example.

KAUFFMANN: Max Ophuls, yes. I can't be expected rationally, aesthetically, to substitute that sheerly cinematic value for all the other things that I've been asked to check at the door.

CARDULLO: And what you say connects with what we said earlier about the academicization of film, in that film critics and supporters have felt the need to justify films *as films* as opposed to films in comparison with literature and paintings and music.

KAUFFMANN: That is true. They've had to plump for, to campaign for the sheerly cinematic as a raison d'être. In my opinion, again a matter of false weight.

CARDULLO: The other aspect of the auteur theory that you might comment on is this idea that you can't view an auteur's film in itself, you have to view it as part of his entire career. Auteur critics do this with John Ford all the time—looking for stylistic signature in every film and becoming ecstatic when they find it, apart from its connection with the rest of the film.

KAUFFMANN: I agree with this idea as a principle; it's the ostentation of it that seems to me odd. Hitchcock directed a film called *Stage Fright*, which is surely by anyone's standard, including Hitchcock's, one of the worst films, mystery films, that he made or anyone has made. But it's seen as virtually equivalent with the best Hitchcock films because it's by Hitchcock.

CARDULLO: It has the Hitchcock tics.

KAUFFMANN: Yes. On the other hand, it would be impossible, and in a sense cruel, to come to *Stage Fright*, just to keep that as an example, *without* keeping Hitchcock's whole career in mind. It's slavishness to doctrine that one objects to, not necessarily to the doctrine itself. The auteur theory is a doctrine that has contributed a lot, I think, to film thinking.

Recently Harvard University Press published two collections of material, edited by Jim Hillyer, from *Cahiers du cinéma*. The first one deals with the magazine's earliest years and therefore is concentrated on the auteur theory. *Cahiers* has since become a structuralist, Marxist magazine; it was in its first ten years or so thoroughly auteur. I wrote a long review of that book for *The New Republic* and I tried to identify the auteur theory with the post–World War II surge of *happiness* about the film as such. This theory originated in France, and it was just happiness that film existed as a fresh art for a new generation that wanted to be rid of the trappings and moral debts of the past. This feeling was conveyed in the course of time to America in a different context. I'll give you a wide analogy: it's like communism coming to this country from another country in which it had some pertinence and application. People gathering to overthrow governments in the Balkans are a little different from people gathering in Union Square here to overthrow the forces of the White House, which they used to do—talk about—in the 1930s. Likewise, transported auteurism became a very different item here. It ceased to be the reclamation of the future by the young and became in this country a mode, a vogue, an academic imperative for a time. Of course, by now, it's quite démodé, auteurism.

CARDULLO: You yourself have several times quoted Bazin's line, "Auteur, yes, but of what?" Auteur critics don't like to think that Bazin had this attitude. But in translating some of his reviews, I've had it reemphasized for me that he knew the differences between films—by the same director and by separate directors—knew that some were better than others.

KAUFFMANN: But he also saw, as I read him, the value of the auteur theory, which was to make us look at the virtues of the text. People have said—I have said, others have said—that there is a certain parallel between the auteur theory and the New Criticism, which was a corrective of the biographical, psychological, and Marxist criticisms that had taken over literature. It said, "Come, let's look at what we're talking about here, which is the text on the page."

CARDULLO: And it did its job.

KAUFFMANN: Yes, and auteurism, I think, helped in the same way.

CARDULLO: There's another side of auteurism that we haven't discussed yet and that you've brought up numerous times in your reviews. In fact, I think you wrote an article on this very subject. That is, crediting the various aspects of a film—cinematography, editing, casting, etc. That is to say, you may have an auteur, but often he's not the auteur of everything you see—obviously he *cannot* be the auteur of everything you see. A great cinematographer can make a filmmaker, as Sven Nykvist has, in part, made Bergman, and a great screenwriter can make a director.

KAUFFMANN: *Matewan*, directed by John Sayles, speaks to this point. The triumph in that film for me is the cinematography of Haskell Wexler, or, to take an earlier example that more people will know, a film by Howard Hawks called *Twentieth Century*. Now everyone says, "Oh, Hawks," and tries to find virtues in Hawks's work in that film. Of course he's a highly gifted director, that's not arguable, but for me the auteur of that film is John Barrymore. Hawks could auteur six ways from Sunday, but the film wouldn't *exist* without Barrymore. The same thing is true, at a higher level, of Dreyer's *Passion of Joan of Arc*. Who'd care for all of Dreyer's miraculous art—and it is marvelous—if it weren't for the central miracle of Falconetti's performance? Of course he helped her with that, so in part you could say that his auteurism reads through her, but she did it.

CARDULLO: Another example is Ted Post's *Go Tell the Spartans*. Post's screenwriter, Wendell Mayes, transformed Daniel Ford's novel, he significantly improved it, and without that script, there'd be no *Go Tell the Spartans*. So the auteur theory is always—was always—suspicious.

KAUFFMANN: The latter-day auteurists, insofar as that's still a tenable term, have tried to make up for this shortcoming by talking about other kinds of auteurs who operate in film, about the actor or screenwriter or cinematographer as auteur. But, centrally, we know that the idea behind auteurism was essentially "the director as auteur."

CARDULLO: I'd like to get back now to the negative description of you by some people as a literary film critic, and I'd like to talk about how that criticism of your work is a product of the kinds of criticism being written today. Why do critics—not daily or weekly critics but academic ones—feel this way about you, why do they describe you as such?

KAUFFMANN: Well, I don't think that they do, so much. The academic critics today, and there weren't that many when I began writing, think of me as an impressionist, just as they think of, to pick a name out of a hat, Irving Howe as an impressionist. That's not to equate myself with Irving Howe, necessarily, although I'm happy to be linked with him.

CARDULLO: And you say it's the film buffs who look at you as a literary critic?

KAUFFMANN: Yes. The academic critics think of me as an impressionist, because I—now I'm putting this in my own terms—deal experientially with film, deal with it analytically in terms of a highly personal set of ineffable standards. That is, I could not possibly codify for you what my beliefs are about film; it's a matter of instances rather than precepts. They could tell you what their doctrine is, what their standards are, to a great extent; I could not, and to them that's a defect.

CARDULLO: To me what they do is a defect because they stifle sensibility when they let doctrine dictate response.

KAUFFMANN: Again, I'm speaking in a brusque way about a lot of bright people, but I have often thought that for the nonbright who are doctrinaire, doctrine is a substitute for talent. And if I'm anything, I'm a critical talent, and I don't think that's a factor in their thinking at all—intellect and erudition, yes, but not talent. I've read more than one book in which I've been mentioned as someone who was a factor in the author's coming to film and taking it seriously and whom, by implication, that author has now passed, outgrown. I don't mind that in the least, I hope it's true, but I don't for a moment subscribe to the idea that the kind of criticism I practice is outmoded or passé.

CARDULLO: I would have to say that the kind of criticism you write, in my experience, is the kind in history that survives, because it has what some would call the impressionist element, what I would call the personal element.

KAUFFMANN: I agree with you. Eric Bentley, too—the best drama critic we've produced in this country—feels the same way about criticism. That's not to allocate immortality to myself, but I agree with the principle you've stated. Although, of course, when we speak of history, we're only speaking of what has happened up to now.

CARDULLO: And Bernard Shaw, as you know, made the same point about criticism. It *has* to be personal.

KAUFFMANN: Well, we both would have thought so, but personality now sometimes evinces itself just in the way an individual handles a well-thumbed deck of cards, critical cards, that have been handed to him by colleagues.

CARDULLO: Is there a critical theory ascendant today in film studies and what is its effect?

KAUFFMANN: Well, there are three theories that are said to be dominant in criticism generally today in this country, three approaches: feminism, Marxism, and structuralism. And I know by looking at journals that, if these three approaches don't prevail in criticism, they're plentifully visible. I have nothing to say against any of them as contributors to enlightenment. It's like being asked to militate against Freud—who wants to? The intelligent person who is alive today and doesn't know Freud isn't exercising his intellect to the fullest extent. I happen to have strong sympathies with feminism, if the feminists care. Marxism has affected me as it must any person, certainly any person my age who's lived through the things I've lived through, and structuralism is an enlightenment in itself. But I simply can't find an intellectual reason or an emotional propellant to make me adopt any one of those approaches as the sole or even primary series of tenets in judging a work of art.

CARDULLO: I've always shied away from such theories because each seems to shut off a whole other world of experience.

KAUFFMANN: Only when you go in and close the door behind you. Not if you take something out of that particular theoretical experience and move on. And that isn't to trivialize the matter, either. I grew up in an age when what are now called macho attitudes were *the* set of attitudes. But I've learned a lot from young women who have been my students at Yale and at the CUNY Graduate Center. That hasn't made me—I will use the phrase—a parochial feminist, but I hope I'm a more understanding human being and critic.

CARDULLO: Could you talk a bit about the structuralist enterprise before we move on to another subject?

KAUFFMANN: Well, like so much in film criticism, it's trying to be like Daddy. Literary structuralism anteceded it and is much greater in every sense—to begin with, it has a greater body of work on which to operate. And film critics are trying to be like structuralist literary critics; the only way they can prove they are adults is to behave like

Daddy, in the approved magisterial fashion. Again, I don't want to adopt a tone that sounds dismissive of a lot of serious and intelligent people, but not all structuralist film critics are intelligent, and even those that *are* seem to me to some extent blinkered, which I would also say of Marxist critics. Structuralism in film studies has a particular application and use because of the operation of the term "genre." In a certain sense structuralism is more pertinent to film than to any other field because genre is a more potent force in film than it is in other arts. It's obviously discernible in drama, literature, and painting, but it has more potency in film, I think, than it has in the other arts. And by its very nature genre is analyzable by structuralist standards because it is a mode of art in which structure is the chief cause for being.

CARDULLO: And structure, for the structuralists, connects ultimately with the structures of society.

KAUFFMANN: As does genre.

CARDULLO: Right, and one of the problems I have with the structuralists is that, as we suggested earlier, they flatten all works of art, popular and high, and examine them as artifacts of the society.

KAUFFMANN: Yes, it's finally, if not primarily, a nonaesthetic enterprise. But the more rounded critic can, again, learn from the structuralists. What I have been saying through our talk makes it sound as if I favor a series of co-optings—embracing and defanging one opposing theory after another—but this is not what I mean.

CARDULLO: No, you're not talking about defanging, but about taking the essence, the best, of a particular approach and blending it into your overall approach.

KAUFFMANN: Of course, the teaching of the kind of criticism I try to practice is very difficult compared with the teaching of doctrinaire approaches.

CARDULLO: Well, if I may say so, if a student doesn't have critical talent—not the ability to learn, but *talent*—that student will find the going rough in a class of yours.

KAUFFMANN: I hope that, in a progressive sense, what you've said is true, that I've helped people to refine their talent. But, as a teacher yourself, you can obviously see that teaching doctrine is easier than developing talent.

CARDULLO: Never having had such a teacher, I've always been puzzled about what staunch Marxist and structuralist critics say in the classroom. If they are as doctrinaire and arcane as their criticism, I just wonder how they communicate with undergraduates about film. Do undergraduates really comprehend their arguments?

KAUFFMANN: I can't answer that question because I've never attended such a class, although I've heard Marxist and structuralist critics speak at conferences and I've read articles by many of them. But my guess is that they're very effective teachers, that they give all their students, undergraduates as well as graduate students, some sense of acquisition, some sense of insight, in reasonably accessible form. Revelation comes more easily through the doctrinal approach than through the generalist approach.

CARDULLO: I guess such teachers are particularly successful at schools like Yale, where you would find the sort of student susceptible to the new, the fashionable, in criticism and theory. I'm not so sure that their approach works at any but the most cosmopolitan universities.

KAUFFMANN: That's impossible to pronounce on.

CARDULLO: I'd like now to discuss a subject that you've brought up a number of times in your writing. I quote from "After the Film Generation": "In recent years, for reasons too complex even to dabble in here, both the flood of serious foreign films and the stream of serious American films have dwindled pitifully." What do you think are the reasons?

KAUFFMANN: This has to be answered very carefully, because one can give an answer that's too simple or that's ludicrously broad.

CARDULLO: Let's set the stage first by saying that we're comparing what's going on now with what was going on in the halcyon days of the late 1950s and early 1960s, when directors whom you esteem, like Antonioni, Bergman, Kurosawa, and Truffaut, were doing what many consider their best work.

KAUFFMANN: Fine. The short answer, which doesn't tell you nearly enough, is economics: everything in film has become more expensive to do, and money is hardly irrelevant to filmmaking. Orson Welles once said that the man who talks about films and doesn't mention money is a jackass, and I would try not to be one. But the economics are connected with other, social factors, I think. One of them is the very success of films. The impact of films has been so strong that, to a certain degree, it's turned people away from films. It's seduced young people into intellectual sloth. The success of film itself, generically, has made many young people feel, first, that merely by going to a film, they're indulging in a cultural act, that to put their behinds in a film theater is to be seated in a wagon to Parnassus, no matter what the film happens to be. Second, the success of film has, I'm convinced, vitiated literateness to some degree. Fewer young people these days are as passionate about reading as they used to be. I think the person who is passionate about reading is passionate about films; and when the act of filmgoing turns you off reading, you also lose your interest to some extent in serious films. Because you begin to associate serious films with laboriousness, with enterprise, with collaboration, audience collaboration with the work being projected on the screen. I think that it's a very serious charge against film that it has in a certain sense vitiated passion for itself, vitiated the very passion that it once aroused in people.

CARDULLO: But how did it do this?

KAUFFMANN: By making people intellectually slothful, by making them feel that by going to a film, they were taking care entirely of their cultural life, no matter what the film is. You're taking care of all your obligations to culture by going to see the latest *Star Trek*, and if anyone challenges you, you can say, "Well, look what X said in the so-and-so quarterly about *Star Trek*."

CARDULLO: I remember that when I was an undergraduate, a professor of mine chastised me for seeing too many films; he said that filmgoing was too passive an enterprise. This clearly pertains to what you've been saying.

KAUFFMANN: Filmgoing is certainly in some degree a passive enterprise, but it doesn't have to be too passive a one.

CARDULLO: He said that the conventional filmmaker did everything for me, did for me what I had to do for myself when reading.

KAUFFMANN: He overstates his case, but his wariness is appropriate— wariness at how film allows you to lean back and have your popcorn and let the images wash over you at the same time that it allows you to feel that you're engaged in the great cultural enterprise of the day. That film allows both these feelings is harmful to it in the long run as an art form.

CARDULLO: I see what you're saying, that film lulls you into thinking you've paid your cultural dues, lulls you into intellectual laziness, so that eventually literary culture itself declines—the very culture that, together with the theater, produced a critic like you. Very interesting.

KAUFFMANN: Let me add just one more thing if I may. I don't know anything about rock music, but I'm told by people who do that rock speaks to them and for them in ways that film may once have tried to do but doesn't anymore. I'm talking now about people of fine intelligence, not just punks.

CARDULLO: We'll get back to the subject of why film is in the state it's in, but what you've said about the dangers of filmgoing is related to the subject of literary culture. For the most part, this culture doesn't exist the way it did in the 1930s and 1940s. A man with your aspirations today has to go to the university; there is no real literary culture to nurture and support him. He has to teach in order to eat, so he usually has to leave a major city like New York, and I think that this may have a deleterious effect on him. I feel myself that, having left the New York area, I'm in danger of becoming too compartmentalized, of separating myself from all different kinds of people and associating with only one kind. I think that, at worst, this is what breeds sterile, academic film criticism. If I may say so, I think you were very fortunate to have grown up in literary New York.

KAUFFMANN: Literary/theatrical New York! All of what you've said is true. One difference between us is that I graduated from college in 1935 and you finished graduate school in 1985—I didn't do graduate work. Half a century, very neat. When I went to the university to study theater and drama, the idea of studying criticism in that field didn't exist; it wasn't ludicrous, *it didn't exist*—it wasn't there to sneer at, even. Criticism was something that sportswriters did when they failed as sportswriters and were assigned by their editors to the drama desk, or it was something that failed playwrights or failed directors did as balm for their wounds. The idea of planning to be a critic and devoting one's self to education for that profession was past even contempt or mockery, let alone aspiration. There's no need to go into all the changes in attitude that have occurred.

CARDULLO: Changes in attitude that brought about all the graduate and undergraduate programs in theater.

KAUFFMANN: And the acceptance of film into the curriculum on the graduate as well as undergraduate level, and the acceptance of criticism as an important vocation in *all* the arts. Of course, it achieved that respectability last in theater and film; long before that it was an honorable profession in literature, painting, and music. By the time you came along, not only was criticism taken seriously, as something to which a sensible person could devote himself, there were methods of education for it. And the upshot of that, it seems to me, is that this very process of education brings about the situation you've just talked about in which in order to go on as a critic, you have to become an educator in order to support yourself as a serious critic. I'm not speaking of this as a defect in a virtue—I don't think it's a defect—but it is a result of a virtue.

CARDULLO: Well, in your day, to judge by what you've done for a living, aspiring writers and critics often became editors.

KAUFFMANN: I've worked at a lot of jobs, including editing, and many a time during those years, I wished I could have taught, but one thing I did not have to do, to sound very parochial: I did not have to leave New York. And in our profession—film criticism, theater criticism—New York is still, alas, the center of activity. We all know that there is theater in other parts of the country, we all know that good films are shown outside New York, especially in film societies, but by sheer weight of numbers—the number of critics and the number of readers—if not other merits, New York is still the court of hearing.

CARDULLO: I'd like to get back to the reasons why fewer and fewer serious films are being made. I'd like you to continue with the point you made about the reciprocal effect filmgoing has on film and literature: the act of filmgoing at once turns a person off to reading and makes him feel that he has paid his cultural dues, with the result that interest in serious literature and serious film declines, serious thinking in general declines, and consequently fewer and fewer serious films get made.

KAUFFMANN: There's a sort of creeping lichen or moss, I think, in our cultural scene at the present time that's affecting standards. What you quoted of mine about the dwindling number of serious films, both American and foreign, could, with slight changes, be said about book publishing—it *has* been said. And this is due to the growth of this lichen of sloth, of passivity, which is the result of several factors. I'm now going to make some very broad, possibly ludicrous statements, but they run through my mind on this matter. Culture, as we have understood the word, means less to young people now than it used to, as a force in their lives, as a necessity in their lives, and film has, in a sense, fed that apathy by its very ease of absorption. It provides an escape from the world.

CARDULLO: It's almost the only culture for some people.

KAUFFMANN: When we go to a film, you and I, the film certainly envelops us no less than it does anyone else, but within that envelopment we discover things; within that envelopment many young people think of nothing. This leads to some very large issues, which I hesitate to mention because what I say will verge on intellectual buffoonery. The decline of culture is connected with malaise in our time, which is connected with theological crisis, which comes home to roost in the existence of nuclear weapons.

CARDULLO: And in the loss of trust in political leaders and in the future. The malaise has to do with the question, "Why bother?"

KAUFFMANN: "Why bother?" or "Let us live from day to day," not in an existential way, but in a hedonistic one.

CARDULLO: Exactly, hedonism is the word I would use.

KAUFFMANN: It's easy to controvert this by talking about individuals we both know who work with energy and initiative to make something of their lives. But broadly speaking, they are the exceptions, which leads me to something positive in the general film situation. In view of the somewhat disastrous experience of filmgoing these days, we must realize that we live by the exceptions. In the film world, the American film world, the situation is such that a film made at the highest technical level, a feature film, now must take in fifty to sixty million dollars to break even. It used to be forty million about eight years ago; I assume it's gone up 20 percent. How much flexibility and adventure can there be if you have to please that many people? One could conclude from this that no good films would ever be made again, but the startling fact is that they come along insistently—I won't say regularly, but insistently.

CARDULLO: And let's not delude ourselves into thinking that most of the films made in, say, 1960 were good. They weren't—most of them were bad; but 1960 still produced more good films than 1986.

KAUFFMANN: Right. We're talking about proportions here. And when you idolize foreign films, you have to remember that, in any year, most of them are so bad they never even get to this country. And half of the ones that do come over are not very good. The inexplicable fact, to speak again of American films, is that *Tender Mercies* comes along (Figure 2). The inexplicable fact is that Jim Jarmusch's two films, *Stranger than Paradise* and *Down by Law*, come along. The completely baffling fact is that a very pleasant, delicate little film like *Roxanne* comes out of Hollywood with a Hollywood star. These things *cannot* be explained. They are the result of human stubbornness triumphing over the dismal state of film production in particular and cultural life in general.

CARDULLO: Let's talk further about some of these exceptional films. I re-saw *Tender Mercies* recently, and it's even better than I thought. I think one of the reasons it's so good is that its production values are simple. Unlike most films, this film is not overproduced. I have not liked Horton Foote's other work for film and for the stage, but he certainly hit the jackpot with *Tender Mercies*, perhaps in part because of Bruce Beresford's direction.

KAUFFMANN: I think one of the reasons it succeeds, besides its chasteness in production, is that it fits a definition I recently read in a book called *The Classical Hollywood Cinema*, by Bordwell, Staiger, and Thompson, a very good, very important book. That definition is of what they called "the art film," simply because they had to call it something; and the art film for them, as opposed to the commercial film, is a film that faces the effects and tries to look for the causes. It's not content to accept things as they are, to reflect what's going on in society, in your words; it must analyze and explore. *Tender Mercies* analyzes and explores what's going on in one person's life. Here's a man who finds himself in a baffling and despairing situation, which I won't detail, and fights his way out of it by looking for the causes. And why the film triumphs for me—I'm talking about it thematically now, not cinematically—is that he doesn't find the causes, the reasons. But he knows that he was right to search for them, and that the search is what reclaimed him as a human being—to the extent that he is reclaimed.

CARDULLO: And he's not even convinced at the end that matters will continue to be as good as they have been.

Figure 2. *Tender Mercies*, 1982, directed by Bruce Beresford. Courtesy of the Museum of Modern Art (New York), Film Stills Archive.

KAUFFMANN: You're right. He doesn't believe in anything. He says that, even though he's fallen in love, has married, and is resting as from a storm in the shelter of this woman's affection, which he repays with his affection, he doesn't trust happiness.

CARDULLO: I like the fact that in this scene with his wife, he keeps on hoeing his small vegetable garden the whole time he is talking.

He doesn't stop once. In a lesser film, this man and his wife would have had a very maudlin conversation, after which they would have embraced and he would have resolved to trust his happiness.

KAUFFMANN: In Foote's other work that I know, people *are* glowingly reconciled at the end and they *do* find answers. This film, *Tender Mercies*, in its quiet way, is stark.

CARDULLO: And the vast Texas landscape in which it takes place contributes to that starkness.

KAUFFMANN: There's a line in *Agamemnon*, spoken by the Nurse, I think: "I have looked into the hand of God, and in it, nothing." That's always seemed to me to be profound, because there's not nothing, there's *the hand of God*, and *in* it is nothing.

CARDULLO: And Duvall has come to that perception by the end of the film. Let's talk a little bit about him, because just as *Twentieth Century* wouldn't exist without John Barrymore, *Tender Mercies* wouldn't exist without Robert Duvall.

KAUFFMANN: I can't imagine the film with anyone else, although it is possible that George C. Scott could have done the role.

CARDULLO: Maybe Jon Voight, too.

KAUFFMANN: But that's not to detract in the least from Duvall's performance. We've both seen Duvall in a lot of things, and I have a very serious grievance against him, which is that he could be acting great roles, greatly.

CARDULLO: On the stage?

KAUFFMANN: On the stage and on film. If Steve McQueen could make a film of *An Enemy of the People*, why can't Duvall do one of *John Gabriel Borkman*?

CARDULLO: He certainly has the influence to get funding for such a project. But I think he actually said once that he preferred the anonymous roles that films afforded him.

KAUFFMANN: Yes, I think anonymous is a good word. The roles he creates can be associated with no one but him: they're not like the well-known, highly sought after roles in the theater repertory.

CARDULLO: That's one of the virtues of film: you do the part and it's done, forever—except in the case of remakes!

KAUFFMANN: I have seen Duvall in the theater and he was wonderful. Not in the so-called classics, but in classics of their day, such as an early production of *A View From the Bridge*, with Jon Voight in the cast and Dustin Hoffman as the assistant stage manager and understudy. Duvall was in *American Buffalo*, you'll remember. The man could do anything; my only charge against him is that he doesn't do enough.

CARDULLO: Let's discuss a few other good films.

KAUFFMANN: I think that in 1982 we had the best farce since *Some Like It Hot*: *Victor/Victoria*. Blake Edwards is a talented man who swings very widely on the pendulum: he can be atrocious, he can be mediocre, and he can be excellent. He is for me the only person now directing in this country who has some feel for slapstick, who can make it vital and irresistible. That plus a finely honed sense of characterization and structure made *Victor/Victoria*, to me, a *very* successful film.

CARDULLO: I'd like you to talk a bit, if you will, about Martin Scorsese's *Raging Bull* (Figure 3).

KAUFFMANN: I think of *Raging Bull* as a picture about immigration. This is a film about Italians in America, also a film about the Irish in America—his wife is Irish. There have been plenty of films about poor men as such using boxing as a way out of the slums. This doesn't seem to be that kind of film. This man might have gotten out of the slum some other way. There is something almost operatic about the character of Jake La Motta, something romantic about his behavior. I'm not referring to his dealings with women, but to his solitariness, his questing, his willingness to take the worst that can happen if by doing that he can gain selfhood and independence in America. For me the film was operatic right from the first shot, before the titles, when you see La Motta shadowboxing in slow motion to the strains of *Cavalleria Rusticana*. This showed at once that Scorsese had an idea, that he wasn't just going to give you another boxing film; and he "proved out" his idea very well. This picture's about an Italian— a first-generation one in this case—about the particular abrasions the Italians experienced as they confronted American society upon immigration. And I think that La Motta's violence comes from his cultural and social situation; it isn't just a question of psychological bent. He is the product of a certain ethnic group that feels it needs to make its way aggressively in America.

Figure 3. *Raging Bull*, 1980, directed by Martin Scorsese. Courtesy of the Museum of Modern Art (New York), Film Stills Archive.

CARDULLO: He even makes his way aggressively within his own circle: with his wife and friends.

KAUFFMANN: He is a fount of rage, outside the boxing ring as well as within it.

CARDULLO: In my opinion *Raging Bull* is Scorsese's finest film, although I don't think a lot of people agree with me. Does it go beyond the ethnic boundaries to address the issue of violence per se in this country?

KAUFFMANN: I don't think it needs to, because America is made up of ethnic components and the American character consists of what ethnic groups have contributed to it. America *is* her ethnic groups, and in its violence, the Italian experience is just the quintessence of the immigrant's adversarial relationship with his new land.

CARDULLO: And contact sports, among which boxing heads the list, are the quintessential outlet for American aggression, which expresses itself all too often, unfortunately, in actual everyday violence. What do you think of Stanley Kubrick's work?

KAUFFMANN: People who admire *Full Metal Jacket*, his most recent film, and earlier films of his like *2001: A Space Odyssey* and *Barry Lyndon*, seem to believe that he is succeeding in making art in a commercial world.

CARDULLO: He tries. I'll give him that.

KAUFFMANN: In the whole time I've been writing film criticism for *The New Republic*, two reviews stand out in my mind as having elicited a flood of adverse letters. By a flood I mean thirty letters. One was an adverse review of Zeffirelli's *Romeo and Juliet*. I stepped on a lot of adolescent toes with that one, and all the adolescents weren't teenagers. The other was a review of *2001*. I got angry letters in response to my piece on *Romeo and Juliet*; in response to my piece on *2001* I got sorrowful letters. Two of them, I remember, from clergymen, who said more or less the same thing: "I pray for you, that in time you'll come to see the light about this film." They seemed to think that Kubrick was doing something important within the bounds of the programmed film.

Kubrick, you know, has since sequestered himself on an estate in the English countryside, and his work shows the effects of his insulation from the world. He makes his films in England, under his total control. He's a great chess player, and he likes to handle every component in a film the way he handles chess pieces. He creates what Leo Braudy calls "closed films." My first clue about what was going wrong in Kubrick's work came when I read that he was through with the actors in *2001* more than a year before the film was released. That meant that, for over a year, he was tinkering with every tiny piece, adding this sound, refining that effect, using the actors only as one component of a machine he was creating. Of course, literally, that's what actors are: one component. But this was, I felt, a deliberate equalization of all the components on Kubrick's part; it made him absolute Lord and God over everything in the movie. *Full Metal Jacket* is one more example of this little private game he's playing with film and the world. And like each of his films since *2001*, *Full Metal Jacket* has an air of smugness about it. It's as if Kubrick is saying, "What I give you, world, you must be satisfied with."

CARDULLO: Which among the current generation of directors practicing throughout the world mean the most to you?

KAUFFMANN: If I were forced at gunpoint to select two, they'd both be German: Hans-Jürgen Syberberg and Margarethe von Trotta. A couple of Sundays ago, I went to see *Parsifal* again—a difficult film, four-and-a-half hours long. It's Wagner's music drama, complete and in German, without subtitles. It's a film that was made, even in Germany, only for those who know and like *Parsifal*, or at least know it. But to me it's a triumph of creative imagination. Syberberg had a recording made of the music drama, and then he made a film, not just of *Parsifal*, but of what *Parsifal* evokes in him—about art and politics and history, about film and theater, about the possible exorcism of the demon Wagner himself. It's a prime example of what in the theater is called concept directing—a director's "statement" of a classic—and because of the fact that it's a film, it points, for me, to something in the future that you might call theater-film. Syberberg's *Parsifal* is far less pure cinema than a superb television film of a production in a hypothetical theater. As such, it is a thrilling conjunction of tradition and innovation.

CARDULLO: I didn't dislike von Trotta's *Rosa Luxemburg*, although I wouldn't rate it as highly as you seemed to in your review.

KAUFFMANN: Well, I think it has severe faults. The subject is an im-

Figure 4. *Marianne and Juliane*, 1981, directed by Margarethe von Trotta. Courtesy of the Museum of Modern Art (New York), Film Stills Archive.

possible one for a film. That doesn't mean one has to admire her for tackling it, but still it *is* an impossible subject and I won't even say she came up with the best possible script. I don't think she did. Nevertheless, once the script became a given, what happened thereafter was enormously impressive: her casting of the roles, the performances she elicited, every aspect of the film's making. Her best film for me to date, though, is *Marianne and Juliane* (Figure 4). To me it's one of the most important films of, let's call it, the post-Antonioni period. You can now call it the post-Bergman period, since he's retired. It's a film about the difficulty of being a liberal these days, the crisis and the drama entailed in being one.

CARDULLO: In Germany.

KAUFFMANN: Anywhere. But especially in Germany, because they have terrorism and as yet, thank heaven, we don't. And they have a different past; intelligent young people have a quite different past to remember in that country.

CARDULLO: I'd like to talk briefly about two other German filmmakers,

Figure 5. *Jail Bait*, 1977, directed by Rainer Werner Fassbinder. Courtesy of the Museum of Modern Art (New York), Film Stills Archive.

Werner Herzog and Rainer Werner Fassbinder, whom I would rate one and two ahead of Syberberg and von Trotta.

KAUFFMANN: Well, Herzog and Fassbinder are the next names on my list. Herzog is a major adventurer in film, and not just physically in the sense that he goes into the South American jungle to make *Aguirre, The Wrath of God*, although that's part of it. He's a magnificent talent, but there's no one film of his that, in my opinion, ranks as high as two films of von Trotta's: *Marianne and Juliane* and a film made just before it called *Sisters*.

CARDULLO: Let's move on to Fassbinder. What's that film of his where a teenage girl and her slightly older lover kill her father?

KAUFFMANN: *Jail Bait* (Figure 5). It's based on a play by Franz Xaver Kroetz.

CARDULLO: A wonderful film.

KAUFFMANN: Fassbinder is such a wild farrago of talent and insanity that it's very hard to talk about his work as a whole. After all, he made forty-one feature-length films, and he was only thirty-six when he died in 1982! For me the two best Fassbinder films are *Effi Briest* and *Berlin Alexanderplatz*, which is a staggering piece of work. If you prefer Fassbinder and Herzog to Syberberg and von Trotta, I can't argue with you: that's just a matter of taste. There's no question that the most fertile source of good films in the last fifteen years has been Germany. In addition to the films of the four directors we've been discussing, there are, to name just two, Wim Wenders's *The Goalie's Anxiety at the Penalty Kick*, from a novel by Peter Handke, and Handke's own *Left-Handed Woman*, also from a novel by him (Figure 6). There's at least one reason for all this German fertility, and it's related to something we talked about earlier: finances.

CARDULLO: Yes, Germany subsidizes the theater and it subsidizes film, directly and through television. It's important to realize that the Germans are preeminent in theater and film partly because of the money the German government puts into both these enterprises.

KAUFFMANN: For four years in the early 1970s, I was on the Theater Advisory Panel of the National Endowment for the Arts, and if I'm remembering correctly, we met six times a year and read long reports and applications and worked very hard to apportion justly a total budget of about three-and-a-half million dollars. The city of Hamburg at that time was giving about six million dollars to its opera house alone.

CARDULLO: And people fill that opera house, they fill theaters throughout Germany—they have to, or the government wouldn't put up the money. There's a demand for art in that country, and the government helps to satisfy it.

KAUFFMANN: But to talk about subsidy for film in this country is ridiculous, because films are so very expensive to make here. To help a filmmaker, you'd have to give him, and all like him, many millions.

CARDULLO: What costs so much? Is it artificial cost—created by the unions, for example—or is it genuine?

KAUFFMANN: Are union expenses artificial?

CARDULLO: They are and they aren't. They're artificial when, to use the example of the New York theater, you have to pay people in a

Figure 6. *The Left-Handed Woman*, 1980, directed by Peter Handke. Courtesy of the Museum of Modern Art (New York), Film Stills Archive.

band who aren't needed simply because their union contract says that if you use a band you have to employ so many band members. I'm sure that this occurs in film also.

KAUFFMANN: Featherbedding, they used to call it, and I'm certain that it goes on a great deal in films. Even if artificial costs such as this represented 50 percent of the budget, which they don't, and you got rid of them, you'd still be left with a budget for an average feature film these days of around ten million dollars. How could a subsidy possibly defray that amount in any significant way?

CARDULLO: German subsidies seem to defray the cost of German films.

KAUFFMANN: That's because the budgets for those films are so much smaller than ours.

CARDULLO: You see, you're making my point for me: that costs are largely artificial in this country. Werner Herzog did not spend as much money to make *Aguirre* as Steve Martin and company spent to make *Roxanne*. A good example of an American film that, relatively speaking, did not cost a lot to make is *Gal Young 'Un*, directed by Victor Nuñez. Yet the production values were very high. How did they do it?

KAUFFMANN: You know very well that they had no actors of any renown in *Gal Young 'Un*, no union costs of any kind, no studio rental charges, etc.

CARDULLO: Well, this is what I'm talking about. Your definition of featherbedding, it turns out, is much less inclusive than mine.

KAUFFMANN: But you can't monkey too much with the conditions of Hollywood filmmaking or you're killing what you're trying to help. Hollywood itself, if the term still means anything, means a certain level of technical proficiency, and you won't help film in this country, or American film in the world, if Hollywood is threatened. We're talking about subsidizing filmmaking at its highest technical level, not about subsidizing so-called independent productions like *Gal Young 'Un*. Which isn't to say that they don't have a place, a very necessary place, but that's not what we're talking about. When we talk about German directors such as Herzog and von Trotta, we're not talking about what we could call independent production. We're talking about central productions in the filmmaking of that country.

CARDULLO: Why not subsidize independent productions to the point that they could compete technically with Hollywood and thus become central to the filmmaking of our country? Film is going to continue to scare away potentially great artists if more independent avenues aren't opened to them.

KAUFFMANN: Or it scares them away from independent filmmaking, toward trying to get into the mainstream.

CARDULLO: Yes, that happened to Nuñez, I believe. He made a big-budget, Hollywood film after *Gal Young 'Un*, it went nowhere, and he hasn't been heard from since.

KAUFFMANN: It happened to a woman named Claudia Weill. She made a good film called *Girlfriends* on her own, so to speak, and then was taken to Hollywood, where she made the dreadful *It's My Turn*.

CARDULLO: And what about Susan Seidelman?

KAUFFMANN: Susan Seidelman made a very good first film called *Smithereens*. Then she made, intentionally or not I don't know, a commercial caricature of *Smithereens* entitled *Desperately Seeking Susan*. And she's gone on to make an even worse film.

CARDULLO: Jim Jarmusch shows some desire to remain independent.

KAUFFMANN: He will not make anything but his own films, and he knows that in order to do this he must work very cheaply. So far he's delivered handsomely with *Stranger than Paradise* and *Down by Law*.

CARDULLO: I wish there were more like him. I'd like now to take our discussion to an abstract level. What is it that film can do that other art forms can't? Why should film be as important as we say it should? Why should more potential young artists be drawn to film, costs aside for the moment? Why should they be drawn to it as art? I think you once wrote, and I'm sure others have written also, that film is *the* art form of the twentieth century.

KAUFFMANN: Yes, and that's because it's the one technology that is absolutely humanist in its outcome, or can be. It embodies all the technological impulses and cravings and interests of our age in the employ, not of machinery, but of the human spirit, the human mystery, optimally speaking. I think that was one of the ideas I was trying to express in my article "The Film Generation."

Now what can the film do? We both know that Grotowski's theatrical mission was to strip away the trappings of the theater, to tread a *via negativa* in order to discover what it is quintessentially the theater can do that nothing else can do, and of course he was thinking specifically of film as the opponent. What is it, he asked, that the theater can do that film cannot do? We're now trying to consider, you and I, what the film can do that neither the theater nor the novel, nor radio nor television can do. Television is a subject complicated by the commerce of the world. It is intrinsically different from film, but it shares so much of the vocabulary and syntax that some of the things I'm going to say now about film could also be applied to television. One thing that film, as a performance art, can do that no other performance art can do is explore interiority. The film can go inside human beings in a way that a play, for example, cannot.

CARDULLO: How?

KAUFFMANN: With the voice, with the close-up, and with the ability to present four states of consciousness, as Fellini does in *8½*: present awareness, memory, dream, and daydream (Figure 7). I don't know any other art form that could do that. A novel could do it, of course, but the words wouldn't have the immediacy and effect of film, the power of the image.

CARDULLO: But some have said that filmic images cannot mean complexly in the way that the words of a novel can. Can you respond to that?

KAUFFMANN: No, because it's not a provable point one way or the other. For me, images have meant as much as words.

CARDULLO: A good example of such an image is that close-up from *Persona* in which Liv Ullmann is kissing Bibi Andersson's neck, both of them with their eyes closed.

KAUFFMANN: Think of the next-to-last moment of *Wild Strawberries*, where Victor Sjöström waves across the inlet to his parents, who see him as a boy.

CARDULLO: I would counter the argument that images cannot mean as complexly as words by saying that images can almost mean more deeply and more ambiguously because they're not as explicit.

KAUFFMANN: That's true, but they can also be more facile than words. Film has a built-in power that is a built-in danger: it's immediately strong in a way that no other art is except music. You often feel that you have to fight your way out of a film when you're not liking it because the images are so strong, so overpowering.

Figure 7. *8½*, 1963, directed by Federico Fellini. Courtesy of the Museum of Modern Art (New York), Film Stills Archive.

CARDULLO: I think that Robert Altman is the filmmaker most often guilty of trying to make images mean what they don't. He even directed a film with that very title, *Images,* and it's terrible.

KAUFFMANN: He and the Taviani brothers are among the worst offenders in this area.

CARDULLO: Yes, the Tavianis' *Padre Padrone* suffers from this defect.

KAUFFMANN: But if we agree that images have an authenticity of their own, then the images of *8½* do for interiority what no other art could duplicate.

CARDULLO: Some surrealist painting does it.

KAUFFMANN: Doesn't do it in motion, doesn't do it serially and cumulatively.

CARDULLO: Right, think of the surrealist films *Un Chien Andalou* and *L'Age d'Or*, on which Salvador Dali and Luis Buñuel collaborated.

KAUFFMANN: Then there's the aspect of, let's call it, isolation: the ability of film to isolate factors in a work. I'll give you an example, a negative example. I once saw a production of *'Tis Pity She's a Whore*, which is a fascinating play. In the last scene the brother, Giovanni, comes in with his sister's heart impaled on a dagger and stands there with it almost until the end of the play. Now that is simply impossible to play these days. There's no way that he can stand onstage with his sister's heart on the end of a dagger and play a long scene with a lot of other people. Everyone in the audience was tittering. First, they knew that it was a fake heart, and second, even if it had been a real heart, the scene wouldn't have held, because obviously the distraction would have been too great. We're conditioned by film now to want what's important to be selected and isolated. The film director could have cut away from that damned heart and dagger so that you wouldn't have had to see them through the whole scene; you would have seen only the face of the brother or the faces of the other people. That's more than a convenience: it's in the nature of the medium to allow you to arrange space and assign prominence. This gives film great power.

CARDULLO: Someone like André Bazin would argue that this power is the dangerous one of manipulation.

KAUFFMANN: Anything can be manipulative. Harmony and counterpoint can be soppy and manipulative. It's true, nevertheless, that film is more powerful in this way than any other art form. The question is, to what use does it put its power? In Bergman's exquisite, strange last film, *After the Rehearsal*, it's the film's power to concentrate on an individual or two individuals, to isolate him or them from context, that makes the drama of the piece—not drama in the conventional sense, but internal drama. I would say that the attributes of film that are most important to me are not the ones of spectacle and motion—the ability to move anywhere and show anything—but the ones of selectivity and interiority.

CARDULLO: Let's talk for a minute about Kracauer's description of film as "the redemption of physical reality." Bazin said something similar, except that, with his Catholic sensibility, he probably put the emphasis on "human reality" rather than "physical reality." How would you characterize this use of the word "redemption"? What are these men talking about?

KAUFFMANN: They're talking about making God's creation more marvelous to us than it is.

CARDULLO: Through the process of framing, which confers a special importance on it.

KAUFFMANN: Yes, through the process of photographing this creation in motion. It's the filmmaker's function, Bazin believed—and I'm putting this very baldly—to celebrate God's miracle—the miracle of the world and human existence in it—by presenting it to us. Merely by reverently presenting it to us whole, in all its mystery and splendor. That's one of the two major options available in film, the other being the "interfering" option, as espoused by Sergei Eisenstein.

CARDULLO: The manipulative one, which uses editing and montage to reconstruct reality.

KAUFFMANN: For example, Margarethe von Trotta could be called a Bazinian and Hans-Jürgen Syberberg an Eisensteinian. There's a historical antecedent for this opposition in the opposed theater views of Stanislavsky and Meyerhold. And one can see all of twentieth-century theater and film—by theater I mean not only the plays themselves but their theatrical production—falling into one category or the other. Of course, there are some admixtures—$8\frac{1}{2}$ is one example in film—but mostly there's a bias one way or the other.

CARDULLO: I'd like to get back to national cinema a bit before we close. There has been a resurgence in British filmmaking recently. Some titles: *My Beautiful Laundrette*, *Prick Up Your Ears*, *Withnail and I*, *Rita, Sue and Bob Too*, *Wish You Were Here*, *The Whistle Blower*. Historically, why hasn't British cinema been able to compete with that of other nations? Is it because of the predominance of theater in England, the existence of so long and rich a theatrical tradition that there hasn't been room for film alongside it?

KAUFFMANN: I don't think it's that so much as two other things. First, there was considerable censorship in Britain before World War II— Eisenstein's *Battleship Potemkin*, for example, couldn't be shown there. Second, American films swamped the market. There was hardly room, figuratively speaking, for British film to breathe. I know that there are volumes of British film history. But look through them and what do you find that's of any significance? I'm not talking about the technological side—Britain had a lot to do with the invention and perfection of the equipment of filmmaking. But it has not had a lot to do with film artistry. The best directing talent it has ever produced, Lindsay Anderson, has in my opinion had a thoroughly unfulfilled career.

CARDULLO: What happened right after the war?

KAUFFMANN: There was a lack of Hollywood films, and for a moment the British were all by themselves. But instead of going on to develop an indigenous cinema of quality, they very soon aped Hollywood and then again became predominantly an American market.

CARDULLO: What happened in the late 1950s to cause a blossoming in British film that coincided with a rebirth of its drama?

KAUFFMANN: Their society was undergoing radical changes that led, in drama, to the plays of the "Angry Young Men," and in cinema to the so-called social realist films of the 1950s and early 1960s: *Room at the Top*, *Saturday Night and Sunday Morning*, *The Loneliness of the Long-Distance Runner*, etc. But this movement played itself out fairly quickly: the substance of the films became thin and their aims were sometimes less than large. For me, some of the films from this period—they come right before it, actually—that stand up best are the Ealing Studio comedies.

CARDULLO: Yes, *Kind Hearts and Coronets*, *The Man in the White Suit*, and *The Lavender Hill Mob* come to mind. What's responsible for the recent flurry of good British films?

KAUFFMANN: I think it's a matter of new talent and opportunities for older talent. Alan Clark, who has been active in British television for twenty years or so and has a very good reputation as a director, finally got the chance to make *Rita, Sue and Bob Too*. The script has some faults, but this is quite plainly a vigorously directed film by a man who knows what he's doing and knows what he wants. What has helped this recent resurgence is the sponsorship of Channel 4 on British television, for which a lot of these new films were made.

CARDULLO: Australian film has been thriving for some time now.

We've had, just to name a few items, Fred Schepisi's *The Chant of Jimmie Blacksmith*, Gillian Armstrong's *My Brilliant Career*, and Bruce Beresford's *Breaker Morant*.

KAUFFMANN: Yes, but what's happening—and I suppose this is inevitable in the world as it is—is that Australia's becoming the source of talent for other countries' films. David Lean used Judy Davis, the star of *My Brilliant Career*, in *A Passage to India*. Schepisi made *Roxanne* over here, Beresford did *Tender Mercies*. And Peter Weir, most familiar as the director of *Picnic at Hanging Rock*, made his best film that I know in this country: *Witness*.

CARDULLO: In conclusion, two related questions. How do you feel, after over thirty years on the job, about writing for *The New Republic*, and whom are you addressing in your reviews? That is, who's your ideal reader?

KAUFFMANN: I can't imagine a better critical post than the one I have at a respected weekly magazine whose readership is in the hundreds of thousands and is at a certain general intellectual level. *Time* magazine has, what, twenty-five million readers a week in all of its editions, but its readership comprises a vertical slice of the population. *The New Republic* gets a horizontal slice, and those readers are a wonderful audience. And after thirty years, the effect is cumulative, almost familial: I started writing for a certain group of people and now I'm writing for their children. At least this is the feeling I get— I hope I'm not under any illusions.

I must note how wonderfully I've always been treated by the people at *The New Republic*. The situation was good under the first owner I worked for, Gilbert Harrison, and it's become even better under his successor, Martin Peretz. Peretz and his staff couldn't possibly be more congenial, helpful, and noninterfering. Writing for *The New Republic* suits me because I'm much more interested in writing for the most intelligent nonspecialist in film than for film people—this is a matter of temperament, not of intellectual decision. And that's the readership that, by and large, *The New Republic* affords me. In a word, I have a dream job. Perhaps I shouldn't admit this, but it's certainly true that I have found my experience in writing for *The New Republic* to be a golden proof of Oscar Wilde's dictum that criticism is the best form of autobiography.

CARDULLO: One more question. How in fact did you become a film critic? What led up to your assuming the film critic's post at *The New Republic* in 1958?

KAUFFMANN: The Mafia. I had been educated for the theater, had worked in it, had always loved films but had never, in a certain sense, concentrated on them. In late 1957 I was a juror in a Mafia trial in New York, a trial that lasted nine weeks, and a practicing film critic, Arthur Knight, was a fellow juror. We lunched together almost every day for those nine weeks, and by conversing with him, I realized how much I'd absorbed about film through the years. Then, while that trial was still on, a writer I knew came around one evening to say goodbye—he was moving to England. He said he had been approached by a magazine called *The Reporter*—now long defunct—to be their film critic, had told them he was moving to England, and had recommended me. I told my friend about my discoveries during those jury lunches. In a few days *The Reporter* called, and I wrote three or four reviews for them. But we didn't get on. It ended with my having an unpublished review on my hands. I sent it, by some divinely lucky fluke, to *The New Republic*, and the then arts editor, Robert Evett, who became a dear friend, welcomed me immediately, lastingly. But if it hadn't been for those lunches prompted by the Mafia, it might never have happened. An ill wind blew tremendous good my way.

Afterword: The Critic as Humanist

Jonathan Kalb

uring my years as a graduate student in criticism at the Yale School of Drama, an irresolvable rift existed between that school and the university's English Department. It was the early 1980s, heyday of deconstruction. We theater types were taught by New York humanists who loudly and publicly expressed their contempt for jargon, their appreciation of individual insight and writerly talent over technique and doctrine. There seemed to be no intellectual ground on which these two sides could even meet to debate their differences. Students tend to distrust such stalemates, and I remember thinking of this one as an exquisite instance of two forms of snobbery—one academic, one professional—each failing to recognize its reflection in the other.

Chestful of earnest heroism, I cast myself as a peacemaking diplomat one spring, spent a fortune on books by Bloom, Miller, de Man and others not found on drama school syllabi, and applied for a job teaching English composition, on the mistaken assumption it would earn me entree beyond the high Gothic walls surrounding the university proper. No rapprochement ever arose, surely in part because that fortune lavished on literary theory had done little to change my attitudes toward theater criticism, but also because no one on the English side ever cared a whit for my mission. No hard feelings. Really, no feelings or thoughts of any sort concerning the episode followed me as I began my critical career. I had put it behind me like a bit of adolescent sexual experimentation until Jody McAuliffe asked me to write the afterword to this book.

Many themes in this volume merit elaboration but, after reading it through, what seems to me most worthy of separate commentary is the repeated implication that good theater criticism is necessarily humanist criticism. Tacit in the majority of essays (some of which extend its application to film criticism), explicit in Stanley Kauffmann's interview, this shared opinion will be, for some, nothing more than evidence of a common political prejudice among the contributors. This prejudice is often associated with Yale Drama School, and indeed a large number of the contributors have intimate links there. Not all of them do, however, which lends support to the idea that there is something else behind the opinion as well, something more substantial that I could not have understood fully back at Yale: the voice of experience. Humanism, as American theater critics understand the term, is as much a response to the real-world conditions in which they must practice their craft as it is an ideological preset. Theater critics function in a strikingly singular milieu, and if stressing that starts to sound like the professional snobbery just referred to, then so be it. Here are some reflections on what turned my nose gradually upward.

Humanism and humanists have been under siege for the past generation in a way that young intellectuals have been forced to face more squarely than our teachers ever were. The old guard of American theater critics, represented here by Robert Brustein, Richard Gilman, and Kauffmann, made their reputations in the 1950s and 1960s when it was still possible to make one's living as a literary journalist. *The New Republic, The Saturday Review, Commonweal, The Nation*: these were only the most famous few of many possible outlets for well-informed, timely commentary. Theater writers generally slouched into academia, if they went at all, often to supplement the New York lifestyle necessary for anyone who wanted to follow the theater. Any child of the first generation weaned on television who is interested in serious theater writing—particularly the kind that appears while shows are still running—has radically different prospects. Most of the intellectually reputable weeklies have now disappeared. The few that still exist pay token fees and, in any case, show little interest in critics outside the old guard. The would-be critic in my generation faces a Sophie's-Choice-of-the-mind: enter academia, thereby sacrificing the feeling of immediacy to a living art, or join the mass media, sacrificing the chance to probe seriously and the self-respect and satisfaction that come from it. Most of my former cronies chose academia, which placed us directly in the path of a machine programmed to annihilate us; the dominance of deconstruction-era politics, which continues to see our "impressionist" methods (the term is Kauffmann's) as irresponsible and naive, was all but absolute when we arrived.

A sampling of the other camp's arguments is in order, though I make no claim to objectivity. "Humanism" first got into academic trouble long before our teachers became its unwitting deputies. Marxist critics lumped the term together with "liberal humanism" and used it to describe a state of mind that could be summarily dismissed as representing the ambitions and world view of only a small, privileged socio-economic class. Here is a typical swipe by Terry Eagleton; the topic is the Cambridge journal *Scrutiny*, whose presiding figure was F. R. Leavis:

> . . . it represented nothing less than the last-ditch stand of liberal humanism, concerned, as Eliot and Pound were not, with the unique value of the individual and the creative realm of the interpersonal. These values could be summarized as "Life," a word which *Scrutiny* made a virtue out of not being able to define. If you asked for some reasoned theoretical statement of their case, you had thereby demonstrated that you were in the outer darkness: either you felt Life or you did not. Great literature was a literature reverently open to Life, and what Life was

> could be demonstrated by great literature. The case was circular,
> intuitive, and proof against all argument, reflecting the enclosed
> coterie of the Leavisites themselves. (*Literary Theory*, p. 42)

One glaring problem in this passage is that Marxist critics, without harping on the word, also habitually make assumptions about
what "Life" is and tend to be quite self-righteous about them, their
assumptions presumably being "un-intuitive" and based on sounder
socio-political analyses than "Leavisites" are capable of. More to the
point, though, in trying to ridicule away a term like "Life" simply because some people use it vaguely, Eagleton shows that his ostensibly
broad-based ideological critique is really bounded by the borders of
literature. Like most specialists in printed art forms, he is oblivious
to the terminological headaches faced by critics of live performance.
To comment on an art that involves living beings and takes place over
time, without ever resorting to the word and concept "life" and the
notion that it is universally shared, is to be hobbled indeed.

The subject gets stickier when use of such terms reflects a flirtation
with faith and religion, as is often the case with Gilman. An example
is this passage from his *Seagull* essay, which might also be seen as a
sort of humanist retort to Eagleton's point about circularity.

> . . . the subjects of imaginative literature, in which I include
> plays as texts (and also in performance . . .) don't exist indepen-
> dently of the writing itself. They're not like prey waiting to be
> pounced upon by a verbally gifted hunter, or seedy rooms need-
> ing to be refurbished by a painter in words. In turn, writing isn't
> the expression or treatment of a preexisting reality but an act
> that discovers and gives life to a "subject" within itself. (33)

There is more than a touch of elitism in this organicist assertion that
great artworks take on independent lives. The "life" inside Gilman's
" 'subject' within" can't be perceived by all onlookers, and certainly
not by those inured to such mysteries by, say, the mental habits of
dialectical materialism. Gilman would remain unfazed by this criticism, however, as would most of the other critics in this book. If
he uses without hesitation a phrase like "fundamental life" (36), if
Kauffmann quotes without historical apology a nineteenth-century

passage about "the energy of life" (67), if David Wyatt grounds his thoughts on Sam Shepard in a notion of "life as an unending and often unwilling competition for space and love" (104), it is because none of them is afraid of generalization. The so-called arrogance of the humanist critic has nothing to do with imposing prescriptive patterns; it has to do with insisting on the value of seeing forests for trees. Some just happen to be more zealous than others about their forests, and they can sound like keepers of a faith. Faith: a bold drive to generalize, based on a commitment to the soundness of one's perceptions so strong that one is inclined to apply them to everyone and everything as a universal organizing principle.

This is my point in a nutshell: one cannot write *well* about the theater without making some provisional assumptions about the universality of one's responses. The theater is too public a forum, too much of its aesthetics is wrapped up in the responses of large groups of people, for a voice with no pretensions beyond its singularity ever to be very illuminating. A theater critic cannot afford to write in constant fear of being associated with Matthew Arnold and his assumption that all hypothetical audiences shared (or ought to share) his middle-class liberal values. No such assumption is necessarily implicit in critical speculation: say, a guess on why the audience laughs at a given point, or a judgment that a given line sounds trite. The theater critic is not in a reading chair, at ease and alone; the job involves observing not only a performance but also a thousand other minuscule signals involving the mood, the receptive spirit, of other spectators. The theater critic describes an experience in a group partly as a surrogate for a group, and any pretension to hermetic, or wholly uncontingent, response is as much a lie as the old Arnoldian claim to speak for everyone. Furthermore, theater criticism deals with the "unreferrable." That is, you can't ask your reader to turn to page 256 of a published text, or to study a detail in a painting. Not only does each split second in a play speed by; it speeds by differently at every performance, so even repeated viewings can't provide unambiguous reference. Theater critics must choose and fix certain split seconds in order to deal with the subject at all, which means necessarily using themselves as examples of how the audience responds.

Critics who do not do this will sadly disappoint their readers. Which brings me back to the topic of forums for publication, another special circumstance for theater criticism. Theater, unlike classical literature, is not (yet) predominantly a university phenomenon. It still lives by its ability to attract large numbers of spectators from the general public—albeit within a narrow demographic range, but that is hardly the fault of the medium per se—and as long as that is so, the question of "appeal" will be a legitimate part of the critic's subject. For one thing, writing about appeal—what makes people go to, or stay away from, a cultural event—often means speculating about universals. For another, the theater critic, especially in a period when serious uses of the stage are waning, has many reasons beyond egotism for wanting to affect appeal, for wanting to make people see more in productions that bring dignity to the medium—and this must be done in journalistic forums such as *The Village Voice*, *The New York Times*, and *The New Republic* if it is to reach a readership that bears some relation to the medium's spectatorship.

Today it is this sort of critic, not the poet, playwright, or academic writer, to whom the classic Horatian directive to teach and delight applies. If the serious theater has any enduring role in our period of massive domination by electronic media, it is to be the proudly elitist medium. Renting a video and watching it on a private box inside a private box is the first and easiest choice after prime-time pap; unthinking "envelopment" by a film in the spirit of "hedonism" (see the Cardullo/Kauffmann discussion, p. 247) is a close second. But something must serve those vestigial "obligations to culture" that Kauffmann speaks of, that part of the common man's conscience that always wants to know he could try harder if he wanted to, the part that feels superior to the glut of programming around him pitched at an eleven-year-old consciousness. That something is theater. In the age of TV and video, theater is a standing opportunity to reach out, a place you have to get dressed and go to, where (unlike the movie theater) something other than passivity will be asked of you. And critics who weather the disapprobation of their academic colleagues in order to write for these reachers are not condescending or making disingenuous nods to populism. Quite the opposite: if they have the humanist spirit about them, they are displaying the Horatian courage of their elitism, daring to guide while fully aware of the complexities of their action.

Of course, in the current American intellectual environment, any assertion of cultural leadership meets skepticism and hostility. The Enlightenment is out, pluralism and diversity are in, and anyone who questions the rectitude of that displacement is truly, to use Eagleton's phrase, "in the outer darkness," oblivious to the barbaric fundaments of all existent institutions, the theater among the worst. If addlepates like Jürgen Habermas defect from the program, that only proves their fundamental indifference to the world's horrible social inequities and dominant metanarratives, chiefly of interest to the white, upper middle-class graduate students who dominate American humanities departments. No values handed down "from above"— that is, from people not previously disenfranchised—are dependably acceptable during these culture wars. The poison spread by centuries of racism, sexism, and classism was so ubiquitous and pernicious, says the theory, that the whole world must be remade ("invented," "written") before we may legitimately speak of meaning again, particularly meaning that aspires to universality. Having courage to generalize and judge informedly, however, recognizing and having the courage of one's unavoidable elitism even in the face of all this loud-mouthed denigration, is not *only* arrogance; it is also a reflection of a risky commitment, an emotional investment in one's subject and one's unique perceptions, without which a strong writerly voice is impossible and a confident teaching manner unlikely.

For some readers, perhaps for many, much of what I have said will sound arrantly patriarchal. I cry no mercy but ask only that my argument not be misconstrued. Nowhere in this essay do I contend that my opinions and perceptions, or those of critics with similar political prejudices to mine, have any stronger claim to universal validity than other people's. Nor do I think that feminist critics—or gay, African-American, Hispanic-American, or any other voices previously excluded from theater discourse—should not be heard and actively welcomed. What I do mean is that any feminist who does not generalize from her perceptions as a feminist spectator will write theater criticism with very little appeal, persuasive weight, and longevity, even among feminists. And that last sentence itself is a give-away. I include myself and feminists in the same human club in order to claim to know something (*not* everything) about their reactions, leaving me vulnerable to the wrath of all who want to define the club in order to exclude me. Intolerance of that wrath is an ideological preset to which I plead guilty.

I am also aware that the United States has produced numerous embarrassing examples of critics who bring shame on the humanist tradition by abusing their authority—a problem that grows more severe every day because of the compromises publications must make in order to survive competition from film and broadcast media. Kauffmann is understandably pleased with the "horizontal slice" of his *New Republic* audience, comprised of "the most intelligent nonspecialist[s] in film" (266); that audience confers on him one of the country's rarest writerly privileges. Most of the rest of us write in much more trying circumstances. Newspapers exert constant pressure on writers to betray their ideas through brevity and oversimplification, and glossy magazines subject them to the irresistible seductions of American fame. Because saying clever and brutal things guarantees the domination of one's opinions over other critics' in the popular imagination, sensationalism is a path to hegemony. To say as many have, however, that *all* theater critics offer a behavioral model based on power politics rather than values and standards, is to make against criticism the same charge Puritans once leveled against the theater: that bad apples *do* spoil the whole bunch. On the contrary: a few abusive parents do not make all parenting pathological.

In the fall of 1992, I changed universities. After two years in the Performance Studies Department at New York University, a department peopled by rich white folks so afraid of ratifying a rich white folks' canon they could never adopt a curriculum, I left to teach at Hunter College—which was like moving from nyu to NYU. It would be hypocritical of me to make too much of my newly democratic surroundings, but I mention them because the move reinvigorated me in unforeseen ways about my humanist leanings. Like much of the City University system at the moment, Hunter is a physically dilapidated place whose demographics reflect those of New York City. My students there generally don't write with the panache of ivy leaguers; they lack experience and hence expertise in the written discourse by which academic achievement is usually measured. They have something, though, that my chic downtown students often lacked: a hunger to know. They burn with curiosity about what their parents and grandparents never read, a daily reminder that not every member of groups previously excluded from Western culture is intent on scrapping past values. My students don't come eager to dump Marlowe, Kleist, and the Wakefield Master from the syllabi without reading them first; they want to know what the fuss about those figures was based on. Hunter students are a bit weak on Derrida, but they have the street smarts to know a hearty historical meal from nouvelle-theory cuisine.

After a decade in the field, then, I have come to believe that the Yale Drama School—while hardly an indispensable fundament, as this collection shows—offered exemplary preparation for an American theater critic. Ostracized by the English Department for not being "real doctoral students," ostracized by the directors, actors, and designers in our own school for being intrusive eggheads, we were treated to a shockingly accurate preview of the environment in which we would subsequently work. Americans—both spectators and practitioners—will follow a good theater critic, but only rarely will they admit it. The most influential among us is a shepherd with a reluctant flock. We interpret that reluctance as the glimmerings of consciousness, though, and push on with our missions, even though the silence around us is sometimes deafening. And we work every day with a basic truth we Yalies would quickly have forgotten had we ever scaled those high Gothic university walls: that is, people aren't interested in your ideas until they feel you have thought a bit about what their full, rightful measure of humanity is.

Notes on Contributors

ANDRÉ BAZIN (1918–1958), the highly influential French film critic and theorist, was the cofounder of *Cahiers du cinéma* and the spiritual father of the French New Wave.

ROBERT BRUSTEIN, critic, actor, director, and founder of the Yale and American Repertory Theatres, has served on the faculties of several universities and was Dean of the Yale School of Drama from 1965 to 1979. He was drama critic for *The New Republic* from 1959 to 1968 and has written many books on theater and society, including *The Theatre of Revolt* (1964), *Seasons of Discontent* (1966), *Theatre* (1968), *Revolution as Theatre* (1970), *The Cultural Watch* (1975), *Making Scenes* (1981), and, most recently, *Reimagining American Theatre* (1991).

BERT CARDULLO is the film critic for *The Hudson Review* and teaches in the theater department at the University of Michigan, Ann Arbor. He edited *Before His Eyes: Essays in Honor of Stanley Kauffmann* (1986) and *The Film Criticism of Vernon Young* (1990) and is the author of

Indelible Images: New Perspectives on Classic Films (1987) and *What Is Neorealism?* (1991).

ANTHONY DeCURTIS is a Senior Editor at *Rolling Stone*, where he oversees the record review section. He is also popular music critic for "Weekend All Things Considered" on National Public Radio. He guest-edited the Fall 1991 issue of *SAQ*, titled "Rock & Roll and Culture."

JESSE WARD ENGDAHL is a free-lance author and film instructor at the Crossroads School. His recent writings on film and travel have appeared in *California Magazine*, *L.A. Style Magazine*, and the *L.A. Weekly*. He has worked as a production assistant and has written screenplays for independent Hollywood producers.

RICHARD GILMAN teaches at the Yale School of Drama. Among his books are *The Making of Modern Drama* (1974), *Decadence* (1979), and *Faith, Sex, Mystery: A Memoir* (1986). "*The Seagull*" is a chapter from a forthcoming work on Chekhov.

JIM HOSNEY currently teaches graduate courses in film history and aesthetics at the American Film Institute in Los Angeles. He heads the Film and Video Program at the Crossroads School, where he also teaches classes in film theory, contemporary American filmmakers, and the European avant-garde.

MAME HUNT has worked on new plays at such theaters as the Los Angeles Theatre Company, the Berkeley Repertory Theatre, and the Goodman Theatre. She has taught playwriting and new play development in Reykjavik, Los Angeles, and many places in between and has worked with some of the finest playwrights in the country, including Marlane Meyer, Darrah Cloud, Thomas Babe, Neal Bell, and José Rivera.

JONATHAN KALB, Assistant Professor of Theater at Hunter College of CUNY, has been a theater critic for *The Village Voice* since 1987. Winner of the 1991 George Jean Nathan Award for Dramatic Criticism, he is the author of *Beckett in Performance* (1989) and *Free Admissions: Collected Theater Writings* (1993).

STANLEY KAUFFMANN, film critic for *The New Republic*, is Distinguished Visiting Professor of Theater and Film at Adelphi University.

Assistant Professor of the Practice of Theater at Duke University, JODY McAULIFFE is a member of the Society of Stage Directors and Choreographers. She has published fiction in *Southwest Review* and is an alumna of the American Film Institute's Directing Workshop for Women.

ALAIN PIETTE is a member of the English faculty at the State University of Mons, Belgium, and the author of a forthcoming study of the Belgian playwright Fernand Crommelynck.

MARY ANN FRESE WITT is Professor of French, Italian, and Comparative Literature at North Carolina State University. She is the author of *Existential Prisons* (1985) and has written essays on Kafka, Pirandello, Ionesco, Genet, Sartre, and others. She is currently researching fascism and the theater in France.

JACQUELYN WOLLMAN received her B.A. in Film from the University of California at Berkeley in 1980. She studied at the Paris Film Center and is presently a Story Analyst for Columbia Pictures.

DAVID WYATT is Director of Graduate Studies in English at the University of Maryland, College Park. "Shepard's Split" forms a chapter in his forthcoming book, *Out of the Sixties*.

Index

Library of Congress Cataloging-in-Publication Data
Plays, movies, and critics / Jody McAuliffe, ed.
The text of this book originally was published without the present
introduction, afterword, and index as vol. 91, no. 2 (Spring 1992) of the
South Atlantic quarterly.
Includes index.
ISBN 0-8223-1404-5. — ISBN 0-8223-1418-5 (pbk.)
1. Theater.   2. Motion pictures.   3. Motion pictures and theater.
4. Drama.   I. McAuliffe, Jody, 1954–
PN2020.P57   1993   792–dc20   93-17308   CIP